FREE FALL

Also by Nicolai Lilin

Siberian Education

FREE FALL
A SNIPER'S STORY FROM CHECHNYA

NICOLAI LILIN

CANONGATE
Edinburgh · London · New York · Melbourne

First published in Great Britain in 2011 by
Canongate Books Ltd, 14 High Street, Edinburgh EH1 1TE

1

Copyright © Nicolai Lilin, 2010
Translation copyright © Jamie Richards, 2011

The moral rights of the author and translator have been asserted

First published in Italy in 2010 as *Caduta libera* by
Guilio Einaudi editore, s.p.a., Torino

www.canongate.tv

British Library Cataloguing-in-Publication Data
A catalogue record for this book is available on
request from the British Library

ISBN 978 1 84767 971 0

Typeset in Sabon by Palimpsest Book Production Ltd,
Falkirk, Stirlingshire

Printed and bound in Great Britain by
CPI Mackays, Chatham ME5 8TD

This book is printed on FSC certified paper

AUTHOR'S NOTE

This book is a story constructed with true details, a distorted reflection of the reality that we experienced.

That is, I changed the names of characters and units to protect those involved; I omitted place names and also blurred the times when the events narrated here actually took place.

N.L.

FREE FALL

I was getting bored at home, coddled by my mom,
Then one fine spring day, the dear Fatherland called me away.
Now I'm not bored one bit, time flies like a bullet . . .

Russian army song

If any citizen, in the absence of legal grounds, fails to appear
at the appropriate commissariat in response to the summons
for military conscription, he will be considered a 'deserter'
and tried according to the law of the Russian Federation.

*From the Russian Federation law on
military service, Article 31.5*

Walking with my shadow on the ground,
going down the rocky road,
boots making me cripple-toed,
and my helmet slipping down.

Rifle thumping on my arse,
girls still on my mind.
I trip on stones and fall behind,
cursing every Russian curse.

Op-lya, the army is me!
Op-lya, the army is me!

*From 'The Army is Me' by singer-songwriter
Sergei Trofimov*

Having a prostitute for a daughter brings a family less
dishonour than a soldier for a son.

Old Russian proverb

When I turned eighteen, I already had a past behind me. But the world had one too, and it was decidedly more complex than mine. My country was turning into a realm of the absurd. Capitalism, so longed for, never came. The mentality of the crook reigned, the mentality of people out for easy money who wished to look smarter than God himself. Or, as my grandfather would say, 'Everyone wanted to take God's beard and try it on for size.'

In Transnistria people did nothing but talk about Western society. The United States and Europe were living examples of economic and social prosperity; everybody wanted to become Western, thinking that if they wore designer clothes, ate fast food and bought foreign cars, democracy would naturally follow, and take root in our great and beautiful Land. It was like an infectious disease, a fever whose origin and character nobody could explain.

Post-Soviet society had erased the values of my fore-bears, the people who had raised me and who, for me, represented the pinnacle of human wisdom. The more this Western euphoria grew, the clearer it became that chaos would rule our days.

It was in this cheerful context, as I was saying, that I turned eighteen.

*

One spring morning, I woke up and went outside, opened the mailbox, and found a white card with a red diagonal line across it. It said that the military office of the Russian Federation was asking me to appear for my physical and to bring my identification documents. It added that this was the third and final time they would send me notice, and if I didn't show up within three days I could expect a criminal conviction for 'refusal to pay my debt to the Nation in the form of military service'.

I thought that the scrap of paper was a joke, a formality, something of little importance. I went back inside, grabbed my papers, and without even changing, headed across town in my slippers to the old Russian military base.

At the door, I showed the guards the notice and they let me in without a word.

'Where do I have to go?' I asked one of them.

'Go straight, it's all the same . . .' the soldier replied unenthusiastically, clearly irritated.

What an idiot, I thought, heading towards a large office where it said: 'Drafts and New Recruits Department'.

The office was dark; you could hardly see a thing. On the back wall was a small window out of which shone a dismal, feeble yellow light. I could hear the tip-tap of a typewriter.

I walked towards the window and saw a young woman in a military uniform at a table, typing with one hand and holding a cup of tea with the other. She took small sips and kept blowing into the mug to cool it off.

I leaned on the counter and peered in. I saw that on her knees under the table there was an open magazine. It was an article on Russian pop stars, with a photo of a singer wearing a crown adorned with peacock feathers. It made me feel even sadder.

'Hello, excuse me, Miss, I got this in the mail,' I said, holding out the card.

The woman turned towards me and looked at me for a second as if she couldn't figure out where she was or what was going on. She snatched the magazine she'd been reading and flipped it over behind the typewriter so that I couldn't see it. Then she set down the mug of tea, and without standing up or saying anything, and without expression, she took the white card with the red line from my hand. She looked at it for a moment and then, in a voice that seemed to belong to a ghost, asked:

'Papers?'

'Which papers, mine?' I asked awkwardly, pulling my passport and everything else out of my trouser pocket. She looked at me with a hint of disdain and said, through clenched teeth:

'Well, certainly not mine.'

I handed over my papers and she put them in a safe. Then she took a form from a shelf and began filling it out. She asked for my name, surname, date and place of birth, home address. Then she moved on to more personal information. After asking for my parents' details, she said:

'Have you ever been arrested or had trouble with the law?'

'Well, I myself have never had trouble with the law, it's the law that seems to have trouble with me sometimes . . . I've been arrested lots of times, I can't remember how many. And I've been in juvenile prison twice.'

She looked up and examined me. Then she tore up the form she'd been filling out and took another, larger one, with a red line running diagonally across it, like that on the card I'd received in the post.

We started again, covering all the personal information, this time including my convictions – article numbers, dates. Then my health: illnesses, vaccinations; she even asked if I consumed alcohol or drugs, if I smoked cigarettes. This went on for an hour . . . I couldn't remember the exact dates of the convictions, so I made them up on the spot, trying to get at least the month right, or general period.

When we were finished I tried to explain that there must be some mistake, I couldn't do military service. I had requested and been granted a six-month deferral, assuring them that in the meantime I was going to finish a course of study and then enrol at university. If everything went as planned, I added, I was going to open a physical education school for children, there in Bender.

She listened, without looking me in the eye, which worried me. Then she gave me a piece of paper. It said that from that moment onward I was the property of the Russian government and that my life was protected by law.

I couldn't understand what all this actually meant.

'It means that if you try to escape, harm yourself, or

commit suicide, you will be prosecuted for damage to government property,' she told me coldly.

I suddenly felt trapped. Everything around me began to seem more serious and sinister than before.

'Listen,' I burst out, 'I couldn't give a shit about your law. If I have to go to jail I'll go, but I will never take up arms for your fucking government . . .'

I was furious, and when I started talking like that I instantly felt powerful, even more powerful than that absurd situation. I was sure, absolutely sure, that I could change this machine that was threatening to regulate my life.

'Is there a general around, or whatever the fuck you call your authorities? I want to see one, talk to him, since you and I don't understand each other!' I raised my voice, and she looked at me with the same expressionless gaze as before.

'If you want to speak with the colonel, he's here, but I don't think that will solve anything. I advise you to keep calm. Don't make things worse for yourself.'

It was good advice, thinking back on it now. She was telling me something important, I'm sure; she was showing me a better way, but at the time I was blind.

I felt sick. How is it possible, I asked myself, that just this morning I was free, I had my plans for the day, for the future, for the rest of my life, and now, because of a little piece of paper, I was losing my freedom? I wanted to yell and fight with someone, to show how angry I was. I needed to. I cut her off, shouting in her face:

'For Christ's sake, Holy Lord on the cross! If I want

to talk to someone, I talk to him, period! Where the fuck is this commander of yours, general, whatever the hell he is?'

She rose from her chair and asked me to calm down and wait for ten minutes on the bench. I looked around and I didn't see any bench. Fucking hell, what is this place? Everyone here is nuts, I thought, as I waited in the dark.

Suddenly a door opened, and a soldier, a middle-aged man, called me by name.

'Come, Nicolay, the colonel is expecting you!'

I jumped up like a spring and ran over, eager to get out of that disgusting little room as quickly as possible.

We went out into a small courtyard surrounded by buildings all painted white, with propagandist drawings and posters illustrating the exercises that the soldiers had to do to learn to march. We crossed the courtyard and entered a room filled with light, with big windows and lots of flowerpots. In the middle of the flowers there was a bench, and next to the bench a large ashtray.

'Wait here. The colonel will call you from this door. You can smoke if you like . . .'

The soldier was kind. He spoke to me in a very friendly tone. I'd calmed down and I felt more secure; it seemed that my situation would be cleared up and that someone would finally listen to me.

'Thanks, sir, but I don't smoke. Thank you for your kindness.' I was trying to be as nice as possible myself, to make a good impression.

The soldier bade me goodbye and left me alone. I sat

there on the bench, listening to the soldiers who had come onto the courtyard for drills. I looked out the window.

'Left, left, one, two, three!' the drill sergeant shouted desperately. He was a young man in an immaculate military uniform, marching along with a platoon of men who didn't seem to have any desire to march.

'Nicolay, you can come in, my boy!' called out a firm male voice. Despite its kind, almost sweet tone, the voice had something off about it, a false note you could hear underneath.

I went up to the door and knocked, asking permission to enter.

'Come in, son, come in!' he said, his voice still kindly and brimming with friendliness. He was a big, strong man sitting at an enormous desk.

I went in, closed the door, and took a few steps towards him, then suddenly I halted.

The colonel was about fifty and was very stocky. His head, which was shaven, was marked by two long scars. His green uniform was snug; his neck was so wide that his jacket collar was completely taut, as if it were about to tear open. His hands were so large that you could barely see his nails, they were so deeply set. A split ear suggested he was an experienced wrestler. His face might have been copied from the Soviet military propaganda posters of the Second World War: unrefined features, a straight wide nose, big resolute eyes. On the left side of his chest a dozen medals hung in a row.

Jesus help me, this one's worse than a cop . . . I could

already imagine how our meeting was going to end. I didn't know where to start; it was like there was no way I would be able to express myself in front of somebody like him.

Suddenly, interrupting my thoughts, he spoke. He was looking through a file similar to the ones in which police keep confidential information on criminals.

'I've been reading your story, my dear Nicolay, and you're starting to grow on me. You didn't do very well in school, in fact you didn't do much at all, but you did play four different sports . . . That's good. I played a lot of sports when I was young too. Studying is for the weak; real men do sports, prepare themselves for combat . . . You did wrestling, swimming, long-distance running and target shooting . . . Good, you're well prepared; I think you have a good future ahead of you . . . There's just one flaw: Tell me, why do you have two convictions? Did you steal something?' He looked me straight in the eyes and if he could have done he would have looked right into my mind.

'No, I didn't steal anything; I don't steal from people . . . I beat up a few guys, twice. They charged me with "attempted murder with serious bodily harm" . . .'

'That's nothing, don't worry . . . I got into fights when I was young too; I understand completely. Men need to make their space in the world, to define themselves. Fighting is the best way – that's how you find out who's worth something and who's not even worth spit . . .'

He was talking as if he were about to give me a prize. I felt uncertain; I didn't know what to say and above all

I didn't know how to explain to him that I had no intention of doing military service.

'Listen, son, I couldn't care less about your jail time, your criminal convictions and all the rest of it; I think you're a good kid, God bless you, and I want to help you out because I like you. I have your whole life written here, from your first day of school . . .' He set the file on the desk and closed it, tying the two ribbons on the side. 'I'll give you two choices, something I do only in exceptional cases, for people I really care about. I can put you in the Border Guard and send you to the Tajikistan border − you'll have a good career, and if you like mountain climbing, it's perfect. Or, I can put you with the paratroopers, a school for professionals − after six months you'll become a sergeant and you'll go far there too. Eventually you could even get into special forces, in spite of your background. The army will give you everything: a paycheque, a home, friends and an occupation at your level. So what do you say? Where do you want to go?'

It was like listening to the ravings of a madman. He was saying things that made no sense at all. The army giving me all the things that I already had! How could I explain to him that I didn't need an occupation at my level, or friends, or a salary, or a house . . .

It was like when you get on the wrong train and suddenly realise there's no way to make it turn back. I took a breath and blurted out my response:

'To be honest, sir, I want to go home!'

He changed instantly. His face turned red, as if a pair

of invisible hands were strangling him. His hands balled into fists and his eyes took on a strange glint, like the sky before a storm.

He took my file and threw it in my face. I managed to put up my hands in time to ward off the blow. The file hit my fingers and came open, and the papers scattered all over the room, on the desk, the windowsill, the floor.

I stood as still as a statue. He kept glaring at me, full of hatred. Then he suddenly began shouting in a terrible voice, which I could immediately tell was his real one:

'You thankless bastard! You want to rot in shit? Then you can rot in shit! I'll send you to a place where you won't even have time to pull your trousers down you'll be shitting in them so much, and every time you do, think of me, you ungrateful bastard! You want to go home? Then from now on your home will be the saboteur base! They'll teach you what life is really like!'

He was screaming at me, and I stood there, completely drained.

'Out! Out of here!' He pointed at the door.

Without a word I turned on my heel and left the office. Outside the door a soldier was waiting, and he saluted me.

'Sergeant Glasunov! Follow me, comrade!' he said, with a voice that sounded like a Kalashnikov when it sends a cartridge into the barrel.

Your comrade is a mangy dog, I thought, but said humbly:

'Excuse me, Sergeant, may I use the toilet?'

He gave me a strange look, but didn't refuse.

'Certainly. Down the hall and to the right!'

I walked down the corridor; he followed, and when I entered the bathroom he stayed and waited for me outside.

I was able to reach a small, high window, and since it had no bars I jumped down without any problem. Out in the yard behind the office, there was no one around.

'To hell with this madhouse, I'm going home . . .'

With this and similar thoughts in my head I headed for the exit of the base. There, the guard stopped me. The soldier was young, maybe my age, very thin and a little cross-eyed.

'Papers!'

'I don't have them on me, I came here to visit a friend . . .'

The soldier gave me a suspicious look.

'Show your permit to leave the base!'

At that my heart sank into my boots. I decided to play stupid:

'What permit? What are you talking about? Open the gate, I have to get out . . .' I moved towards the gate, going past the soldier, and he pointed his machine gun at me, shouting:

'Stop or I'll shoot!'

'Get out of the way!' I replied, grabbing the gun by the barrel and ripping it out of his hands.

The soldier tried to punch me in the face, but I blocked him with the butt of the rifle. Suddenly someone hit me on the head from behind, hard. I felt my legs wobble and my mouth went dry. I took two deep breaths, and at the third I passed out.

I came round a few minutes later. I was lying on the ground, surrounded by soldiers. The sergeant who was supposed to be watching me was there too, looking worried and telling everyone in a conspiratorial tone:

'Nothing happened, everything's fine. Listen, nobody saw anything, I'll take care of him.'

It was clear that he was afraid of being punished for his carelessness.

He came over and kicked me in the ribs.

'Do that again, you bastard, and I'll kill you myself!'

He gave me a few more kicks, then gave me his hand and helped me up. He took me to a kind of house with barred windows and a steel-clad door. It looked just like a prison.

We went inside. There wasn't much light and everything seemed dirty and grey, neglected, abandoned. There was a small, narrow hallway, with three steel-clad doors. At the end of the hall a soldier appeared, who looked about twenty and a little thin, but with a kind face. He was holding a big set of keys of various sizes and kept shaking them, making a strange noise that under the circumstances almost made me cry out of sadness and desperation. With one of his keys the young soldier opened a door, and the sergeant ushered me into a very small, narrow room, with a little barred window. There was a wooden bunk attached to the wall.

I looked around and I couldn't believe it. Just like that, I'd ended up in a cell.

The sergeant looked me in the eye and said:

'Stay here and wait!'

I looked right back at him, without concealing my hatred.

'What the fuck am I waiting for? What's the meaning of all this?'

'For the end of the world, you piece of shit! If I tell you to wait, you wait and don't ask questions. I'm the one who decides what you have to wait for!'

With that, the sergeant gestured to the soldier to close the door and marched off triumphantly.

Before locking me up, the soldier came closer and asked me:

'What's your name, kid?'

His voice seemed calm and not mean.

'Nicolay,' I replied softly.

'Don't worry, Nicolay, you're safer in here than with them . . . Rest up; in a few days they'll take you to the train that will take you to Russia, to your future unit . . . Have they told you where you're going yet?'

'The colonel said he's assigning me to the saboteurs . . .' I replied in an exhausted voice.

There was a pause, and then he asked excitedly:

'The saboteurs? Holy Christ, what happened? What did you do to deserve that?'

'I had a Siberian education,' I replied, as he closed the door.

*

I was locked in that cell for three days.

There were lots of other people in the temporary prison, and every now and then I could hear them. Some would groan; many were silent; one was always begging for food. They passed us our rations, horrible stuff, in vacuum-packed bags. You couldn't tell what was in them; the biscuits were all crumbs, probably smashed by something heavy. As the guard later confessed, the people 'waiting for the train' like me got the packs that had been damaged in transit.

'But this food is disgusting, my friend, give me something better, just once. I don't know − a piece of fruit?' I was always asking the guard for extras, and once in a while he'd get me an apple, a peach, a couple of prunes.

'Don't be picky, kid. You have to get used to eating whatever's around . . . Those dogs, in the place you're going, they definitely won't be waiting for you with piping hot dinners! You'll see, the day will come when you'll remember these biscuits as being the best thing in the world . . .' He wasn't being mean, although it was obvious that he was a little scared of me.

Every so often he'd open the little window and chat with me for a while. He asked me where I was from, about my family, and why my parents hadn't paid the recruitment office to get me exempted from service. I was honest with him; I told him about my life, and about my neighbourhood, Low River, and before long a sort of trust had been established between us.

I took care of my business in the latrine in the corner by the window. I was already familiar with the smell − it was the same as jail – but here I had no cellmates who smoked who could give me a match to burn some paper.

I asked the guard if he could give me anything and through the window he tossed me a bag of white powder, a bathroom disinfectant. I used it, but within half an hour the chemical odour became so strong it hurt to breathe – it was as if they'd thrown me into a vat of ammonia. I nearly passed out and I cursed with every breath.

On the evening of the third day, the guard told me that our train had arrived and would take us away that night.

I had decided to try to escape during transit.

I thought that if they put me in a jeep, I could jump out as it left the base.

At about midnight I heard a great racket, a car engine, and some voices. They started to open the cell doors one by one, calling out our names. Soon they opened the door to my cell, and in the corridor I saw a young officer staring at me. From the little stars on his epaulettes I could tell that he was a lieutenant. He called my name, his voice calm. When I replied, 'Yes, that's me!' he responded in a tired but amicable tone:

'From now on, boy, it's better if you learn to reply like a real soldier. When you hear your name called, you should only say "Yes, Sir!" You understand?' He looked at me with humility; it almost seemed as if he were asking me to do him a favour. Since I was thinking of escape, I decided to play along. I stood up nice and straight, like I thought soldiers were supposed to stand in front of a superior, and with a voice full of energy I said:

'Yes, Sir!'

'That's it, very good. Now go to the door, there's a truck waiting for you.' And he turned to the next cell. I stared hard at his back and yelled:

'Thank you, Sir!'

He waved his hand lazily, without looking at me, as friends do when they part ways after spending the day together.

From the hall, I could see a military truck in the court-yard, and two soldiers with their rifles aimed at me.

'You! Get in the truck. Now, now!' one of them shouted in my face.

I knew very well that once I was in there I wouldn't have another chance to escape. I froze, as if struck by lightning. I still couldn't believe that what was happening to me was real.

'Get in the truck, I said! What, are you deaf?' he taunted, pointing his rifle at me.

I had no choice, and so I got in. Twenty men climbed in behind me, then the armoured door closed and the truck took off.

Inside it was so dark you couldn't see a thing. Some of them were speaking, asking questions: Where is the train? Is it far away? As if wherever the train was made any difference. Some of the men were calm; they said they already knew where they had been assigned. One said:

'I don't care. My father knows the commander at the base they're sending me to. He set it all up; I'll hide out for my whole term of service. I'll pass the time with the country girls . . .'

As I listened to them talk, I realised that none of them

felt responsible for his own life. I was surrounded by children. For many of them, military service was their first opportunity to be on their own, without their parents coddling them. It was a new experience, they said, an adventure. I couldn't believe my ears. They were losing two years of their life doing something that none of them would ever have chosen to do, and in spite of all that they were happy.

After a few hours, we reached the railway station. It was enclosed by a red brick wall with heavy barbed wire on top. It reminded me of the sorting yard in the central prisons. The train was there on the tracks, with a long row of sleeper cars. Floodlights from the towers illuminated a square full of young men, like me, dressed in civilian clothes. Some carried bags, as if they were going on a holiday. There were guards everywhere, some with dogs; it was just like when they'd taken me to jail. I lost all hope of escape.

My only thought at that moment was procuring a toothbrush and a few other things I needed – I'd left the house without imagining I'd end up here, and I hadn't brought anything with me. I went up to a guy with a backpack and asked him if he happened to have a tooth-brush. He looked at me strangely. It was clear that even though he was taller than me and definitely seemed stronger he still didn't know a thing about the crude realities of life. I smiled at him.

'Listen up – give me your toothbrush, toothpaste, towel and soap . . . I want to show you a trick!' I tried to sound friendly.

'What trick?' he asked.

'A funny trick, trust me,' I said, forcing myself to chuckle, as if I actually wanted to astonish him with some sleight of hand.

'Give me your stuff while there's still time!'

He looked a little suspicious, but in the end his child-like curiosity won out, and he reached into his backpack, which was full of all kinds of stuff his mummy had packed for him to help make him comfortable during his tour, and pulled out a small bag. I snatched it out of his hands and slipped it under my jacket, and walked away as if nothing had happened.

'Hey, what about the trick?' the idiot asked, a smile still on his lips. Poor fool, he still hadn't realised that I'd ripped him off.

I glared at him, and in an ugly voice replied:

'Get lost or I'll rip your eyes out, you piece of shit!'

Filled with shame and fear, head hanging, he walked back over to the others in his group.

As soon as we reached the yard we lined up in fours. There were a few hundred of us altogether. The soldiers passed by and took away whatever they considered 'useless', which was nearly everything. Bags, backpacks and any other possessions were immediately confiscated.

'Money, watches, jewellery, cigarettes . . . everything out of your pockets!' the soldiers yelled.

The others looked around, disorientated. The most fragile ones burst into tears after a soldier yelled at them. I was angry, but at the same time I almost felt like laughing at their behaviour.

At last the doors of the train opened and they ushered us on one at a time. Two soldiers made another sweep, throwing everything they found on the floor in a corner: watches, chains and other items, until a giant pile formed. I had put the bag between my legs, inside my underwear – to be more precise, I'd hidden it under my balls. The soldiers didn't even touch me; I raised my arm to show that I didn't have anything in my trousers, and they let me by.

I took a place at the window, just as I had done in jail. I had learned that that was the best spot, the safest.

The train hadn't even pulled away and the complaints had already begun. One guy was whining about the guards hitting him because he hadn't boarded the train fast enough, others because they'd lost the things they had brought from home. It was clear that they had never felt the sense of vulnerability and powerlessness that you feel in the face of the system, when you are crushed by the reality of power.

After a two-day journey, we reached a place similar to the one we had just left. There were lots of soldiers in the yard wearing various uniforms. It was midday, and all the men had come to the windows to get a look.

And they began to chatter:

'Look, the tankers! They're here for me, I'm going with them!'

'The ones in blue berets are the paratroopers. Look, that guy has a bayonet hooked on his boot!'

'Well, the infantry still have the smartest uniforms!'

The cheerful voices made me nauseous. I wanted to get off that damned train as quickly as possible.

The officers opened the doors and let us out, and then they began to call us, one by one. The first on the list were the ones headed for the infantry, so the yard was immediately half emptied. Then they called the artillery, and almost the entire second half left. After that, they called three groups simultaneously: paratroopers, tankers and motorists. Then there were about twenty of us left. Some officers in blue, navy and white uniforms came; they were the *spetsnaz*, the autonomous special units of the infantry, and they took most of the rest.

There were three of us left. A man in civilian clothes came, gave us a melancholy look, and said:

'Saboteurs, let's go!' Without waiting for us, he turned and started walking towards the car, an armoured military off-road vehicle parked on the other side of the yard. We didn't look at one other, just followed him, and after a moment an officer ran after us with a folder full of papers. Each unit's representative had signed a piece of paper covered with stamps and other scribbles before leaving with his group. Now the officer, still running, yelled at the top of his lungs:

'Zabelin! Give me your bloody signature for once, you bastard!'

The man in civilian clothes casually kept walking. The soldier gave up, and, cursing, gestured contemptuously in our direction.

'Your unit is bullshit; you're just a bunch of amateurs!'

The man in civilian clothes stood by the car with the keys in his hand, staring at us.

'All right, boys, I'm Senior Lieutenant Zabelin, in charge of the saboteur training unit . . . Which of you boys can drive?

'I can, Senior Lieutenant Sir!' I replied, with the voice of a young communist – full of energy and faith in the Nation's future.

He gave me a funny look:

'Tell me, how many times have you been in?'

'Two, Senior Lieutenant Sir!' I replied, without missing a beat.

He whistled, and then asked:

'Did you steal? Deal drugs?'

'No, Senior Lieutenant Sir!'

'Well then,' he said, raising his voice, 'are you going to share what the hell you did that was serious enough to get two juvenile convictions?'

'I impaired some people's health, Senior Lieutenant Sir!'

'You *impaired some people's health*? What language are you speaking, boy! Can't you explain yourself any better?'

It was like talking to my late, great uncle Sergey. He used the same expressions, and his voice wasn't cruel or fake like that of other soldiers.

'I beat up and stabbed two people, Senior Lieutenant Sir! But I did my time and I've learned my lesson!' I kept playing the good soldier, responding in the way I imagined that soldiers were supposed to respond: fast, like tap-dancing with your tongue.

'Good boy! I like you!' he said, amused. 'Now take the keys and be careful with the transmission, it's an old car . . .' Then he paused, looked at all three of us and said in a normal voice, without any trace of mockery or arrogant bullshit or anything of the sort:

'Never call me "Senior Lieutenant Sir" again, is that clear? From now on, you're saboteurs. We don't have ranks, just names, remember that. So I'm "Comrade Zabelin" to you. Let's go, get this thing started . . .'

The saboteurs' camp was in the paratroopers' camp. It was a base within the base, with fences, checkpoints and everything. The paratroopers went about their daily lives and we never encountered them.

Our barracks were long, arranged on a single storey, and in the middle of the hallway there was an entrance that led underground.

During the first week they subjected us to various trials; they wanted to assess our health and endurance. Zabelin was our only drill instructor; there were a dozen sergeants who assisted, but he saw to the training himself. They woke us up during the night and made us run, armed and with full backpacks as if we were in the field. We would leave the base in total darkness, Zabelin at the head of the ranks and a few sergeants at the side and the back, and start running like a pack of animals. It was extremely difficult; we had to move in the dark down dirt paths in the woods, run up and down hills, and every metre of ground we covered cost us enormous effort. Lots of guys got hurt; one fell and broke a leg; another didn't see a ditch and fell in, shattering one of his vertebrae. You couldn't see a thing, and Zabelin didn't let us use any lights.

'You have to move in the dark like animals. Darkness is a saboteur's best friend; you have to take advantage of it. It's your lover, your partner . . .' he would always say when anyone tried to complain.

We also had to learn how to orient ourselves in the dead of night; it was important to know where base was at all times, to be able to load our rifles, arrange things in our packs. Even in the barracks our windows were always covered by heavy shutters made of dark wood. We ate, did our business, showered, dressed, dismantled and cleaned our weapons, all in the dark.

Zabelin respected me because I had learned to run in the dark without being afraid to fall, I handled exertion well, I could go a long time without drinking water, and especially because I never asked pointless questions, which he hated more than anything.

After a week, we began target practice. Beforehand, Zabelin asked if any one of us was handy with weapons, if we had shot anything. A few of us said yes, so he ordered us to take up the AKSM-74 Kalashnikov assault rifles, and gave us each an entire clip. I had a head start; in addition to the target shooting I did in a city sports team, I had lots of hunting experience in Siberia with my grandfather Nikolay. Whenever I went to visit my grandfather, even when I was still just a kid, my father often let me shoot his Kalashnikov.

When it was my turn, I made a spectacular shot. Instead

of just hitting the bullseye, I knocked it down, breaking the pedestal that secured it to the ground.

'Siberian, what the hell are you doing? Why didn't you aim for the centre?' Zabelin pretended to be angry with me.

'There's no point in shooting straw targets with this cannon, Comrade Zabelin!' I replied, like the ideal soldier. 'If you want me to hit that bullseye give me a slingshot, at least then it would be fun!'

My comrades broke into laughter. Zabelin laughed, too:

'All right, let's make a pact: if you can knock down the rest of that pedestal, I'll send you to a place where you can do whatever you want!' His tone was very cheerful.

'Consider it done, Comrade Zabelin!'

I levelled the rifle, fixed the stump in the crosshairs, lowered my aim by half a finger and fired, very delicately pressing on the trigger. The pedestal lifted off the ground completely, and fell with a bounce.

'All right, Nicolay, you've earned a spot in the sniper course. Starting tomorrow you'll be working with Comrade Sergeant Yakut!'

From then on, every day for four hours, I would leave the main group and follow individualised training with a small detachment composed of twelve men. The sniper instructor was a sergeant of Siberian origin, like me, and so they called him Yakut, after the region he came from.*
He was sharp and knew all there was to know about war.

---

* This nickname derives from 'Yakutia', a republic in Eastern Siberia.

He'd fought in several armed conflicts and was an expert in 'micro expeditions', brief and highly risky engagements in special war operations. He seldom spoke, and spent most of our lessons teaching us the basics of shooting with precision rifles. He explained how to make the most of the telescope and how to pick out and hunt down other snipers. The principle wasn't difficult; you had to move slowly without letting yourself be seen, be patient, and be extremely alert – like a hunter.

After a month of training exercises, I'd figured out a way to escape from the base. So one night I grabbed a few of my things and crossed two fences watched by the sentry. Like a shadow, I crept along the walls, but when I finally emerged outside the base, thinking that I'd made it, there was Zabelin, eating an ice cream.

'Want one?' he asked casually.

'Might as well . . .'

I couldn't imagine what he had in mind, but something told me he wouldn't get me into trouble. I followed him to where he'd parked his car. We drove into the city, although it must have been two or three in the morning, and we stopped at the sort of diner frequented by truckers, a place where people would sneak off to their cars with prostitutes.

We sat down at a table and, without exchanging a word, ate a meal together. He washed his meat down with long sips of vodka. He offered me some too, but I declined

– I didn't want to get drunk. After eating in perfect silence, Zabelin ordered two lemon ice creams. Once the obese, exhausted waitress had set them on the table, he finally began to talk.

'Nicolay, I don't know what kind of mess you were born into or raised in, but I can assure you that here, in the army, nobody cares who you are. You don't exist. Here you're a number, and if you make one mistake they erase you, just as they would erase a number. I'm certain you could become a good saboteur, and I think that this is your only chance to save yourself. You're going to find yourself in serious trouble, but if you follow my advice you'll thank me for it one day . . .' He spoke softly, without a sign of irritation, still calmly eating his ice cream.

I was eating my ice cream too, and I wasn't thinking about military prison – where, if he wanted, he could have sent me without much difficulty. The only thing that mattered to me at that moment was figuring out how he'd caught me, when I thought I'd been careful and invisible. He kept talking:

'You running away from my unit makes me look bad. If this story got out I'd have problems with superior command, and I don't want any problems with them, understood? You know, don't you, that all deserters get sent to military prison? You know what that means? Well, don't think that just because you've been in juvie a couple of times you've seen all there is to see in this world . . . The point, dear Nicolay, is that starting tomorrow I'm going to send you on clean-up duty for three days. You'll help the team that runs the military prison here, not far from our base. When you return, you can decide whether to run away or stay here and do your duty like the rest of us . . .'

We returned to camp. I went to sleep in the barracks and in the morning a sergeant woke me up with a taunt:

'Let's go, Count of Monte Cristo, they're hauling you off to jail!'

I got dressed while my comrades were still sleeping, and went out to the yard. A car was waiting for me, with three soldiers and a lieutenant. We introduced ourselves, and after the military formalities we left for the prison.

Zabelin hadn't exaggerated when he'd told me about the prison. In the yard, a few soldiers were walking in a circle, wearing faded old military uniforms; huddled together they looked like an indistinct dark grey blob. They had big white numbers on their backs, and they were frighteningly thin, shuffling around hopelessly, dragging their feet in imitation of a military march. It was the most horrible place I'd ever seen in my life.

A soldier holding a baton stood in the middle of the circle and barked out commands:

'Left, left, one, two, three!' He had an iron whistle in his mouth, tied to a little strap around his neck.

When he whistled, everyone immediately dropped to the ground, their bodies straight like logs, their hands on their heads. Yet one of them remained on his feet.

The soldier screamed at him, his voice almost hysterical:

'You! Did you not hear the whistle?' Then, seeing that there was no reaction, he moved quickly over to him. The prisoner's knees shook so hard you could almost hear them knocking, but he kept on his feet. 'For fuck's sake, are you deaf?' the soldier said, standing right in front of him. And without warning, he unleashed a series of blows with the baton, on the man's back, neck, head. The man fell to his knees and wet his trousers. He was crying, begging the soldier not to beat him anymore. But the soldier's only response was to laugh in his face.

'You piece of shit traitor, you pissed all over yourself! How dare you?' He gave him another volley of blows. The prisoner was on the ground now, the soldier's boots kicking him.

The most chilling thing was that the whole scene had taken place in absolute silence. No one breathed, as if the yard were completely airless, without oxygen, without anything at all. It was like we were trapped inside a bubble that kept us from understanding what was going on.

My task, along with six other men, was to do the cleaning and take the food to the blocks where the military prisoners were being held. None of them was mentally stable; it was like they were in a catatonic state. They didn't respond to questions; they behaved like animals, scurrying from one side of the cell to the other and then freezing the moment you looked at them, as if they were afraid to be caught moving. They lived according to the simple orders dictated by the whistle; they would eat in their cells, then march out to the yard, take their blows, undergo humiliation and torture from the guards, and then go to sleep at night only to wake up the following morning and start it all over again. They couldn't communicate with each other, and any activity that would let them think was prohibited. They were unrecoverable, so deeply traumatised that – as one of the guards later confirmed – once they left prison, they never managed to reintegrate into society again. Many of them committed suicide; some wandered the streets until winter came and the cold killed them.

After three days in that prison, I decided not to tempt fate again, and so I returned to the routine of boot camp.

We saboteurs had an unusual uniform; we wore civilian clothes, things from home. As we would be conducting missions behind the front lines, travelling through territory under enemy control, it was essential that we be able to pass unrecognised. 'The most important thing,' Zabelin always said, 'is your shoes.' He explained to us that in wartime many soldiers complained of foot pain because of their boots, and he made us wear trainers so we would always be comfortable and light on our feet.

Zabelin had taught us the precious rules of 'saboteur survival and solidarity', as he called them. They were like commandments, and each of us had to learn them by heart. The idea was to create a sense of unity, to make us into our own clan within the army. The rules were very precise: saboteurs obey no one outside their commanding

officer; under no circumstances may saboteurs be transferred to other units of the armed forces; in armed combat,
saboteurs are forbidden to leave their dead on the ground.
If a group suffered serious losses and was left isolated
from the rest of the unit, they were not allowed to retreat
from the line of operations. The only valid alternative was
the most drastic: suicide. Each of us carried a personal
hand grenade, which we were supposed to use to blow
ourselves and the others up should the unit be surrounded
by enemies and run out of ammunition. They were extreme
rules, and I didn't like them very much. I didn't understand
why we would have to kill ourselves, just because the
saboteur strategy had no retreat plan, unlike every other
unit of the Russian army.

What's more, unlike the rest of the Russian army, we
had nothing to do with military law. Every Russian soldier
is required to memorise if not the entire military code, at
the very least the principal articles. But as for us, we've
never even touched our books, just as none of us has ever
learned to march or salute properly.

Our weaponry, however, was better than the rest of the
army's. The paratroopers were equipped with Kalashnikov
assault rifles, models with folding stocks and silencers
which were attached in place of flash suppressors. With
the silencer fitted we used ammunition with less gunpowder
– the bullet would explode with less power so as not to
exceed the speed of sound, and thus the weapon effectively

turned out to be almost silent compared to the rifles they used in the infantry.

In actual war, I was soon to discover, you would detach the silencers; they were cumbersome, and during a mission it was hard to get the right ammunition. The charges you could find on the front line were the usual Kalashnikov ones, whereas you had to 'reserve' the special stuff at the warehouses, which wasn't very convenient. This is why everybody would replace the silencers with flash suppressors picked up from wherever, often taken from an enemy. If you were lucky, you could find nice handmade models that worked to perfection – that is, that completely concealed the burst of flame created by the shot.

My comrades and I used two precision rifles. One was the classic Dragunov with a long barrel, useful for covering long distances. With one of these, its release modified and reload slowed down, an expert soldier – if he had the right cartridge – could shoot up to a kilometre away. It was a rifle used primarily as a field weapon, good for operations in wide-open spaces or at the foot of the mountains. The other rifle was a variation for special units: a VSS with a folding stock, a scope that detached easily for transport and an integrated silencer on the barrel. I liked that gun; it was light, precise, and it never betrayed you. The scope in particular was very sturdy and even if it slipped or hit something heavy it didn't break. The VSS didn't make any noise, but it only worked with a certain type of cartridge. It was able to cover a maximum range of three hundred metres, and it was useful for urban combat, where the gunfights were at very close range. You could also use it for reconnaissance, scouting and sabotage operations. The back-up groups for the assault squads often used it to keep watch over enemies without being seen.

We learned to parachute jump; first in broad daylight, and then after some practice, only at night time.

The idea of jumping out of a plane scared me, and I had no desire to try it. The first time, Zabelin had to force me to jump, dragging me to the side door and pushing me out into the air. The parachute opened by itself. I felt something hard yank on my shoulders and my neck went *crack* – whiplash, as I found out later – and in a few seconds my legs hit the ground. My left knee, which I landed on with my whole weight, blew up like a balloon. In the two weeks afterwards I did the planned jumps, even though my left leg hurt like hell every time I landed. That way, at least, I learned to land as gently as possible.

Night jumps were very dangerous. The ground beneath us was dark, and even if we asked what altitude we were flying at – to figure out how many seconds to wait before opening the parachute – nobody ever told us the exact height, and we often hit the ground sooner than we expected and got hurt. I landed in the trees twice, and it wasn't much fun. I didn't like parachute jumping at all, and I never learned to handle it without anxiety.

*

In this way, a couple of relatively peaceful months went by. By then, we were all so used to night drills and all the other arduous aspects of the saboteur's life that we hardly noticed them anymore.

But I had noticed that Zabelin often brought up the subject of war. He talked a lot about Afghanistan, Afghan fighters, Islam, Muslim society and their philosophy of life, but most of all he talked about military tactics. Knowing that we were right in the middle of the Chechen-Russian conflict, I began to worry − I had a million doubts about what our commanders were *really* thinking, and I didn't like it at all.

One by one, they started to pull people from our unit, and my comrades disappeared into thin air. They asked one man to report to the colonel's office and soon afterwards we were all told that he had been transferred to a fixed post, where he was to spend the rest of his military service.

After three months of field training, it was my turn.

That morning, they called me to the colonel's office. There were two other guys from my unit with me, and we were all anxious. Where are they going to send us? our eyes asked one another.

The office was luxurious, full of valuable antique wooden furniture and leather sofas and armchairs. A lot of military stuff hung on the walls: flags, insignias, photographs, even some antique weapons. The colonel was a

nasty, beefy man who was bursting out of his uniform
and had a face the colour of beetroot. He was accompanied by three officers, two of whom had a very dodgy
look about them – as my dearly departed uncle would
have said, 'they were born thugs'.

After the formal introductions, they invited us to sit
down on the sofa, right in front of a big television. As
we sat down, I searched the eyes of my comrades. Unlike
me, they looked happy; maybe those idiots were expecting
to see *Cinderella*. The colonel himself put on the video-
cassette. The first image that appeared on the screen
showed the flag of the Russian Federation, which waved
proudly amidst smoke and fire, riddled with holes and
torn in one corner as if mice had nibbled away at it. At
that instant I felt panic rise within me. I couldn't show
my desperation, but my whole body screamed silently. I
knew immediately, I was sure beyond a shadow of a doubt:
they were sending us to Chechnya.

A male voice, strong and determined, and an equally
determined female voice, spoke theatrically over images
of war, their words snaking between the charred bodies
of our soldiers, the children looking out from the rubble
in the streets, the civilians marching off in rows, forced
to abandon their homes . . . The shots documenting the
chaos of battle were interspersed with clips taken by
Chechens and Arabs as they decapitated one of our soldiers
who'd been taken prisoner, while the tanks burned on the
road in Grozny. Then Russian hostages who had been
released showed the camera the stumps of their hands,
fingers and ears, which had been cut off by their

kidnappers in order to blackmail their families. The image of a Russian transport plane shot down by the Arabs at the base of the mountains and our soldiers' bodies strewn all over the rocks was accompanied by the words: 'The terrorists have no respect for the living or for the dead: an aeroplane carrying our soldiers fallen in battle was shot down by Chechen-Arab guerrillas, so our men were killed a second time.'

Sadness came over me. I was going to a place where every human value I had ever known would be meaningless. I couldn't turn back; I would be forced to accept the rules of the game, of which I was now a part. I thought of the stories told by my grandfather Nikolay, who had travelled all over Europe during the Second World War. I remember vividly how this strong man – who, when I was little, had always seemed so real and pure – could handle the difficulties of everyday life without batting an eye, but when the word 'war' came out of his mouth, he would suddenly become sad and almost seem to wilt. I thought back on the war in Transnistria, when I was still a little boy, and the only thing that came to mind was the frightening number of bodies on the streets of Bender, my hometown.

Meanwhile, the voices on the film went on with their insane story, explaining, in the same flat tone they used in propaganda announcements for the masses, that the Chechens were the bad guys and the Russians the good guys; that truth, power and even God himself were on our side, and that the only good thing a Russian could do in this life was kill as many Chechens as possible, and

exterminate all their allies, the Arab terrorists, fundamentalist Muslims and 'all the weak elements under the influ-
ence of their propaganda'. There was no way I wanted
to get into that mess, but the reality was clear. When the
film concluded, with a shot of the same flag as the beginning, I had already lost all hope.

The three officers began to explain to us the reasons why
we had to go and risk our lives, and my comrades seemed
hypnotised: they were sitting on the sofa with foolish half-
grins on their faces, and they punctuated the officers' every
statement with enthusiastic nods of affirmation.

'So, boys,' the portly colonel broke in, 'the Nation is
asking you to do your part! Are you ready?'

These words cut me like a knife. I couldn't feel anything;
my head was about to blow off and shoot ahead by itself,
like an old locomotive speeding downhill, detached from
the rest of the train.

All three of us leapt to our feet, and together, in perfectly
idiotic unison, we yelled with all our might:

'Yes, Comrade Colonel! We will serve and honour the
Russian Federation!'

'Good thing . . .' he said ironically, switching off the
television, his fat finger pushing so hard on the remote
control that it went *crack*.

Once we were out of that office, they didn't allow us to
return to the barracks. They led us to a room where we
waited to hear our fate.

After a few hours, Zabelin arrived. He was in good spirits, even whistling a little tune. My comrades asked him loads of questions: 'What are they going to do with us?' 'What's going to happen to us?' He hated stupid questions, as I said, so he looked at them with a smile and said:

'Did they have you watch that video? You'll be in next year's version . . .' At which they stopped asking questions.

Zabelin took me aside and whispered to me. 'Nicolay, I put in a word for you with someone I know; he's called Captain Nosov,' he said, looking at me sternly. 'He's an old friend of mine, an expert saboteur. You'll be on his independent team. Do what he says, and if you're lucky, you'll go home alive and in one piece.' Then he shook my hand. Before leaving, he told us all to go to hell, an old Russian saying for good luck.

Half an hour went by and then a soldier came in, with three new uniforms. They had the paratroopers' insignia printed on them, and naturally they came with the blue beret so loved and sought after by every paratrooper. He brought army boots too, which weighed at least a kilo each. Another soldier set down three knapsacks identical to the ones in which they had brought our provisions, and said:

'You have to wear uniforms because during the trip you'll be with the paratroopers. Put your clothes in these backpacks, and when they leave you to your units you can put your civvies back on.'

I put on the uniform and looked at my reflection in the window. I didn't like seeing the gear on me – it seemed unnatural. My comrades, however, were amused by the situation. They adjusted one another's berets, struck model poses, as if they were getting ready for a party or an award ceremony.

We had a few hours' flight to Chechnya. On the plane with us were soldiers who belonged to other units in the paratrooper force. They were joking, laughing, shouting, talking about the political situation and the war. To buck up their courage, they said the Chechens were 'a bunch of fags — they can't even keep their guns up'. Another threw out some serious insults towards the Arabs.

I would soon discover that in this war, for the sake of practicality — and thinking back on it now, it's a very shameful thing — all our enemies were called 'Arabs', whether they were Chechens, Muslims, Afghans, Taliban, terrorists, or fighters who had sided with any political creed. The word 'Arab' was the way we indicated the enemy.

There were two lieutenants next to me who seemed not to give any weight to the ruckus. They let the soldiers talk, and the atmosphere was upbeat, almost party-like.

We landed at night. They separated me from my comrades and pointed me to the armoured car headed for the mobile immediate-response unit, where the team of saboteurs under Captain Nosov was stationed.

I sat on top — sitting on the roof was known as riding the armour — along with a group of soldiers I didn't know. As the car made the long journey in the dark, I realised that the others were speaking to me with some disdain.

They were part of a special group from the Ministry of Internal Affairs, and evidently I, the newcomer, was not welcome.

The first thing I noticed when we got to the base – and this would sink in over the days to come – was that everything worked opposite to the way it did at boot camp. There was no light to be seen at the checkpoint, there was no sign of recognition for entering vehicles – I only realised that we had arrived because in the dark I saw three soldiers cupping their hands to try to conceal their cigarettes. Smoking at the checkpoints was prohibited, especially at night – the risk of being spotted, even from a distance, was extremely high.

They took me to an ugly building, a military container for the transport of supplies that had been turned into a sort of cabin, with a small window and a rough-hewn wooden door. They handed me over to a soldier in civvies carrying a cut Kalashnikov with a folding stock. He put away my papers, and without even glancing at them, handed them back as soon as we were alone.

'My name's Pasha, but everyone calls me "Moscow". You're with us. Come on, put your stuff on the bunk in the back and take off that uniform, I'll give you a jumpsuit. Have you got trainers?'

I looked at my papers in disbelief. According to regulation, all documentation regarding soldiers had to be kept in the office of the unit to which we were assigned. Giving them back to a soldier was strictly forbidden. So I introduced myself and immediately asked,

'Hey, what's the story with the documents, why did you give them to me? Where's the secretary?'

He looked at me as if I were from another planet.

'Who am I supposed to give them to, babyface? We haven't got offices or secretaries, so everyone's his own secretary around here. We're saboteurs, a mobile unit. Today we're in one place, tomorrow in another. We're independent, get it?' he said, chewing on a hunk of black bread. The smell of burned grain was overpowering and it reminded me of *kvass*, a drink that my grandmother made. 'Follow me,' Moscow said, before I could respond.

The cabin was full of men in everyday clothes – some were sleeping, others eating or chatting. I was surprised by the number of weapons lying around – there was a Kalashnikov at the foot of every bunk, and there must have been at least twenty more stacked against the wall, not counting the rifles that some of the men were holding. On the ground lay crates full of new cartridges, still covered with a thin coat of grease, and a crate with several hand grenades. Other ammunition was scattered around, along with a couple of rounds for RPG-7 grenade launchers. In one corner there was a stack of bulletproof vests, modified just like Zabelin had taught us in boot camp; they were short, with the bottom cut off in front so you could move your legs more easily and use the sides as pockets for ammunition. From two normal jackets you could make one good one, and at chest height, in the hand-sewn pockets, you would always insert a double set of iron plates.

I would soon learn that the saboteur base never stayed in the same place for long, and from time to time they would put us with units that needed our assistance. In the intervals between one operation and another we would sleep in the place we called 'home', that is, the temporary barracks, where the only things we never ran out of were weapons and ammunition, which were scattered everywhere and even got mixed up with our food.

Moscow led me to the back of the base. Next to a tumbledown wood cabin, there was a steel vat filled with water, and a pole with the flag of the Russian Federation, just like the one I had seen in the propaganda video, was attached to it. From the vat, you could see a man's head, half-submerged, making bubbles as he breathed out of his nose.

'Ivanisch, the new guy's here . . .'

The head in the water lifted and I saw the face of a man in his forties, clean-shaven and with the expression of someone who wants to steal something. It was Captain Nosov, and in a very calm, low voice, one of those voices that can frighten you, he asked me:

'So, you're the hotshot delinquent? Zabelin has told me a lot of things about you . . .'

I was surprised, because I had no idea what Zabelin could have written about me, but I gave an affirmative response all the same.

'That's me, Comrade Captain!'

Nosov looked me straight in the eye.

'Forget all that "Comrade Captain" crap. Here, we're just one big family, call me Ivanisch.'

'All right, Ivanisch . . .'

'How is that old Zabelin?' he asked me, as he kept working in the vat. 'Has he gone completely deaf yet?'

I didn't know what he meant; it was as if we were talking about two different people. 'Deaf?' I asked, confused. 'He hears everything just fine. He's good, actually. He said to tell you hello.'

The captain gave me a serious look.

'Boy, I was side by side with Zabelin in Afghanistan for a long time. In Kabul they tried hard to destroy us, and after a bomb went off he nearly lost his hearing. As the years have gone by it's got worse. Shit, don't tell me you didn't notice!' he concluded, smiling.

Images of Zabelin as I had seen him in the three months spent in training camp flashed through my head.

'I really didn't, I didn't notice. I'd never have thought,' I replied. Only then did I realise what a tough guy Zabelin was. He had been able to hide from all of us something that should have been so obvious.

'You think that if he were all in one piece they'd keep him in that shithole? Zabelin's a professional saboteur. If he were completely fit he'd be here with us right now.' Nosov said this with anger. Then he stood up and stepped out of the vat, resting his feet on an empty wooden crate, the kind they use to transport Kalashnikovs.

'Soldier, towel!' he thrust out his arm, waiting for Moscow to pass him the green rag that he'd already been

brandishing for a while, almost like a votive offering, the
ones they would put at the statues of pagan gods in ancient
temples. Just then I realised that it wasn't a towel but a
flag; it was green, with different-coloured stripes and some
Arabic writing in white. Nosov took the flag and started
drying himself, making the strangest faces.

I couldn't help laughing. His face turned serious and
he asked:

'What the fuck are you laughing at, delinquent? I put
my skin on the line every blessed day to conquer these
shit flags – I have the right to use them to wipe my ass,
since they're no good for anything else.'

Moscow laughed too, and bit off another hunk of black
bread.

Nosov cut us short:

'Listen, boy, this is how things work around here; until
you've had some experience in the clean-up crew, our
family won't accept you for military operations. Now
go and eat, rest, and starting tomorrow you'll go and
clear the fields. Just the other day we finished a mission
close by, so you'll have some work to do. Then, we'll
see.'

He started getting dressed, throwing the green flag to
the ground. It was soaking wet; it had become a useless
scrap of fabric, destined to be buried in the mud.

Moscow and I went back to the barracks, and on the way
he told me how things worked in the unit. From what I

understood, the two most important rules were: don't try to escape, and eat at every opportunity.

'What's this business about the clean-up crew?' I asked impatiently. 'What fields am I supposed to clear? It's not like I have to go pick tomatoes, right?'

'Really? You haven't figured it out?' he said, giving me a sad look. 'You have to collect the bodies. They make you do it so you get used to contact with dead bodies, so you won't have a hard time at the crucial moments. We've all been there, friend – you'll be on clean-up duty for a couple of weeks.'

The next morning, following Moscow's directions, I reported for duty at a big military truck. There, on the wooden benches placed along the walls, sat ten others. I said hello and took my place.

The clean-up crew was composed of twenty people or so. Calling them 'soldiers' didn't really seem right; they were like gravediggers, except they wore uniforms and drank a lot of alcohol.

Our job was very simple. We would go wherever battles had taken place, often major clashes, and gather all the bodies – human and animal – that we saw on the ground. We would toss the bodies into the truck, then jump in with them and take a pleasant ride back to camp.

My first 'pick', as we called them, was in a half-destroyed and long abandoned village.

They gave me a pair of thick rubber gloves that went

all the way up to my armpits, typically used in the chemical protection units. Then they gave me a long rope with a slipknot at the top, like the kind people hang themselves with. One guy explained succinctly how to move the bodies:

'You take two of them, tie their legs together with the rope and then drag them to the truck. Don't go through their pockets and don't take anything from the bodies, otherwise you'll be in deep shit. If you find any weapons, take them to the sergeant.'

The battle had taken place a few days earlier. There were bullet holes everywhere, and the streets were filled with craters from the explosions from mortar fire and hand grenades. At the entrance to the village there was a Russian armoured car, gutted and burned. The wheels didn't have tyres anymore, the back doors were slightly ajar and you could see a leg dangling out and an army boot. It was strange, like looking at a painting. I had the impression that I was entering a dimension where time had stopped: everything was dead, nothing living could pass there.

I took a few steps in the direction my new comrade had pointed and I saw a corpse in a ditch near the main road that led to the centre of the town. It was striking, because it didn't resemble any corpse I'd ever seen before – and I've seen quite a few dead people in my day. The ones I'd found the most revolting had been the bodies of the drowned that I'd pulled out of the river – unfortunately, some of them had even been friends – and the thing that had struck me most was the smell. When they were still in the water you

didn't notice at all, but once they were brought to shore
they started to stink so badly just being near them made
you want to vomit. The bodies of the drowned get terribly
deformed; they swell up, full of rotting parts and leaking
fluids, until they look like a big ball of gelatin. When I was
a boy, in the summer of 1992, after the war between Transnistria and Moldavia, I saw many war corpses in the streets,
but I'd been almost indifferent to those bodies. I was too
occupied with trying to find the weapons and ammunition,
and I hadn't given the dead much thought.

My first body in Chechnya, however, made a different
impression on me. I felt pity, because it seemed like he'd
been taken by surprise, at a moment when he hadn't
expected anything bad to happen. He lay straight, his legs
extended, his hands joined over his heart, as though before
dying he had tried to keep his soul from coming out. His
face was completely white; his skin looked like marble,
all taut over his bones, but the veins on his neck and
temples were black. His eyes were wide open, so dark
you couldn't tell their colour. His mouth was slightly open
and you could see his teeth, stained with blood.

I studied his body for a moment and then I grabbed
him by his bulletproof vest near his neck, and tried to
pull him to the road. At first glance he had seemed hefty,
but when I pulled him up out of the ditch I was shocked.
He weighed almost nothing; it was like moving a wet rag.
I carefully examined his uniform, which in certain spots
was paper thin, as if beneath it there were no longer a
body but only the impression of a human being, the depth
of a piece of cardboard. Standing there, motionless, with

that poor man in my arms, I felt a sudden hard, violent tug coming from inside his body. Terrified, I instinctively slackened my grip.

The body dropped, and from the vest − where, a second before, my hand had been − came a giant sewer rat. His tail was greasy and disgustingly hairless, the skin glistening. As he came into the light of day, the rat gave me a look full of hatred, and then slowly crept back down into the ditch. Frozen, I tried to comprehend what I had just seen. Behind me, I heard the voice of someone else on the clean-up crew:

'Never grab them by the vest, they're full of rats. They're dangerous, those beasts − they eat human flesh, so they're strong and aggressive. Last year a rat almost tore three fingers off one guy in a single bite. Follow my advice; just grab the bodies by the legs and before you tie them, tap them with your foot a couple times, and those pests will run away.'

I couldn't tell whether the man was messing with me or telling the truth. Either way, from that day on I did as he said.

When the truck was full, we climbed in and sat on the benches at the sides. The corpses were piled on top of one another in front of us. They made us eat in front of the bodies so we would get used to their presence. Sometimes, when the truck went around a corner on the trip back, the corpses fell on top of us. It bothered me the first few times, but after a while I got used to it. I'd shove them off and put them back on the pile. I learned to treat bodies like objects of no importance.

After two weeks of corpses and rats, they told me that I could officially become one of the saboteurs.

Everything in the saboteur unit seemed chaotic. At first glance one might think that we were a group of regular guys, people who had nothing to do with military life and had somehow ended up in the middle of a war. In reality, we had our own philosophy, a series of very precise rules and most importantly our own way of understanding war. The only thing the superiors really cared about was the outcome of a sabotage operation or the continual patrol of the territory. Other than that we could act however we liked. We were autonomous – we just had to do our job well.

The group was very close knit; we were more like a family than a military unit. This happens with people who have to be together no matter what – when you share tough times you develop a sort of collective brain, an ability to understand the world by putting aside your personal point of view and using the mentality of the group.

Often the drafted soldiers – especially the younger ones – were really angry, because they felt trapped, exploited by the regime. These feelings formed a wall of hatred between people, and made day-to-day life difficult. Especially in the large army units, where hazing was very common, there was no communication between the soldiers and none with the officers. This is why internal disputes were so frequent, and when disciplinary measures were taken many soldiers became deserters – and some committed suicide.

The effects could clearly be seen during war operations. Many units weren't able to carry out their assigned tasks because the soldiers didn't know one another or were afraid of their comrades. They were subject to frequent breakdowns; they felt alone and they didn't trust anyone.

Among the saboteurs, on the other hand, hazing didn't exist. We were like brothers, because each of us knew that in hard times it's always better to have a brother by your side than an enemy.

I had been with my team for just a few days when I witnessed the tragic end of a group of infantrymen. Ten young soldiers were killed by one of their own, a machine-gunner who lost his mind during a mission and started shooting at everyone who tried to come near him.

When war gets tough, and emotions run very high, the stress can push you over the edge. It happens to everyone sooner or later, and it happened to me too. In times like that it's important to have the support of people who will stand by you. You need someone who will give you a word of encouragement, listen to you, or keep you from feeling alone and abandoned. If there's not a solid bond among your comrades, the person in trouble can become very dangerous – then everything ends in tragedy, just as it did with that machine-gunner.

I remember that for an instant I had him in the cross-hairs of my rifle. I could see his face, he was desperate, his eyes were crazed and he kept on shouting something

incomprehensible, shooting and crying. I followed him
with my scope but I couldn't bring myself to kill him – it
seemed unnatural to shoot one of my own. In the end,
since he wasn't responding to our requests to stop fire,
the paras were forced to shoot him down.

We knew that to survive we had to trust our comrades,
but we also had someone else to lean on: Captain Nosov.
He was like an older brother. We knew that whatever he
did, he did it to save our skins, so that we could return
home to our mothers alive and in one piece.

Nosov belonged to the generation of those whom the
old generals referred to as 'gladiators', so called because
many soldiers from that draft had never experienced a
time of peace. They had gone to the war in Afghanistan
as young men, and had embarked on a long, sad life,
bouncing from one war to another without rest, taking
part in every bloody conflict that broke out in USSR territory before and after its fall.

He had fought in all the post-Soviet wars; for a time
he had even been stationed in the former Yugoslavia,
where he was an instructor for the special units of the
Serbian army. When the Chechen conflict broke out, he'd
been one of the first Russians sent out there.

He was an expert saboteur, old Ivanisch, and every time
one of us mentioned his name it was evident that the
soldiers in the other units knew and respected him. Our
enemies knew him well too, because when he fought in
the war in Afghanistan, Chechnya was still part of the
USSR and many Chechens had actually done their military
service under him. It was incredible to think that the same

soldiers – now grown men and professional soldiers – were now fighting against us. It often happened that one of the Chechen prisoners would recognise among the Russian soldiers an old friend from military school with whom they had once fought.

Sometimes Nosov would tell us war stories, and what struck me the most about him was the tenderness of the words he used to describe all the brutality and horror of social collapse. It was like he was talking about something very dear to him, like family. At times even the enemy seemed like a fundamental part of his existence, as though without it his life would make no sense.

In my head, I had extremely contradictory images of our captain. Sometimes he seemed too brutish, almost inhuman, while at other times I felt that he cared more about us than he cared about himself. In time I would come to understand that for Ivanisch a single person was less important than the whole unit. Our personal histories didn't interest him. He saw in each of us a role; we were part of a mechanism intended to carry out specific tasks. This was his way of caring about us; he couldn't allow himself to get too attached to the individual.

Nosov didn't like to talk about himself or his family; we knew only that he had a sister named Rita, and that once in a while she would write to him.

He burned those letters right after reading them, and if the circumstances allowed it he would immediately ask one of us – often me – to write a reply. He always said the same things; he told her how charming the places we found ourselves in were, how the sun went down, how beautiful the rivers that flowed high in the mountains were. He explained how hard life was for the people there, and then every so often would ask us to add something of our own, 'for beauty's sake', as he would say. In every letter he would reassure his sister, telling her to 'keep clear of the war' — of course he didn't write that he was actually part of an active unit on the front lines; instead, he invented little stories about us, the men who were guarding a warehouse with him, in a safe place, on some Russian air base.

All we knew about Nosov was that he didn't have a house, a wife or children. His relationships with women were limited to the little parties organised by his officer friends, where young nurses and cooks would go. He himself called those soirées 'bordellos', and after every one they had to carry him back to the unit. He'd come in very drunk, semi-unconscious and with scratch marks from a woman on his face. All the officials said that Nosov was a hit with the ladies because he had a 'big calibre'.

There weren't many of us; perhaps that's why we became close to one another so quickly.

The first time I felt a strong sense of solidarity was during one of my first battles. We were walking close to the wall of a house when we were attacked by surprise. As we tried to cross the yard a group of enemy soldiers lying in wait on the roof of the house across the way opened fire on us. A hail of bullets came down around us, and pieces of brick flew off the wall and ricocheted. We took off running. In the chaos, however, we managed to keep calm; nobody changed direction or passed anyone else, and we moved as we always did; three covered, the others ran, then switch . . . We were in complete synchrony, linked parts of a single organism. As I ran with the others, that feeling gave me courage.

Of course, living together wasn't easy at first − each of us had led very different lives, until we found ourselves in hell alongside a bunch of complete strangers.

My comrades came from all over Russia, and obviously each had his own story behind him, but we had all been marked by the same things: run-ins with the law, unstable families, difficult personalities . . .

The oldest comrade was Moscow, who, as you can tell by the nickname, came from the nation's capital. He'd been called to arms two years late, because as soon as he had come of age he had run away from home to avoid military duty, but ultimately even he, like me, had been caught and sent to war.

One of our other brothers was Shoe. He had two juvenile convictions for burglary under his belt. His name was really Viktor, but he had earned his nickname because he never wanted to take off his shoes. Nosov was always yelling at him, telling him that if he didn't wash his feet, sooner or later the smell would poison the entire unit. Shoe was always cheerful and had an athlete's physique: he was nimble like a mouse, and he could fit through even the narrowest of spaces.

Another was Zhenya, aka Deer, so called for his hunting

skills. He came from the region of Altai, in southern Siberia. His parents were scholars; his mother was an archaeologist or anthropologist, something like that. Deer was a normal guy, but when he got mad or didn't believe what you were telling him his eyes became two slits so narrow that they disappeared.

Then there was Spoon, whose real name was Roman. He was physically strong, a little wild in his way of doing things. He would eat whatever he came across; he was always hungry. He was originally from a remote village in the woods at the foot of the Ural mountains. He got his nickname because of his surname, which in Russian sounded very similar to the word 'spoon'.

Finally, there was big, bulky Aleksandr, who was from St Petersburg. Even though he was incapable of stringing together two words that made complete sense he always talked a lot, mostly about wanting to become a footballer (his nickname, in fact, was Zenith, from his favourite football team). He was our machine gunner, and he always carried his RPK 7.62-calibre gun. Nosov would joke that Zenith was 'Mother Russia's last shot'.

As for me, in Chechnya just as in Transnistria, everyone just called me Kolima. I was the sniper; I had to protect my comrades during transfers, participate in operations as a storm trooper, and find and eliminate the enemy snipers collaborating with other units.

In short, we of the 76th division were a group of men each cut to his own cloth, and despite the differences in age, background or social class, none of us ever felt alone. In fact, if I look back on it now, the only thing that truly helped us endure the war was finding in the others friends to lean on. Friends who strived every day with all their might to do the same thing you were doing: trying to stay alive.

We brought back trophies from every mission: the weapons and ammunition taken from the enemy. For this reason every saboteur had a couple of American and European guns, the most prized of which were the Colt .45 ACPs and their American clones. Having a weapon like that meant a lot; it meant that the person carrying it was a cutthroat, and commanded respect from the others. If a young soldier found a pistol like that, a senior soldier would swipe it from him, and thus the weapon would pass from hand to hand, until it wound up in the hands of the commanding officers.

The Austrian Glock and its variations, however, were the weapons of choice for conscripts and contract soldiers. People also liked CZs and other German guns. Among the terrorists, besides an unbelievable number of Russian-made firearms, like Makarov 9s, Stechkins and Tokarev 7.62s, European or American guns were always going around, generally ACP 45s, PARA 9s or 9x21s. I myself took a 9x21-calibre 98 Beretta FS from a dead man's body, a beautiful, very handy weapon, more precise and secure than Russian pistols.

The assault rifles, as I said, were modified. We also used drum magazines with a higher number of charges than usual, and we would tie normal magazines together so that when we ran out of shots we could replace them in a second.

The enemy's bayonets and knives were almost always American, and when we could we took them for ourselves. We liked those weapons a lot because they were useful and easy to handle, whereas the Russian bayonet seemed like a sort of universal tool you could use for anything – even plumbing, if you wanted – except close combat.

From the body of the first enemy sniper I killed, I took a Canadian-made knife designed for the American army. It was an all-black bayonet, nice, light, easy to carry and to hook to your belt. A year later, when I walked into a fight with a young Arab – our group was on a mission in a small city that we were liberating – that bayonet saved my life.

That one was a close call.

I was on reconnaissance in the basement of a city hall building. It was too dark to see anything, but all of a sudden I heard a noise. It was clear that the other guy had noticed my presence too. Shooting blindly, we used up our entire magazines without landing a single shot.

After that, the poor bastard threw a hand grenade, but it only made a terrible noise. With a heavy head and a constant whistling in my ears, I pulled out my bayonet and leapt into the dark where I thought my adversary was. We hit each other again and again; I hit him with the knife, while he tried to strike me with the butt of his empty gun.

When I finally made it out from underground, and my comrades brought out the man's body, I saw that I'd practically ripped him apart. He was missing a few fingers; his whole face was full of open bleeding wounds. I had even gouged out one of his eyes. I don't remember how I delivered the final blows, but on one side he didn't have a single centimetre of living tissue left.

My muscles were frozen with emotional exhaustion, and for a good half hour I wasn't able to open my right hand, the one that had been gripping the knife. It had been clenched so tightly it almost seemed as though an invisible hand were holding it shut.

Even if keeping the enemy's weapons was prohibited by Russian military law, we didn't care. As our captain would always say:

'If they want us to play their game, then they can at least let us use the toys we want!'

After I'd been with the saboteurs for a while, I realised that Captain Nosov had his own personal theory on war. It was based on his experience in Afghanistan; he often said that it was very similar to the war we were going through in Chechnya, because in the end the enemy was the same. His interpretation of the facts, when he commented on what happened during our operations, was decidedly anti-government. In short, as any Russian soldier worthy of the name would say – always ready to defend the nation's honour at all costs – Nosov 'whistled like a traitor'.

Our captain was convinced that the war in Chechnya was nothing but a farce, a performance that Russia had put on all by itself, making use of its friends in the Arabic world and even paying the mercenaries to fight against us. Since I had always kept my distance from political discussions, the captain's claims weren't always clear to me. His theories completely overturned my beliefs about the governing structures; Nosov often talked about the power of ex-KGB agents, asserting that somehow a group of veterans within our secret services had the Russian government under their thumb.

I was very curious and asked many questions, because I truly wanted to know what was going on, in this place I'd been thrown into. So the captain tried to explain everything to me in the simplest way possible:

'Look, to understand the reasoning behind this conflict you have to know how the "chaos-effect" works. I'll give you an example: you have a store full of delicious chocolates and a customer wants to buy them and take them home, but the law prohibits taking them away. They have to be consumed there, without leaving the store. But this guy knows a lot of other people who, just like him, want your chocolates, and they're all prepared to pay you any amount to be able to take them away and eat them on their own time, or maybe even sell them to someone else. However, the law against the consumption of chocolate outside the store isn't something you like either, because you're interested in selling as much as possible. At this point Moscow comes into play, who in our story takes on the role of a representative of the law. He's always there in your store, watching and making sure nobody takes any chocolate home. Obviously, you don't like Moscow either. Do you follow me so far?'

Although it was a rhetorical question I nodded, and Nosov went on with his story:

'So imagine that I come along and propose that you play a trick on Moscow. I send a couple of friends to your store, you send a few of yours, and one day our friends start a fight there. While they're beating each other up – they break some tables, a few old chairs and maybe even one of the windows – Moscow, as a good representative of the law, steps in to calm them down and tries to re-establish order. In that instant, I take all the chocolates I want from your store, pay you how much I owe and run away. Thanks to the chaos-effect, our dear friend Moscow didn't see a thing, and you and I got something out of it – and the next time, potentially, we can do it over again. The situation with the war in Chechnya is very similar, except that instead of you it's the leaders of the Arab community, who control the drug trade, human trafficking, gun running, petrol and so on. The chocolates, in other words. Instead of me there's the Russian secret service, who after the fall of the USSR took control of all illegal trafficking on national territory. Moscow, on the other hand, represents legal society, that is, the few who are still trying to somehow obey the law and have faith in institutions (this also includes the representatives of those countries that receive the traffic). And the idiot friends who come to fight in the store to trigger the chaos-effect are the Russian army and the mercenaries. The moral of the story is very sad; without realising it, we're creating chaos to divert attention from the serious things going on in this place. The war we're fighting is just a cover for the trafficking run by the corrupt people in the government.'

It's not as though I knew much about the trafficking, but, explained in this way, the situation seemed a bit clearer to me.

Another issue was the mercenaries in Chechnya. It seemed impossible to track down the primary financial backer behind the armed terrorist groups. It was often the Islamic religious leaders themselves, the imams, who would use their places of worship as storage depots or makeshift field hospitals for their wounded. But they were just small fry, the latest cog in a complex machine.

I remember that after one of these discussions I said to our captain, my face serious:

'Ivanisch, if you know that this war is wrong, if you really think it's a joke, then why do you keep on fighting in it?'

He looked at me with an astonished expression and said in a playful tone:

'Because I have nothing better to do. I'd be useless at home. The only thing I know how to do is war.'

After that remark, which for Nosov was clearly in jest, I reflected at length on how stupid we'd been, we Russians, over the course of history. For centuries we had pursued

various political ideas – often going against the natural
laws of humanity – only because we weren't able to get
out of the system, which kept us trapped inside a constantly
shrinking circle.

Just thinking about it made me want to run. But it was
physically impossible to cross the security lines that separated us from the other world, the peaceful world. And in
any case, that would have been suicide – the images of
military prison were still branded onto my mind.

THE PARA-BATS

My dear Mama, I'm writing you a letter:
'Hi mum, I'm good,
the sun is shining, everything's fine,
on the mountains as always there's fog . . .'
Mama doesn't know what we do on those mountains,
she don't know a thing about our troubles.
The years of our youth are spent
in the Caucasus, where there's always war . . .

The sound of bombs in the background, our brigade
    advances,
over there you can already hear the shots.
The sound of bombs in the background, the tracer
    bullets fly,
and the whole earth shakes from the cannons.
The helicopter goes off, and we must go on,
I hope you make it back, brother . . .
The helicopter goes off, and we must go on,
It'll be hard, and some'll never make it home . . .

Too young when we came here
to the Caucasus, where there's always war.
We'll never forget these terrible years,
and our friends left behind forever . . .
When we come back we'll sit down together,
and before our third glass we'll be silent.
The fallen in battle, the ones who made it home,
Now our souls are one . . .

Russian military song from the period
of the Chechen conflict

We don't need a soul, we've got blue berets instead,
we swoop from the sky like angels, with parachutes
    instead of wings,
we leap onto the ground like demons in battle,
we don't care about a thing, we just want victory . . .

From the Russian paratrooper anthem

There's fog over town, the ataman's smoking his pipe,
and his Cossacks keep drinking their vodka.
The sentinels curse, the osaul's dead drunk,
and the room's filled with the empty bottles.

And while the enemy's calm, the town celebrates,
we fill up with vodka, turn our nose up at death.
But if that bastard the enemy should harm our people,
the ataman, always first, will raise his sword high.

In the streets the accordion plays and the vodka flows,
the Cossacks will never tire of spirit—
'One litre, two litres, three litres, four . . . that's nothing, give
    us some more!'
But the little old ladies can hardly distil it any more.

And while the enemy's calm, the town celebrates,
we fill up with vodka, turn our nose up at death.
But if that bastard the enemy should harm our people,
the ataman, always first, will raise his sword high.

And when the war comes, when the enemy's near,
when his army wants to defeat us,
whatever they do will be pointless, we'll kill 'em all!
Sword against tank, the Cossack will go . . .

'The Cossacks' Song' by the rock group Gaza Strip*

---

* Young Russians love this group for their use of swearing; this song
is also popular among soldiers in the army.

We were supposed to get there at about eight in the morning.

The spot was a couple of tree-covered hills where three huge enemy groups had set up camp a few days earlier. Figuring out how many units those groups were composed of seemed impossible; the information was pretty vague and contradictory. Different numbers came from commanding headquarters on different occasions: first it was a matter of a thousand terrorists, then fifteen hundred, and finally almost three thousand. Every hour the number went up like we were at an auction. But one thing was certain: lots of them were Arabs and Afghans, poor people recruited to fight, almost all of them drug addicts. Before going to battle they would do so much heroin that, when they ran out of ammunition, they would shuffle up to our soldiers like a bunch of zombies, their arms dangling and their eyes bulging. Those poor guys had come so far just to fight us a couple times and then die so miserably.

Their leaders, though, were professional mercenaries who had fought in several wars – in Afghanistan, in the former Yugoslavia, in all the conflicts that the Muslim world had taken part in. They were cowards, they'd take those soldiers to the battle site completely high on drugs and then abandon them. Their only interest was organising direct encounters and then vanishing, taking off. The only thing they were capable of was throwing the clueless to the wolves and making a nice chunk of change off it, which – as our captain Nosov said – 'came straight from Red Square'.

But if those desperate men were in the hills it was because of a plan developed on the desk of one of the strategists at general command – after a month of intense fighting, our men had pushed them there. They couldn't move quickly because the mountains started just beyond the hills, and going through the valleys in large numbers would mean incineration by helicopter fire. Therefore, the only thing the Arabs could do now was try to escape, in small groups of fifty to sixty men.

At the same time, also thanks to the decision of some genius of military strategy, part of one of our units – about sixty men from the 72nd paratroopers – had been sent by night to the area to occupy a strange, pointless position on the side of one of the hills. They were young men from the latest draft, accompanied by about ten officers and expert sergeants; they had no reserve ammunition, but in exchange they had quite a burden on their shoulders – they carried their tents and coal stoves for camp like mules. Someone had decided to transport the heavy artillery and ammunition by helicopter, to lighten their load and allow them to reach their post as quickly as possible.

Yet even that midnight, as they were crossing the first hill, a group of scouts and paratroopers ran into an enemy group. They fought a series of short battles, but unfortunately couldn't retreat, because in the meantime other

Arabs had already blocked their way from the other side. Any subsequent change in position looked more and more like a hopeless attempt to flee – they had no choice but to run, and so at five in the morning they found themselves smack in the middle of the valley, in a small young wood, surrounded by at least two thousand of the enemy.

The gunfire lasted barely ten minutes, after which the paratroopers ran out of ammunition. The Arabs, however, kept shooting at our men with mortars and launching hand grenades repeatedly and ceaselessly (incidentally, as we realised later, amidst all the chaos some of their own men had been wounded by shrapnel from their grenades). The surviving paratroopers, in the desperation of the battle, jumped into an exhausting hand-to-hand fight, using the knives and small folding blades they had on them.

But the agony of our men didn't last long, and within half an hour they were all dead.

The signal reached us saboteurs at six in the morning. Some big shot in the paratroopers' command insisted that the ones to go down into those mountains and eliminate the first enemy group – which had a two-thousand man cover – should be us.

Our intervention was to serve as an 'opener' – it was just the start to a big operation. We had to go there by helicopter, block the pass in the valley and attack them by surprise. There was only one objective, and it was very clear: 'to eliminate all enemy human units', as our executive orders usually put it. According to the signal, the group we were to face had left for the valley that divided

the mountains and it included some professional mercenaries and commanders of military terrorist operations.
The leaders, to be precise.

Some men from the armoured infantry base, at the foot
of the mountains, were supposed to pick us up right after
the battle was over and then the paratrooper unit would
take care of the rest. In short, what they had in mind was
some sort of revenge.

None of us was keen on the idea of going to fight in
a place where there were two thousand enemies. We knew
how things had gone in the last few hours, and we hoped
that we wouldn't end up like the others – victims of a
strategical error on the part of our command. Every time
we had to work behind the front lines, in enemy-controlled
territory, we felt like we were playing Russian roulette.

The preparations were always the same; we had to check
our weapons, ready our jackets and fill them with ammo.
Usually each of us brought sixteen long magazines, four
or five hand grenades and a pistol with a few spare
cartridges. We never carried our guns on our belts, as is
usually done; we put them under our jackets at waist or
chest height, where we had hand-sewn a special pocket
ourselves. It was important to have our bodies free to run
and move without making noise. Before heading out, we
would always jump on the spot a few times or make a
few sudden moves, so we could tell if anything was loose
that could make a lot of noise at the wrong moment.

Our rifles were also modified to be as silent as possible when we moved. The first thing a saboteur had to do with his Kalashnikov was saw off the little iron hooks for latching the gun to his sling. Usually the metal parts kept touching and made a lot of noise – at night, especially in humid air, that noise could be heard up to twenty-five metres away. We used the classic Kalashnikov sling – or alternatively a mountain climbing rope, the ten millimetre ones – and wrapped electrical tape around it several times to attach it directly to the folding stock and the grip, which was plastic on the new models and wood on the old ones. The tape blocked all sound, and it was very resistant. In city battles, where you always needed to have your hands free and your rifle handy, we would often tape our Kalashnikovs right on our chests, against our jackets. I always wore my bulletproof vest wherever I went – it was like a sort of underwear. I even wore it to the bathroom, whether I was on base, with my comrades, or on a mission in the middle of the woods.

Once we were ready to go, we all sat in a circle and had a few minutes of silence. It's an old Russian tradition, called 'sitting on the road'. They say that before embarking on any journey, or beginning anything, carrying out this simple ritual brings good luck.

Later we would be transported to wherever our assistance had been requested. Many times, we jumped out of a plane, primarily at night – that's why our parachutes were black, and the other paratroopers called us 'bats'. At the end of a mission, attack, or any other military operation, to show the others that we'd been the ones who took care of the mess, we would draw a bat some-where. It was a kind of signature, a sign of recognition and valour.

The other military corps had symbols too; every wall in the cities where there had been battles was covered in tags, often along with messages. The soldiers expressed their feelings in sentences like: 'If I die, don't wake me up' or 'Once all my ammo's gone, remember me with kind words.'

In special operations, like ambushing nerve centres or freeing hostages, our captain would leave in plain view a white glove, which was part of the uniform saboteurs wore during military parades.

That time, Nosov explained the situation to us in detail, and he figured we could even capture a few hostages because, as he said:

'The guys up there' – that is our superiors – 'like to push around prisoners of war.'

We set off in two transport helicopters, plus an assault helicopter for protection from possible ground attacks. As a means of transport, helicopters, like everything in war, weren't very safe. There was always the danger that somebody could shoot off a flare and down it, even if they crashed more often because of mechanical problems than from enemy attacks.

We reached the spot at the prearranged hour, around eight in the morning. We found a group of night explorers and special infantry units waiting for us near the woods. They were all people ruined by war – they were very cruel, and after their operations you would often find among the bodies men who'd been tortured, their fingers or ears cut off; cases of violence against civilians were frequent. Within the infantry division, *dedovshchina* was extremely common, even during war; the older soldiers exploited the new conscripts and would force them to go through countless humiliations. This is the reason why the infantry has always had the highest amount of suicides and deserters — many of them can't stand the injustice, and they suffer more from that than from the reality of war.

As soon as we landed, it was clear to both groups that we would have to collaborate — the infantry, like the other units in the Russian army, weren't too fond of us. Other soldiers were always obliged to follow the orders given by any higher-ranking official, whereas we never were. This is why we'd clashed with the officers of other divisions many times, especially the younger ones who would give us orders that we never obeyed. Our freedom from military hierarchy wasn't liked by anyone.

As the first order of business, we set a trap for our enemies. According to command's predictions, the Arabs would arrive around nine-thirty. We covered the positions on one side, at the point where the valley narrowed, while on the opposite side two of our men placed the anti-personnel mines and fastened hand grenades to the trees. A string was stretched taut across the ground, and as soon as someone passed by and broke it the bomb would explode.

We still had half an hour to go before the enemy's predicted arrival, when our sentinels suddenly rushed back to us – we'd sent them to explore three kilometres ahead.

'The column is composed of sixty-three armed men,' said one of them, with extreme precision, 'and it's advancing very quickly.'

'We saw lots of mercenaries . . .' another added.

We were happy. Killing mercenaries meant taking home lots of trophies – American things and other various trinkets. The night explorers immediately started fighting over who would get to keep the hiking boots. Usually the Arabs wore boots produced in the West with high-quality materials, and every infantryman dreamed of having at least one pair.

The column moved along at a clip because they feared direct conflict and they wanted to get out of the area as quickly as possible.

I was positioned a little higher than the others, hidden behind a large tree, where I had established my line of fire. From that spot, the view of the valley really opened; I was able to survey almost a kilometre and a half of the area.

About fifty metres below me was the night explorers' sniper, a professional soldier with whom I had divided tasks – he would cut off the column from behind and I from the front; that way nobody would be able to escape.

The strategy we used was very simple, and, as far as I knew, had been perfected during the war in Afghanistan, against the Taliban. On one side of the space where the battle unfolds, it's open fire; on the other side, there are the mines. This way, the enemy is disorientated and he's forced to move away from the bullets to find a comfortable position and respond to the fire, but he steps on a mine and blows up. A mine causes a lot more damage than any other heavy weapon, because it's absolutely unexpected – a blow from a mortar or grenade launcher is very loud – and even if in the din of the gunfire it's hard for the untrained ear to tell one sound from another, if you're quick enough and hear the explosion, you can manage to avoid the worst.

For us snipers, chaos was the ideal atmosphere in which to work without being discovered. As long as the surprise-effect lasted and the enemy showed fear, we would knock down every subject that looked dangerous, like the ones with grenade launchers and heavy artillery, snipers, sharp-shooters armed with rifles that had optic and dioptric devices, the soldiers with equipment to communicate with the field, the expert commanders and mercenaries, easy to recognise from the superior quality of their dress, arms and ammo. Lots of Arab commanders loved the U.S. Marines' bulletproof vests, which were easy to spot from afar since they were less heavy and bulky than Russian ones. They always had the best weapons, usually 7.62x39-calibre AKS-47s, with American-made scopes or dioptric lenses mounted on top. They were always the first to hit the ground.

Sometimes, however, it wasn't so easy to push men onto the mines. Lots of them tried to turn around and run or would throw themselves forward. At first you had to concentrate your fire on the first and last in line, continuing to reduce the target range but being careful not to hit the people in the middle. This way, human instinct would take over − seeing others fall dead in front of them and behind them, the men would head for the opposite side of the road, and would end up on the mines. After a while, we would also aim at those remaining in the middle, and one after the other they would all set off our fatal traps. Stepping on a mine meant blowing up on the spot.

The mines we used were in part Russian-made, in part taken from the enemy. In the Russian army, it was hard to get anti-personnel mines for normal operations; according to regulations, it was supposed to be expert military strategists who mined an area following a specific plan, established with command. The use of mines or other explosive devices was defined as 'tactics of terror', and since the whole world knew that we were fighting against terrorists, we were supposed to be different from them. If any enemies blew up on a mine and command asked us for an explanation, we all said they'd been put there by the Arabs − nobody could say precisely who, when, or how it had been planted.

To avoid potential problems at the administrative level, all the units would take some of the mines planted by the strategists and keep them for when we would need them. We often bartered with officers or the soldiers who ran the explosives depot; they would give us some of their stuff − mines, bombs, grenades and other explosive material – and in exchange we would bring them the weapons we had taken as trophies.

Much later, when I was back home, I was watching television when I heard a correspondent talking about how the Chechen war had been fought.

He said that the Russian soldiers had scrupulously followed the moral principles of modern war, and that in our army the use of anti-personnel mines was officially prohibited, for any military operation.

If I think of all those mines we planted that went unexploded . . . Who knows how many people still risk stumbling onto our traps.

Back to that morning when we had to avenge our paratrooper comrades . . .

After we were all in position, hidden in the thick of the woods, the only thing left to do was wait. Our ambush was ready, and before long the enemy would come. The sentry had said that the column was composed of over sixty people, whereas there were only twenty-five of us, even counting the infantrymen and explorers. But we had the surprise-effect on our side, one of the most powerful weapons in military strategy.

The first to appear was a group of five scouts; they were Arabs with long beards. They looked hastily and distractedly to the sides of the path, and continued on without stopping. We let them pass and waited for the rest of the group.

Shortly afterward, no more than three hundred metres away, the column we'd been waiting for appeared. We gave the entire group enough time to enter the valley and then, as planned, our machine gun started shooting at the last ones in the row. Those machine guns were 'toys' to the night scouts – they were extremely powerful weapons, beasts that could shoot up to six rounds a second; the bullets were large calibre, capable of splitting a body as if it had been chopped in half with a giant axe. We only had a light 7.62-calibre RPK machine gun, manned by Zenith. As the Arabs began to move towards the mines, our machine gunner went to work on the rest of the group.

I followed right after Zenith's gun, aiming for the front of the line. In the first ten seconds, nobody responded to our fire; enemies fell to the ground one after another without having time to react.

Through the lens I saw human bodies disintegrate with the machine gun blasts – arms flew off, faces blew up; I shot at the torso, as they teach you to do with moving targets. After I hit them they would keep running for a couple metres and then suddenly drop, as if hit by a powerful gust of wind.

Then some of the Arabs took positions on the ground, shielding themselves behind their comrades' bodies, and started shooting at us. The bullets went just above our heads – they were experts, they aimed towards the shells from the precision rifle my comrade in the infantry was using. He had a weapon without a silencer, whereas I had an integrated silencer and the sound produced by my rifle was no louder than a handclap. People who have grown up in war-torn areas can hear and recognise every single noise. From a mere series of blasts at several metres' distance they can get a clear idea of the type and number of weapons, and are even able to figure out their location.

While some enemies were shooting, others began to retreat to the other side. After a few seconds the mines began to explode – two bodies dissolved instantly, sending up a little red cloud, as if their blood had turned to mist. Someone shouted something in Arabic, and everyone else who had been running towards the mined area halted in their tracks.

About twenty were still standing but they didn't know what to do. The machine gunners had let up and our guys with normal rifles took down the enemy with precise, targeted shots. One of them started to zigzag; they shot at him several times, following his moves, but he seemed able to dodge all the bullets, he was so fast.

Just then I heard Captain Nosov yell at me:

'Kolima, see him? Take him down, but don't kill him!'

So I used the basic technique for catching a moving target; I aimed my rifle on his path. Even if he continually changed direction from right to left, there was a constant in his movements because he always passed through the middle. I calculated where he would pass about ten metres ahead and waited. When the objective came into a quarter of my crosshairs, I pulled the trigger. The bullet hit him at leg height, blowing off a piece of his knee. He dropped straight to the ground, yelling and flailing his arms.

'Holy shit,' said Nosov.

Before making a move my comrades and I waited a little, looking around, but none of the enemies gave signs of life, except the runner. He was lying in a pool of his

own blood, and he was conscious. His backpack was
nearby, and he was trying to grab it to get his rifle, but
his movements were slow. That enormous hole in his knee
must have hurt like hell.

When we went down, the infantrymen went to inspect
the area of the massacre. Everything was soaked with
blood and dust; our steps were heavy because we felt a
swampy mass underfoot, like mud. There were body parts
everywhere – arms, legs, heads shattered like ceramic vases.

We realised that one guy had survived. Miraculously,
he was still alive and in one piece; perhaps when the chaos
broke out he had hidden and we hadn't caught him. Yet
even if he didn't have a single wound, he was completely
disorientated – he walked in circles around his dead
companions, disarmed, his hands raised towards the sky,
speaking in his language with a desperate tone. He wore
a military uniform with the insignia of one of the many
fundamentalist organisations involved in the war in
Chechnya; he had a long beard and a small cap completely
covered in medals, the kind that Muslims usually wear.
It struck me, because there in the woods among the corpses
he truly looked out of place. I sensed that it would have
been better for him if he were dead.

An infantryman seized him by the beard and with the
butt of a pistol smacked him in the face. He let out a cry
full of pain and fell to his knees, speaking in a feeble voice
full of humility. He was probably asking him to spare his
life. But the soldier kicked him again in the head with his
heavy boot, and the Arab was left on the ground.

That instant, a small digital videocamera fell from his

clothes. The soldier picked it up and tried to turn it on, but Captain Nosov started shouting.

'Soldier! Who gave you permission to touch the technical evidence or mistreat my prisoner?' Nosov was famous for picking fights with everybody; even the guys in the other units were afraid of him. The rumour was that no matter what he did he never got punished. He had fought in Afghanistan, and so for many he was a veteran worthy of the highest respect.

We ourselves had once been witness to a very personal event in his life. A young nurse, who worked on a base where we were temporarily stationed, just so happened to fall in love with him. When we transferred, as we saboteurs always did, the poor girl killed herself with an injection of morphine.

We hadn't heard anything about this story but one day, three months later – we were on the front lines, fighting in a small city – a young investigator came from the military law office. He delivered a letter to us and started asking questions about our time on the base where the nurse had worked. In particular, he was interested in finding out whether our captain and this woman had engaged in 'relations prohibited by military code'.

Obviously we all said we didn't know a thing, though someone recalled Nosov coming down with something while we were stationed on the base. So – we told the investigator – a nurse in fact did come to our unit, but nobody could remember her in any detail. The investigator asked a few more questions and then left, giving us the letter. We never saw him again.

We all went together to deliver the letter to Nosov right away, and the captain asked me to read it. Before taking her life, the woman had written that she couldn't imagine a future without Ivanisch. She called him a 'heartless man' and concluded by saying that he was 'as crazy as he was handsome'.

After I finished reading – the captain had remained stock still the whole time, without batting an eye – Nosov didn't do anything in particular. He looked at us for a moment and then whispered a single phrase:

'If someone is weak, they should stay home.'

At his officer's command, the soldier rushed over to our Captain, saluted him, and handed him the video-camera. A device like that must have been worth a lot, and for low-ranking soldiers could even present a risk. To prevent anyone killing them for it, officers would immediately take any object of value off their hands.

Nosov carefully opened the videocamera, turned it on, and after a few seconds called three of us over:

'Strays, take everything out of that piece of shit Arab's pockets and wrap it up for consignment. We're taking him home with us . . .'

He showed us part of the film. The Arabs had captured two of our paratroopers; one already half dead, the other seriously wounded in the stomach but still alive. One Arab said something incomprehensible, and all the others started yelling and chanting religious phrases. Abruptly, merci-lessly, one of them cut the heads off the paratroopers. Then they danced around with the heads in their hands, with our soldiers' lifeless bodies in the background. One came up to the videocamera and said something in their language. Then the video broke off.

Before tying up the Arab prisoner, we inspected him thoroughly. He had a small fabric bag hooked to his belt: inside there was a portable computer, a map with some notes and a series of Afghan and Russian passports, all with different names but various photos of the same face.

Nosov was satisfied.

'This time we got the good one . . .'

Meanwhile, the infantrymen took the shoes and other things that could be of use from the bodies. It was like being at an outdoor market – they kept shouting things like:

'Forty-six, boys, who wears a forty-six? I've got a good pair of shoes here, come and get 'em!'

'Help me cut open this bloody jacket – there's a Colt under there, I can see the butt but I can't get it off this fucking fatso!'

'Hey! I've got two full Beretta clips! Does anyone need them?'

'Fucking hell, this guy's shoes were practically new and even the kind I like – too bad our guns blew all these holes in them . . .'

'Guys! I have a cool designer* bayonet over here! Who wants to trade for a pair of shoes?'

In this way, in fifteen minutes the infantrymen had picked the dead clean, leaving them barefoot and unarmed. We'd made an agreement with the infantry;

---

* This was what we called military supplies – ammunition, weapons, clothing – that came from a foreign country.

since they were only rarely involved in operations like that and they needed shoes, guns and so on more than we did, they were free to take their trophies. They would leave us the rifles, scopes and infrared laser pointers, which the Arabs had in abundance, given that the United States systematically and with great generosity refurnished them with all the necessities.

We took the new Kalashnikovs to reinforce our equipment and put everything else in a pile with a hand grenade underneath, which would render the weapons completely useless. I kept for myself a Finnish-made precision rifle, equipped with an American scope and ten full cartridges.

When we were getting ready to go back to the base, Nosov went over to the guy I had hit in the knee. He was hardly moving. His face had gone white, he was losing a lot of blood and if it went on that way he wouldn't last much longer.

The captain looked at him with a wry grin and said:

'You had some fun here in the valley, huh?' He placed his foot on the wound, right where the white bone was poking out, and pushed down with brute force. The poor wretch shouted hopelessly, it seemed like he was going to explode from pain any moment. Nosov laughed softly, looking him right in the eye.

'Piece of shit Arab, you made a bad move coming here. They told you a load of crap about the Russians . . . You think that your people killed the infidels, right?' Nosov didn't raise his foot from the man's knee and his entire body was shaking. A dribble of dark spit trickled out of his mouth, as if he had eaten dirt. He didn't have the strength to scream, he just made a quiet moan, like the cry of a sick dog. The captain pulled his knife out of his jacket, and stroked it as he continued his speech.

'I know you think you're going to your nice little Muslim paradise now, but you can't be so naïve as to think that they'll let you in without you suffering a little here on earth . . .'

We had all realised that something truly horrendous was about to happen, but we were paralysed.

A young officer in the infantry, who seemed to be the most cruel of their group, stood there like a statue; open-mouthed, as still as if he had seen a ghost.

Nosov exposed the Arab's chest, ripping off his military jacket. The man stared at him without saying anything, his eyes bulging with terror.

'Thank goodness I'm here, always willing to help you good people, to oil the gates of the garden of your god. So when you finally open it, it won't bother you with its squeaking . . .'

Nosov bent over him; he put one knee on his chest, the other on his legs, then stuck the knife in his belly and began to cut.

The Arab howled so loud that his voice gave out soon after; he just let out a sort of prolonged, inhuman whistle, like a machine with metal parts grating against each other.

Our captain continued carving into his chest, accompanying his work with a song, a kind of saboteur anthem:

'A bayonet in the back, a bullet to the heart,
the wolves will pray for our souls!
The dead aren't warmed by triumph or glory,
Blood runs in our veins, the blood of the Russian,
today we will satisfy death, God forgive us!'

The louder the Arab wheezed, grimacing with pain, the louder Nosov sang, while he continued carving with patience and calm.

'Born and raised there, where the others will die,
that's why fate made us saboteurs!
The Motherland, great Russia, even she is afraid of us,
we are her true sons, for her we'd drown in blood,
but our hearts burn with true love!'

When he was finished, the captain got up slowly, and with a sadistic smile said to the rest of us:

'We were here, the saboteurs!'

The man's entire torso was skinless, from his navel to his neck. The Arab had lost consciousness, but you could see he was still breathing softly.

Next to him, on the ground, there was a layer of skin. Nosov had cut it in the shape of a bat, just like the ones we drew on the city walls.

The captain said to the infantrymen:

'Go ahead and take it if you want, keep it as a souvenir. That way you can tell everyone that at least one time in your pointless lives you knew some real men . . . Remember that being cruel doesn't mean cutting the noses or ears off the dead to make a necklace or a keychain . . . You don't rape women or beat children. Try to look your enemy right in the eye when he's still alive and breathing, that's enough . . . And if you have the balls to do something else, well go ahead . . .'

We said nothing, mulling over what had just come out of our captain's mouth. The infantrymen seemed frightened, some had stepped back, pretending they hadn't seen anything.

The silence that had fallen around that inhuman torture was broken by Shoe. With an almost indifferent and calm expression − as if he were on vacation − he proclaimed:

'Well, not too bad, Ivanisch, that bat almost looks real!'

A young officer from the infantry pulled his gun out of his holster and went over to the Arab, aiming at his head. Nosov gave him a dirty look.

'What are you doing, son?' he asked, calm.

'Enough, I can't take it − I'm going to kill him . . .' The officer was shaken up. His hand trembled as it gripped the weapon.

'This guy stays as he is,' Nosov yelled, 'and in fact I hope he lives till his friends get here . . . They think they're cruel? They don't know shit about cruelty! I'll teach them personally what it means to be cruel!'

Then he went towards the prisoner on whom we'd found the videocamera and the passports. He was all tied up, ready to come with us. Nosov grabbed him by the beard and dragged him over to his freshly skinned companion:

'Look, and look hard, Arab . . . You don't know who

you're playing with! Pray to your god that command is interested in you, otherwise I'll skin you alive and make my guys belts out of your hide!'

After about ten minutes, the helicopters came. We jumped on while the infantrymen stayed behind, waiting for two special infantry units to close off the valley.

We headed back to base, tired and loaded with useless stuff as usual, this time with an Arab prisoner to boot, who, while we were up in the air, suddenly started to cry.

Moscow, feeling sorry for him, gave him some water to drink, and the captain smiled.

'Give him a drink; I'm sure his throat is all dry . . . What a shitty day, boys, surrounded by a bunch of homos . . .'

When we got to base, there was already a delegation waiting to pick up the prisoner.

Captain Nosov spoke to the colonel while his men loaded the Arab onto another helicopter. The colonel called Nosov 'son', and the captain called him 'old man'; you could tell that they were buddies.

The colonel said:

'The infantrymen complained, saying that you made a bloodbath, you tortured a prisoner . . .' He wasn't at all angry; he spoke with a mixture of complicity and irritation.

Nosov, as always, was playful and in good spirits:

'You know how they are, old man, those guys shit

themselves as soon as they get wind of an Arab . . . They need to be shown that we're the dangerous ones – they should be afraid of themselves, not those ignorant, incompetent, drugged-out religious fanatics . . .' Whenever he spoke, Nosov had a mysterious power; his words carried a strange certainty. The colonel thought for a moment, and then, smiling, clapped a hand on his shoulder:

'Son, you'd certainly know better than anyone else. But remember, if anything ever happens, I'm always here . . .'

As the helicopter ascended, the colonel smiled from the window and waved. Then he made a sign on his chest, as if he were drawing our bat with his finger. Still smiling, he clenched his fist, as if to say 'Keep it up!' We all broke out in big grins and waved back at him, as if he were our own grandfather who had come to visit us.

I thought a lot about what happened that day. Sometimes I regretted not having killed that poor man I'd shot in the knee. But later, after some time had passed, I came to understand the insane logic that guided our captain's actions, and I realised that, yes, it was true that he made some extreme decisions, but he did it so that we could keep fighting the war the way we did.

We owed our reputation to Nosov's great skill in handling complex situations well in the face of the realities of war.

And if his choices didn't always conform to human morality, it was only because they reflected the horror and the difficulty we endured every day in the war, trying to stay alive, strong and sound.

FIRE ON US

. . . for this offensive special commitment is required of the soldiers and officers in the assault units and of all the active units on the front lines. Given the high priority of this operation, the nature of the task does not call for the capture, arrest or transport of terrorists or any other member of an illegal armed group. All human units who pose a threat or cause difficulty in carrying out orders during direct combat must be physically eliminated; whatever weapons or ammunition they may have must be destroyed on the spot or used by the active units to carry out the received order. Any form of communication with representatives of illegal armed groups is prohibited, as with civilians or any individual who does not belong to the units working in the area. Respond to any requests from terrorists for medical aid, negotiation, conversation, or unexpected offers to surrender to the law of the Russian Federation with gunfire.

Part of the order transmitted via radio to all the units involved in the offensive in the city 'N' in the Chechen Republic, 1999

Pummel, throttle, crush . . .

A favourite saying of General Aleksei Yermolov*

---

* Charismatic nineteenth-century Russian nationalist and representative of imperial tsarism in the Caucasus. He applied a policy of terror and repression towards the Caucasian peoples, especially those of the Muslim faith, forcing them with violence to adopt Christianity.

If you only knew what a friend I lost in battle . . .
It happened not forty-two years ago, but just the other day . . .
In the middle of the mountains, in the sand, where the
    heat burns all,
      sparking my memory, now far away from youth . . .
Can you hear me, my friend?
My dear friend, in the end we were able to climb,
climb to that height that cannot be measured in words,
under which you fell . . .

What a friend I lost in battle . . .
As kids we would read war stories,
he certainly couldn't have imagined
I would have to drag his body behind the rocks . . .
Thirty metres away, only thirty metres,
but how far that road was, between night and day . . .

Sand and stone,
sad light of the unknown moon over our heads.
Honour to the flag!
Farewell my friend, you will be with us forever more.
Forgive me, you were killed and I was only wounded,
in the Afghan mountains, in Afghanistan.

If you only knew what a friend I lost in battle . . .
The damned dust filled our eyes,
and our BTR was in flames,
in the sky, like a dragonfly, the helicopter circled
and like voices from the past, everywhere you could hear
    shouts of 'Go!' . . .
Like a nerve, he broke like a painfully stretched nerve,
and from the slope straight towards him a bullet took
    flight . . .

Sand and stone,
sad light of the unknown moon over our heads.
Honour to the flag!
Farewell my friend, you will be with us forever more.
Forgive me, you were killed and I was only wounded,
in the Afghan mountains, in Afghanistan.

Song by singer-songwriter Alexander Rozenbaum,
dedicated to the veterans of the war in Afghanistan

And even if we don't yet know the sweet touch or allure of a
    woman,
even if we've never experienced the pleasant torments of love,
at the age of eighteen we're already used
to gun fights,
to bloody battles that never end,
and we know exactly what it means
to cross the line of fire.

Those days blazed, those nights went up in smoke,
and death flew through the air, laughing and touching us all.

We don't want any honours or promotions,
we've already got what we need to feel worthy.

*From the song of the Russian army veterans who
were involved in the Chechen conflict*

One morning — really early, it must have been four a.m. — Moscow woke me up. My comrades and I had slept in the courtyard of a half-wrecked building in a public housing district on the outskirts of the city. We'd been embroiled in a series of bloody skirmishes with the enemy for days. My group and I had been fighting on the front lines but luckily we were all still in one piece. We hadn't taken any losses, but we were dead tired.

It seemed like the battle was never going to end. Every second was crucial, every action was important and required great concentration, and at the end of the day we felt like juiced oranges. During battle, we had a clear objective: to push the enemy to the other end of the city, where the armoured infantry units were waiting to eliminate all of them . . . It was an exhausting task, and Captain Nosov had given us permission to take a break, to go behind the line to rest amidst the rubble, in the area guarded by our infantry.

Before falling asleep, some of us said that maybe the mission was over; we were all hoping we wouldn't have to set foot in that godforsaken city again. Then, sleep came.

A little while later — at four, as I said — Moscow woke

me up by tapping my chest with the butt of his Kalash-nikov.

Slowly and reluctantly I opened my eyes and looked around. I struggled to remember where I was. I couldn't put anything into focus.

'What's going on, how long did we sleep?' I asked Moscow, my voice worn-out.

'We didn't sleep for shit, brother . . . And it doesn't look like we'll be going back to sleep any time soon.'

The order from command called us back to the front line in the northeast area of the city, where a cluster of enemies had got through a breach in our ring of troops. They had American-made armoured cars, off-road vehicles, and they were equipped with heavy weapons: grenade launchers, 120mm cannons and a pair of multiple launch rocket systems called 'Grad', which is Russian for 'hail'. That night those bastards had attacked the weakest point in the ring – the Arabs, besides being numerous and well armed, had surprise-effects of their own. Nobody had expected a move like that; usually the cities where operations took place were surrounded so that the enemy couldn't get out. We had never seen anyone trying to come in to take part in the battle.

This event caused an immediate scandal. Command was furious. The infantry had been given orders to contain the attack, but manpower was limited and they had no heavy artillery to back them up. They managed to retreat without too many losses, and this in itself constituted a good outcome. The helicopters came late, after the greater part of the enemies had already infiltrated the city. Firing from the sky, our men had only managed to take out the tail end of the group.

The security service was supposed to answer to superior command about how the enemy had been able to approach without being seen . . . For the moment, however, the only ones paying the price for that extremely grave military error were our boys on the front line, who were losing their hides out there.

As they entered the city, the enemy tried to split up our troops, but our men held strong, so the Arabs targeted a district in the northeast under infantry surveillance. The infantry was forced to change positions quickly because they were suffering numerous losses and had taken cover in a building, effectively trapping themselves. As a matter of fact, the enemy had managed to surround the building and then ceased fire, waiting for our men to wear themselves out and use up all their ammo.

The troops that had fought the Arabs as they entered the city attempted another attack, yet due to the darkness and the enemy's powerful defences, they retreated too, and had many losses. At that point they were waiting for the paratroopers and special forces, which included us saboteurs. With the infantrymen surrounded by the enemy, we kept in constant radio contact. Their situation was tough, ammo was running out – to them, every minute seemed to last an eternity . . .

As Moscow explained, we were going to help out with

the counterstrike, which was planned for six in the morning.

Just two hours away.

This whole mess had begun four days earlier. We got to the city after the operation had already started, and as we got closer to the fighting I realised that the site we were headed for was a real bloodbath. A 'triple ring' of our troops had closed off some areas of the city. No one could come out; everything was all ready for the artillery unit to do their job. But they couldn't go ahead with the offensive, because according to the information from the explorers who'd gone ahead, the concentration of civilians was too high. Dropping bombs and missiles would cause a massacre.

The situation was deadly serious – city battles are among the bloodiest and most unpredictable, but when there are civilians in the mix it turns into a big meat grinder, and everyone loses all sense of what they're doing.

The infantrymen had come in with two explorer groups. They were just past the first district when direct combat broke out. The infantry, detached from the main forces, handled the first skirmishes, neutralising the nerve centres where troops were concentrated. We came in after the motorised infantry platoon (even if there was nothing platoon-like about them but the name – in reality it was only three groups, a hundred and twenty soldiers on twelve light tanks), followed by two special units armed with light 120mm cannons.

Our job was to attack the most resistant positions, neutralise the snipers, and as official orders from general command said, 'secure the quality of the movement of the main troops and support the liberation and transfer of the civilian population into the federal territories'. We had a support team behind us – the special paratrooper assault unit called 'Thunder'.

Their unit, just like ours, was completely independent. They travelled in armoured cars and had about ten tanks. They were perfect cut-throats, true assassins – wherever they went, they always wreaked havoc.

We saboteurs, on the other hand, travelled in a BTR armoured personnel carrier, also known among the soldiers as a 'coffin', because its thin armour often got pierced in battle, even under fire from a mere Kalashnikov. To survive a surprise attack it was important to travel on top and not inside; at the first sign of gunfire you could jump off the car and take a defensive position. In the city, however, the BTR had its advantages; having wheels and not tracks, it moved faster and handled better than a regular tank.

We had two of our own drivers; they were hotheads, pros who would have taken us to hell and back without batting an eye. The older one had been in Afghanistan, and he told us that even though he had nearly burned to death in the BTR many times, he had never left it in the road – he'd always managed to get back to base, even with the wheels in flames.

*

According to commanding orders, we were supposed to use a strategy called 'passive advance'. The units enter the city one at a time, occupy a position other than their own and then defend it until another group comes to take over. Then they advance, gradually approaching their actual combat position. Our objective was to reach the 'line of fire', but we had to cross half the city to get there; we would stay in constant radio contact with command. This strategy is particularly effective in urban combat, because even at the most difficult and dangerous points it ensures the creation of a safe zone, which is invaluable for the assault units who always need to be restocked with weapons, to stay connected to the support troops and have a path for transporting the wounded.

When we entered the city the first skirmishes were already over. We went through streets full of dead Arabs and Afghans, with the bodies of some of our infantrymen and a few civilians. Many civilians came out from cellars or other hiding places and ran in the direction we were coming from. These were simple people who had lost everything. Their life was an endless nightmare; the way these people lived – or rather, *subsisted* – in war was terrible.

From the start of the First Chechen Campaign, the civilians hadn't seen a single day of peace. Those who weren't able to flee to Russia or the nearby republics, like Dagestan, Ossetia or some other place, had been forced to witness the sad spectacle of two armies destroying their homes, killing their families, and making their existence a hell on earth. Each of their faces was marked by signs of fatigue and a fatal indifference towards everything.

In war, the living made more of an impression on me than the dead. To me, the dead looked like a bunch of receptacles that someone had used and then thrown away – I looked at them as I would broken bottles. Whereas the living – the living had this horrible emptiness in their eyes: they were human beings who had seen beyond madness, and now lived in the embrace of death.

It was terrible to see old people with children in their arms running in the opposite direction as we marched by, without stopping for a second or turning around. Our paras showed those people the way out, gave them some food even if they had very little, since they were assault troops and only carried their weapons and the minimum needed for survival. Some civilians would take the food and recount what they had gone through during the terrorist siege; others would reveal where the snipers were and wish the soldiers luck. There were many people in tears, hysterical, desperate.

At one point a woman appeared, filthy and with a tangle of hair on top of her head as if it had exploded; in her arms she was holding a little baby covered in blood. The woman walked towards our car with crazed eyes, shouting, asking for help. When she was a few metres away, I could see that the baby had been dead for some time. Her belly was split open, a big black hole that the mother had tried to plug up with torn pieces of rags and sheets. I felt horrible.

Nosov yelled to the civilians:

'Someone help her for the love of God! Take her out of here, or she could get run over!'

A pretty girl emerged from the crowd. From the look of her she seemed Chechen. She put her arm around the woman and said gently:

'Let me hold your baby, let me have her for a while, so you can rest. We still have a long way to go . . .'

The mother gave the baby's body to the girl, who took that blood-encrusted corpse and hugged it in her arms as if it were still alive. Only then did the woman move away from our cars and return to the line, and as she walked she repeated mechanically:

'We have to find a doctor, when we get out of here, we have to find a doctor for my baby . . .'

Our captain looked at each one of us. We tried to appear calm, but the tension was evident. We couldn't wait to throw ourselves onto the line of fire.

'Relax, boys, relax. We'll get to them very soon . . .' His words were full of contempt – it sounded as if he'd spat them out. It spurred us on. Maybe because he was able to transmit his rage in a dignified way, putting into words the emotions we all felt.

Once a medical officer said something about Nosov that, when I thought about it later, really seemed true, right on the mark. I was at the hospital where I had gone for treatment after my first wound. The friendly surgeon and

I were discussing the likelihood of making it out alive from this bloodbath we'd ended up in. I was complaining, saying that it took a lot of luck not to get hurt in war, and then he said to me:

'If you want to save yourself, friend, you have to do what your captain did.'

'What do you mean?'

And, smiling, he said:

'All you have to do is marry the war, love her, and she'll love you forever . . .'

Personally, I wasn't so worried about facing the enemy. What really tormented me was the reality of the situation. No matter how many Arabs I killed, I knew I couldn't change the fate of the war, or of any one of us.

Our column advanced quickly. The battle was getting closer and closer – there was the constant sound of machine gun fire, hand grenades blowing up, grenade launchers being shot . . . A disorientated group of enemies would pop up here and there – we killed them without even getting off the cars. The heavy guns on the turrets took care of them. Like rats gone berserk they ran in every direction; they hid in the houses, but none of us went after them – we left them to the infantry, we couldn't lose time on them. A real battle awaited us further on.

Meanwhile command kept sending directives over the radio, keeping us apprised of the situation. Just when we were almost at the line of fire, three more orders came, one after the other. First they told us to join up with a paratrooper unit poised to penetrate the defence in one area, but we had no support. The order was immediately cancelled because in the meantime the paras had come across a group of explorers and infantrymen and had already taken positions to break through the line, so we were no longer needed. A second later we heard that the affected area had been attacked and breached by the 102nd paratrooper division, who were on the road. The third order – to advance and wait for exact coordinates – came when we were at the line of fire. The battle was right there in front of us, we would find our men along on the road, busy defending the positions they'd occupied in civilian buildings and homes.

We had to drive through a small public housing district. All the buildings were destroyed, and our support units had set up an emergency hospital right there in the ruins, plus a few distribution centres for food and weapons.

I passed through that district, filled with our infantry and medics going to and fro, each with a specific task, and I felt like I had gone behind the set of a theatre. On stage the show went on, while in the wings there were many people working, putting something big into motion, something very important that many people placed even above their own lives.

A guy in a medical unit uniform asked us if we had enough medication. He was holding a box full of individual medical kits. We only had one kit for each of us, so Nosov told him:

'Sure, son, toss a few over, you never know . . .'

The skinny kid threw ten medi-kits, held together with a rubber band, over to our car. Then he yelled:

'Lots of snipers on the roofs, too many . . . watch out for the snipers on the roofs!'

Nosov grabbed the first aid kits and replied:

'Thanks, kid, and if there are snipers that's too bad for them . . . We've got a Siberian sniper with us!'

Then Moscow, giving me a hard tap with his shoulder, yelled to the medic:

'Hey, man, you know how they shoot in Siberia? They can hit a squirrel in the eye from three hundred metres away!' Everyone burst out laughing, making faces at me, since I was the centre of attention.

The only thing I was thinking at that moment was not coming to the same end as that Siberian squirrel . . .

It was true, the most dangerous people in urban combat were the snipers. If an expert marksman learned how to act, move, hide – and was fast and patient enough – he became the perfect assassin and could even change the course of a battle. One of my tasks during combat was to locate and neutralise these sorts of dangers. It wasn't easy – even locating a sniper's position required weeks of preparation, lots of work, camouflage, exhausting waits. All this just to fire a single bullet. But the shot had to be precise and definitive.

Mercenaries from various countries were recruited as

snipers, lured by the good pay. I often encountered Ukrainian, Lithuanian, Estonian snipers, very competent marksmen from the former Soviet Union sports scene. They could shoot with precision, but many lacked the basics of military strategy. My hunting education in the forests of Siberia, which I received as a boy from my grandfather Nikolay, turned out to be extremely useful, and I learned everything else at training camp thanks to Yakut, the Siberian instructor I mentioned earlier.

The snipers were the lords of the battle. In my experience, anything was preferable to going up against another sniper, because I could never be sure what I was dealing with.

We stayed there for a few minutes, just standing on the line of fire. Nosov made two requests for orders via radio, but command didn't know where to send us – it seemed that our men were making progress on every front, and help from the saboteurs was no longer needed. After a while, they finally gave us some coordinates – we had to go to a building where our infantry were outnumbered and undergoing a series of violent attacks from the enemy.

We rushed over to the location: a large, five-storey building, half-burned out and full of broken furniture. Through the shattered windows – and through the holes in the walls from mortar rounds and cannon balls – you could see bits of paper flying through the air like ghosts stirred by the wind.

Our infantrymen greeted us with camaraderie, the only thing that truly unites all soldiers, especially at the toughest times. Their lieutenant had a shoulder wound, and even though his soldiers kept telling him to take cover in the cellar, where the other wounded soldiers were, he went on fighting in the battle anyway. In fact, he was shooting as if he weren't injured at all, and gave orders to set up the defence, addressing his men with professionalism. He was young, he couldn't be over twenty-five, but you could tell he had already 'smelled the gunpowder', as we would say. The infantrymen listened to him and obeyed him like a father; there was a very familial atmosphere in their unit.

First off, Nosov gave him some advice on how to plan the resistance:

'We need to concentrate forces on the sides of the building and leave the middle free.'

The lieutenant agreed, and we all took strategic positions, keeping watch over not only the building itself and the space in front, but also the three roads that led directly to the area occupied by the terrorists.

At four in the afternoon the enemy troops began moving towards us. Gunfire had become very intense in the left wing of the building, where our captain was; a young infantryman, their gunner, was dead – a bullet had gone through his skull.

Nosov recognised the enemy's tactic. They were trying to provoke fighting in one spot in order to gain free access from the opposite side. Next door there was an abandoned house, and if we didn't stop them they would make it a fortified position. Nosov called me to organise a sortie. In a room on the second floor with windows overlooking the courtyard – a big open space with a few trees and bushes, behind which were two of the infantry's light tanks – we had a quick huddle. Nosov said:

'They're definitely going to put something in that house, maybe a heavy machine gun. And once that thing starts working on us, they'll hit us with the grenade launchers too . . .'

'We could beef up our defence with another machine gun on the third floor, and then concentrate the fire on them,' the lieutenant proposed.

'That won't work, we'd only drag it out . . .' Nosov retorted, serious. 'If they have a machine gun, and I'm sure they do, after a few hours of direct fighting they'll realise that we don't want to attack their positions, and they'll call reinforcements to break our defence . . . These people are desperate, our paras are hunting them down.'

So the young lieutenant asked:

'What do you have in mind?'

Nosov had a half smile on his face, which we all knew very well. It meant that he'd already come up with a plan, which (as he would always say with conviction) would work one hundred per cent. In fact, he replied:

'I've already come up with a plan, which will work one hundred per cent . . . You and your boys keep responding to the fire from the left side of the building, but don't shoot at the house next door. Actually, act like you've completely given up on that position. My guys and I will cross the street, shadowing the fence at the back of the building. We'll come through the rear, where there's the curve that goes right to the side of the house . . . If they're there like I think they are, we'll get rid of them and go back to the main road – no doubt some of them will come after us, so your boys'll have to cover us, otherwise we'll lose our hides . . .'

The lieutenant looked at us for a second, trying to figure out if our captain was joking or not. We were already getting ready, removing all the inessentials so we could run faster, and when he saw that we were serious, the lieutenant, a spark of daring in his eyes, said:

'Then let's do it, boys! God bless us!'

We headed out behind our captain.

Usually in city operations we were only armed with Kalashnikovs, each of us always having a couple on him. I had two rifles: a VSS, which I kept slung at my back along with five clips for a total of fifty rounds, and my trusty AKSM, which I carried by hand. This was the paratrooper assault rifle, a model with a short barrel, reinforced compensator, folding stock and dioptric sight, the one with the red dot that we jokingly called 'Lenin's lamp'. This time, however, the operation was particularly dangerous, and Nosov had also brought along a loaded grenade launcher, plus a backpack with another three rounds. Two of our men had 7.62-calibre submachine guns.

We were all wearing light jackets, with jumpsuits underneath, trainers on our feet and no helmets on our heads, just regular beanies. Mine was grey with a pom-pom on top. The other units made fun of us, calling us 'bums' since we wore whatever we came across. Obviously it bothered them to have to wear uniforms; they would rather have been able to do as we did – when it was hot we could wear shorts. None of us shaved, we all had goatees or at least a few days' stubble, and we often kept our hair long. By our looks we were more likely to be taken for a group of terrorists than a unit of the Russian Army. We did it on purpose, obviously, because we often ended up going behind the line and having to blend in with the enemy, even though every so often one of our own shot at us, thinking we were Arabs.

We slowly walked across the courtyard, which the infantry was watching over. The dead bodies of enemies were left on the side of the road. We sprang over to the fence. We could hear the infantry shooting as well as the Arabs, who were attacking the left side of the building. The road made a curve that would lead us to the house, our objective.

From there, however, we could see that two hundred metres ahead, right in part of the yard where our troops were, another group of enemies was hiding behind a half-charred armoured car, shooting now and then at our soldiers.

'Let's cross the road without firing,' Nosov said. 'One of you cover, everyone else run.'

I positioned myself to cover the others. My comrades hunched down and sprinted almost on all fours, and when they had all reached the opposite side of the road I followed. Together we went behind the trees, and then emerged in front of a small building, some kind of old bar, from inside which we had a clear view of the house.

We stopped in the bar to figure out whether there was movement around the house. Nothing happened for fifteen minutes; nobody came, every so often in the distance we saw enemies running over to the building occupied by the infantry. The lieutenant's men shot a few rounds at them, a few Arabs fell to the ground lifeless. A group of enemies continued moving about in a seemingly chaotic manner: they came out into the open clearly with the intention of attracting the infantry's attention, shooting blasts of fire at them almost randomly, without aiming, then going back to shelter.

The captain commented:

'They think they've really got us – look how they're jumping around, they look like mountain goats . . .'

We kept quiet, waiting. At a certain point, however, the situation around the house changed. Two blacks, Africans, came up to the building shouting. One went inside and started kicking in all the doors. More men popped out from a road carrying a heavy machine gun and a cylinder grenade launcher, an American-made weapon. Another little group followed them, carrying the cases with the cartridges, protected by men armed only with Kalashnikovs.

The two black men almost started arguing at the entrance, without being afraid of being hit; sure they were safe behind the house. One of them motioned towards the street and was saying something, the other guy was yelling.

Nosov said:

'Boys, at my signal . . .'

We readied our rifles, aiming at the targets. The captain settled the grenade launcher on his shoulder and went to the window. My comrades stepped away from him so they wouldn't get burned when the grenade exploded.

'Fire!'

In an instant, the spot where the two black men had been arguing had become a hole in the pavement. Meanwhile we had taken down, one by one, almost the entire group. Not expecting an attack from our direction, those poor devils hadn't even been able to make a move. Only one volley of bullets reached us, but it went too high and immediately drowned in our fire, as violent as a hurricane.

The cases with the clips began to explode one after the other, making a racket.

'Let's go back, before they all get here!' shouted Nosov.

We went out from the bar and ran across the main road to the building. From the third-floor windows came the volley from our machine gunners to cover the area behind us, as we had arranged earlier.

Suddenly Nosov stopped in the middle of the street, and amidst the shouts and shots of the enemy – who had seen us and was fast approaching – launched a grenade at the armoured car where the Arabs were hiding. The car blew up, then I opened fire on the enemy, and Moscow and Shoe joined in. In the meantime, Deer and Spoon had already reached the building, and together they fired from the second-floor window. Zenith had taken cover by the building's entrance, and from there opened fire with a grenade launcher hooked to his Kalashnikov, hitting one man full on – we saw bits of his body go flying. Nosov started running again and in a moment we were all back in the building. The infantrymen were looking at us like we were crazy.

As always, our captain asked:

'Everyone in one piece? No holes?'

We were all down on the floor, trying to catch our breath. To be able to answer Nosov, first we had to figure out what our status was, check to see if there was anyone injured or anything. A bullet had split the sole of my shoe, right at the heel. I slipped it off with my knife and showed it to the others.

'For the love of God, Kolima, stop playing these jokes . . .' Spoon said to me, smiling, and everyone started laughing.

Just a few centimetres further up, and that bullet would have hit my ankle.

From that moment on, the battle was like a volcanic eruption. The Arabs, after having lost the machine gun and grenade launcher, were furious and started throwing themselves on our position almost hysterically, attacking repeatedly without stopping even for a second. Fortunately the infantrymen were 'well dressed', as we would say when someone was armed to the teeth; they had three machine guns and every single hole in the wall under surveillance.

We took positions on the second floor. With two other machine guns, my comrades had emptied four cases, ten thousand rounds, in half an hour. I took out three snipers who were trying to climb onto the roof of the nearby apartment building; one of them, before I was able to pinpoint him, had seriously wounded one of the infantry sergeants, hitting him right in the chest. Unfortunately, he died two hours later in his comrades' arms, down in the cellar where there were another seven wounded.

In the subsequent four hours, after nightfall, there was nothing to indicate the presence of live Arabs. The whole street in front of the building was filled with bodies; everywhere you looked you saw nothing but corpses. None of our men shot anymore, and you couldn't hear anything in the vicinity either.

We arranged rest shifts, while some ate and others stood guard. I was able to close my eyes for an hour or so. Hearing only the voices of the guys rehashing the details of the various battles or talking about their families, the houses they were born and grew up in, all the conversations blended together in my head . . .

When I got up I took over from Moscow, and he instantly plopped down on the empty crates of machine gun clips; he was asleep in seconds. I drank a broth made with bouillon with some dry black bread and pieces of stew from the American cans of preserved meat that our men had found on the Arabs.

Nosov was telling a story. I had missed the beginning

because I had gone out into the yard to relieve myself, but it was something about a personal experience of his in Afghanistan. Everyone was listening raptly, and he spoke gently, remembering the men who had been in that war with him, every so often adding a fond phrase like 'May his be the kingdom of heaven' after someone's name . . .

At some point, on the road in front of the building – making a terrible noise as the bodies of the dead were swept aside – about ten armoured cars and light tanks arrived. It was our paratroopers, and they were about to make another advance into enemy-controlled territory.

They asked us to come along. We gathered our things promptly, waking Moscow and the others who were sleeping. We said a quick goodbye to the infantrymen, with whom we had fought very well. We jumped onto our BTRs and were on our way to the line of fire yet again.

The young infantry lieutenant and some other guys from his unit appeared at the third-floor window. As he had done earlier that afternoon, the lieutenant shouted:

'Good luck, boys! May God bless you and forgive you!'

We waved goodbye, although we couldn't see them in the dark, and Spoon replied:

'God willing, we'll see each other again, brothers!'

Our car went after the column of paras.

*

In the dark, the city looked like a cemetery. No lights, no movement – the only things visible were the yellow headlights of our armoured cars illuminating the road. The sound of our engines made us sleepy, but we had to stay awake.

I looked up and the sky seemed empty, everything seemed empty. I felt abandoned, alone, trapped in a godforsaken place from which there was no possibility of return.

As we approached the line we could hear the sounds of the battle. The skirmish seemed really serious: heavy machine gun blasts, grenade launcher shots, tank cannon blasts . . . Our order was to be as careful as possible; we were in full battle mode. But I felt like I was going to pass out from exhaustion. After all the shooting, my head kept feeling heavier and heavier.

We had fought for two days without pause. Sometimes by ourselves, other times with the paras or infantry explorers, who didn't even have time to retreat before they had to keep up the defence in other areas. We had pushed ourselves so hard without ever really resting. Sometimes during transport we were able to get a few minutes of shuteye, just to fool our bodies into thinking they had slept a little.

Our infantry had sustained many losses; the enemy was fighting with desperation, because they knew there was no way out. The streets our cars went through were filled with bodies, the houses were crumbling under cannon fire – in the midst of that chaos it was impossible to coordinate ourselves. The paras accidentally opened fire on the infantry units twice, killing a few of our own.

By that point the end was near; the battle for the liberation of the city was becoming increasingly fierce. You could feel the hate, fear and death in the air. Everyone was exhausted; many were overtaken by fits of rage, even the simplest of conversations became a form of violence. Everyone's nerves were at breaking point, and I was seriously on the verge of losing it.

As we were going down a road where the paratrooper assault units had just finished a battle, I saw an American-made armoured car in flames. Black smoke rose from the tyres, and the internal mechanisms made soft popping noises, like when coffee boils on the stove.

On the front of the car, on the windscreen, wire-bound to the chassis like Christ on the cross, there was a bare-chested Arab covered in blood. His face had been completely skinned: you could see the muscles and bones; the eyes, big and round, seemed made of glass. On his head he wore a blue beret with the paratroopers' insignia, and a battle knife had been stuck between his teeth, affixed to his jaw with the wire. Someone had taken a big strip of cardboard from the boxes of food rations and hung it around his neck, then used his blood to write: 'Allah isn't great, 'cause he has no blue beret.' Beneath there were the names and nicknames of some of the paras who had fallen in the battle.

Passing that tremendous sight, the paras who were with

us in the column stood on top of the cars, removed their berets and saluted their fallen friends, shouting their beloved slogan in unison:

'Angels in the sky, demons on the ground!'

Torturing prisoners was prohibited by military regulations, and according to the law any perpetrators of such an act were to be tried in court and at a minimum sentenced to serve in military prison. Of course, I've never heard of any of our men who had tortured or disfigured prisoners' bodies being reported or turned over to the authorities.

Once, our paras, in a town that had just been liberated, captured an Arab; after cutting off his nose and ears, they gouged out his eyes and filled the sockets with gunpowder. Not content with that, they kicked his arms until they were broken and then shot him in both heels. In that piteous state, in agony but still alive, he was left right in the middle of the main street.

Only afterwards did it come out that the Arab was a big shot — a terrorist wanted by the secret service, who had experience in the Yugoslav wars and a close network of important connections; some people even said that he had studied law at a university in the United States . . . This story quickly reached the ears of a general in central command, who went personally to the front line to track down the culprits. When the general asked the entire para-trooper division (composed of almost six hundred men, all assembled before him) who was responsible, everyone

– including officers and lieutenant colonels – stepped forward. To prevent a nationwide scandal, the general went back to command and swore never to stick his nose into the affairs that took place on the front lines . . .

Battle command is very different from the commanders who plan the war on paper from the safety of an office, calculating operations based on the moral principles of Russian Army regulations. The officers on the front lines had many bloody wars under their belts, and had a completely different way of understanding military code. The men in command, when they learned of enemies being tortured and killed, said we were a 'bunch of maniacs', 'sadists with inhuman conduct'. The truth is that it was impossible to remain a human being after even just a month on the front lines. And many of us were there for the entire duration of our military duty, over two years, and then some re-enlisted and stayed even longer as contract soldiers.

In the face of the horrors we went through every day on the front, some lost their soundness of mind, others risked losing it, and many just died. The soldiers often had to be cruel – it was a matter of survival.

At the sight of that poor wretch tied to the car, I must admit that there were a few sniggers among us. A column of infantrymen and some explorer units was behind us; one of their cars stopped, an officer came out with a pair of pliers and tried to free the body.

There he was, about to cut the cord that bound the dead Arab's hands, when our Nosov noticed what was going on. He immediately kicked our car's turret and shouted:

'Halt, skulls!* Halt!'

The car hadn't come to a full stop before Nosov jumped down. Running up to the officer, he started yelling:

'Soldier! What the hell do you think you're doing with those pliers?'

The officer gave Nosov a sideways look, then said contemptuously:

'Who are you, and why aren't you acting according to regulations? Identify yourself! Name, rank, and unit!'

'Captain Nosov, saboteurs . . .'

The officer, who was a little younger than Nosov but a rank higher, eyed him from beneath the brim of his hat:

'Captain, I order you to return to your vehicle – you're blocking the column!'

Nobody had ever dared talk to our captain like that before.

Nosov ripped the pliers out of his hands and threw them into the rubble, screaming at him like a madman; in fact, even we were startled.

'Boy, you get back in your vehicle and never dare give orders to a saboteur again! When you were still jerking off or taking it in the arse from your schoolmates I was already burying my brothers in Qandahar! Who gave you permission to untie him?' He pointed to the Arab's flayed

---

* This is what we called the armoured car drivers.

body. 'Did you put him there? Well, when you've got the balls to do something like that then you can take him down . . .'

The officer tried to reply, serious and impassive:

'Captain, I must inform you that when we reach our post I will be forced to report your conduct to command!'

'Your piece of shit post only exists thanks to the sacrifice of those boys!' Nosov snarled, pointing at the names of the dead paratroopers written on the piece of cardboard. 'Go ahead and inform whoever you please, do whatever you want; I wipe my arse with your regulations . . . If I see you laying a hand on any other monuments around here, I swear on the souls of my dead brothers that I will shoot you!'

After these words Nosov gave the officer an impertinent military salute, turned around, and headed back to the car.

The officer stood there for a second, without moving, thinking about what he had just heard, returned the salute, albeit belatedly, almost instinctively, then returned to his car.

Throughout this whole incident, what struck me the most was what our captain had called that disfigured cadaver. He called it a *monument*.

Many veterans of the war in Afghanistan, especially the older paratroopers, would leave these 'monuments' in the streets after a particularly difficult battle. They were terrifying sights, always the body of a dead enemy that the soldiers would savage in a frightening way. But the real horror in this ritual lay in the fact that in order to make these 'monuments', soldiers used people who were still alive.

One time, after a skirmish in which a para group attacked and liberated a fortified area, we found a prisoner in this sort of condition who was still breathing. They had cut the skin on his torso and back into strips, in imitation of the stripes on the shirt the paratroopers wear, which back home they call a *telnyashka*. They had nailed the poor devil to a door, heavy tent stakes sharpened into points struck through his hands. Nearby someone had written the motto, also in blood: 'We may be few, but we wear the *telnyashka*!'

However terrible this was, it had become a kind of custom for them, a matter of dignity and prestige, which the paras always tried to honour without anyone ever daring to go against it.

Our column kept scouting the liberated areas, headed for the line of fire. The line kept moving forward, and after every operation we would always lag behind, so every time we would have to catch up to it again. We forged ahead like waves of water, so as not to give the enemy a chance to rest, make a move, organise an attack against us. We were always fighting, always.

Every now and then we would run into various support units; the carriers restocked our supplies, took care of the injured and accompanied the soldiers who were going to rest.

A kilometre away from the front we had to stop; the car couldn't go any closer, otherwise, in the midst of battle, it would have been torched in seconds. Running with heads down, taking cover behind a light tank, we began moving towards the site along with the paras.

The road was narrow, and the enemy was shooting at us crossways. I could feel the bullets ricocheting off the armour of the tank and then dispersing in every direction. We couldn't stick even our noses beyond the tank, the gunfire was so heavy.

After a while the tank stopped, and the turret turned towards the shots. A cannon blast went off, and at the same time, a volley of bullets from the heavy machine gun, which was next to the cannon inside turret. The explosion was so violent and sudden it made me fall down; my head spun.

When we reached the position, we realised it was an inferno. The paras were agitated and running all over the place, by that point not even covering themselves. Our task was to liberate a house; they had tried to attack it twice, unsuccessfully, and were now waiting for support from us and the tank. We all advanced together, breaking through the enemy defence.

We had been able to push back the enemy's defence almost twenty kilometres. Command was happy because usually only five kilometres at most would get liberated in a day, whereas we had been really fast. But every time we concluded one operation, our assistance was needed elsewhere. They ordered us to take out snipers positioned in various buildings, to launch assaults on buildings, help surround enemy-controlled areas, sabotage their equipment . . . We were exhausted. The paratroopers took turns, whereas we saboteurs hadn't slept for three days. I felt so tired that I didn't have any strength left to eat.

After a short skirmish on a narrow road – where we had destroyed a nursery school, our tanks razing the playground completely – we found ourselves who knows how running through the rooms of a destroyed building, shooting the enemy from such a close range that we could almost reach out and touch them.

I ended up on the top floor with Shoe, to try to eliminate the last big gun. We launched two hand grenades.

In the dust coming down from the ceiling we couldn't see anything, and we ran right into four enemies who, like us, were circling around like blind kittens in the grey, dirty cloud which smelled like rubble and burnt explosives.

There in Chechnya I had never shot anyone from such a close range.

Meanwhile on the second floor our captain had taken a prisoner and downed eight enemies, all by himself.

When I came out with Shoe I was completely dazed. Captain Nosov was asking Moscow to keep an eye on the Arab prisoner while he, Spoon and Zenith went to check on the basement.

I sat down on the stairs next to Moscow, across from the terrified prisoner, who kept on trying to communicate something to us. Moscow wasn't listening to him; he was sleepy and worn out, as we all were. As soon as the captain turned his back, Moscow pulled out his gun, an Austrian Glock, one of his 'trophies', and with a derisive scowl shot the prisoner in the head and the chest.

The captain turned around and without saying a word looked at him with pity.

Moscow went and sat down next to the dead man and closed his eyes, succumbing to a wave of exhaustion.

Looking at all of us as if he were actually meeting us for the first time, the captain said:

'This is too much, boys. Everyone to the carrier, to rest behind the line.'

In single file, like zombies, we headed for our cars. My head felt so heavy that I was convinced if I stopped at all it would explode.

We went behind the line, into the area guarded and defended by our infantry. We fell asleep instantly – I didn't even have the chance to finish taking off my coat and side bags before I fell into oblivion, like a dead man.

It wouldn't seem so, but the scariest time of all in war is when you're resting. In those moments you become aware of all the horrors of the situation you've found yourself in. While you don't even have the time to think during operations and just worry about the essential actions needed to carry out an order, everything that would have an impact on your spirit – impressions, doubts, feelings of guilt – comes to the surface when you stop to rest. Then you can't help but despair, because you'd like to rest and forget the war for a few hours, but you know it's not possible. You spend a lot of time half-awake and half-asleep, reliving what you've just gone through and thus fuelling your tiredness even more.

The only time when you can really rest is when you simply pass out, as if someone had pulled your plug all of a sudden. That's how I felt then.

. . . A little later, Moscow woke me up by tapping my chest with the butt of his Kalashnikov.

Slowly and reluctantly I opened my eyes and looked around. I struggled to remember where I was. I couldn't put anything into focus.

Moscow's face looked tired. He was chewing on a piece of bread. It was dark outside, impossible to tell the time. I checked my watch, but I couldn't even see the numbers; it was like everything was shrouded in fog.

'What's going on, how long did we sleep?' I asked Moscow.

'We didn't sleep for shit, brother . . . And it doesn't look like we'll be going back to sleep any time soon.'

I put my face in my hands, trying to muster the strength

to get up and start thinking. I needed to sleep, I felt utterly exhausted. My clothes were dirty and damp, my jacket smelled like sweat and dirt. I was a wreck.

Moscow went to wake the others:

'Come on, guys, we're leaving now . . . They need us.'

They were all in despair – they didn't want to get up. But griping and cursing, they got to their feet.

Captain Nosov was going around with the handset to his ear and an infantryman with the field radio in a backpack was running after him like a little dog. The captain was getting angry, he kept repeating to who knows who, on the radio, that we had got rest for the first time in three days, that we were beat. All to no avail, because after a while Nosov said, in a tone that recalled the sound of tap shoes:

'Yes, Comrade Colonel! I confirm, order received!'

So they were sending us to the front lines again.

I didn't even want to think about it.

I went to the metal vat filled with water. I plunged my hands in; the water was nice and cool; it gave me a light shiver. So I dunked my whole head underwater, and lingered for a moment, holding my breath.

I opened my eyes inside the vat and saw complete darkness. Startled, I pulled my head out immediately and gasped for breath.

The darkness I saw in the vat gave me a bad feeling, it seemed as if death might be like that – dark and airless.

I stood over the vat, and watched the reflection of my face and of my life up to that point dancing on the water. But I stepped back immediately – I didn't want the water to become still, too much like a mirror. According to an old Siberian tradition, looking in the mirror before facing a risk brings bad luck.

And from what I understood from the bits of the radio conversation between Nosov and some unknown colonel, we would be facing many a risk indeed . . .

We all sat in a circle, next to the car, as we always did before leaving for a mission. Moscow explained the situation: during the night a group of enemies had broken through the ring we had around the city, and some of our infantry were trapped in a building surrounded by Arabs . . . We had to free them; the attack was set for six in the morning. Only two hours away.

I chewed on a piece of buttered bread, trying to re-establish contact with reality. Moscow was talking; I was taking little sips of boiling hot soup from a cup made out of an old tin. I was slowly waking up.

Fifteen minutes later we were in the car, once again headed for the line of fire.

During the trip Nosov gave us his take:

'First our command makes a mistake by leaving a weak spot in the ring around the city. Then the Arabs come in and make trouble, and even if they don't manage to advance or to do anything serious they take our soldiers hostage . . . Our nearby troops can't make it in time, and now it's up to us to break through their defence for the second time. And if we don't attack now, our men will die for sure . . . It's a farce, the colonels in command know very well that prisoners get killed, but it's in their interest to look like they tried to save them . . .'

To tell the truth, at that moment I understood absolutely nothing about the situation, I was just trying to rest as much as possible so that I wouldn't collapse later during battle. None of my comrades said anything; the captain went on talking by himself, pondering military tactics, making comparisons to similar cases he had encountered in the past.

At some point Moscow turned to me and whispered with irritation:

'I really hope this is the last time. If they ask us to do anything else, I'm going to tell them all to shove it.'

I was in total agreement.

We soon reached our destination. The car stopped in the courtyard of a small building defended by our men. The yard was full of equipment randomly strewn across the ground. On the opposite side there was a road that separated our territory from the territory held by the enemies. We jumped out of the car and began gathering Kalashnikov clips, tying them together with the wide bandages from our medi-kits, attaching them to our vests.

The captain ordered:

'Prepare ten clips for me too, boys!'

Then he went off to the tent in the middle of the yard,

which was surrounded by sandbags stacked up to a man's height around the perimeter. It was the mobile command base, where there was usually some low-ranking officer, a major or at most a lieutenant colonel.

Our captain was very critical towards the men in command – he called any contact with them 'listening to babies cry', referring to the story in the Gospel about the massacre of the innocents. There was something about their behaviour, he told us, that he had never really been able to understand, and when he had to deal with them face to face they always ended up arguing and he would insult them. As he admitted himself, that's precisely the reason why he never went up in military rank – sometimes he would jokingly add the word 'eternal' to his title of captain; he was aware that nobody in command was very fond of him, either.

That day, I could tell just from the way he stormed over to the tent that Nosov was going to get into trouble the moment he walked in there.

Not even ten minutes had passed before we started to hear shouting coming from the tent, along with a string of accusations and insults, with which our captain was always very generous.

Right after that Nosov came by the sandbags, and called me over, his voice breaking:

'Kolima! Come here, I have a job for you!'

I could imagine what it would be, so I walked towards the tent with some reluctance. Inside there was an infantry major sitting at a table, improvised from empty cases for heavy machine gun rounds. He had a battle knife in his hand, which he was using to show Nosov various points on a map that was spread out in front of them.

On the map, our area was surrounded by empty shells and various calibres of cartridge, which were supposed to represent the different military units. Next to that was a package of black bread, open, and a piece of paper with a pat of butter on top, a Kalashnikov survival knife stuck inside. There was also a big pot full of black tea, which was so hot it was steaming, and in fact its smell filled the entire tent. In one corner, on top of a zinc case, an infantry explorer, a private, ate silently. Next to him, leaning against the case, was his precision rifle: a VSS with an integrated silencer, exactly the same as mine. He was a sniper too.

The major was angry with Nosov, but he paid no attention and made himself at home. He spread some butter on a thick hunk of bread and passed it to me.

'Here. Eat while you can . . .'

I didn't need him to tell me twice, and in a single bite I'd chomped off half the piece. Then the major took an empty tin from a pile of rubbish on the ground and poured a drop of hot tea in it. He rinsed out the tin with a vigorous swish and dumped the dirty tea on the rubbish. Finally he filled the tin up with tea and said to me:

'Drink up, soldier, don't just eat stale bread!'

I liked him right off the bat, this major; he had a very friendly demeanour and he treated me like a son. It was clear that he found himself in an awkward situation, that's why he was trying to get some support.

While I drank the tea, with the residue of the oil from

the tin still floating on top, Nosov bent over the map. He said to me, without ever looking up:

'Look, Kolima, your colleague here has managed to find the spots where the Arabs are. You have to memorise them, study them carefully . . .' I turned towards the explorers' sniper, who still hadn't said a word.

'You left the area by yourself? How did you do it?'

The guy gave me a serious look, and while he was still chewing, he said:

'I went into the sewer system. In the yard, behind the house where our post is, there's an entrance to the sewers. Our lieutenant ordered me to search it and, if possible, follow it all the way to you guys.'

It seemed incredible, looking at the guy. Alone, with a precision rifle and a few clips, that boy had gone through over a kilometre of sewer. Even if they were completely dry, since in the city the water pipes weren't working and there was no drinking water, the biggest danger in the sewers was the mines. During the First Chechen Campaign, all the sewers were mined – first by the enemies, then by us – to keep anyone from using them as underground passageways from one part of the city to another. Nobody dared go in there, the risk was too high.

'That's some luck, brother! You weren't just born with a bulletproof vest, you had a full-on jacket!' I said, looking on the map at the path he had taken.

I had only been in the sewers once. We were clearing out a neighbourhood in the Chechen capital, the city of Grozny. To get closer to the position of an Arab sniper

I had to take down, I went through nearly two hundred metres of sewer, but it was nice and wide, and there was no danger of being discovered. The city was under the control of our troops, and two soldiers from the strategic unit had already passed through that same tract of sewer and deactivated the mines they found on the path.

The Arabs had several models of explosive devices at their disposal, many of which were Italian-made, coming from San Marino. They had different mechanisms, but were all deadly weapons. Some of them had been scattered throughout the city we were supposed to attack, thrown in the street in order to attract our soldiers' attention. They were made to look like mobile phones, watches, videocameras, and unfortunately sometimes toys or boxes of crayons. We all knew about these dangerous surprises, and if during the First Chechen Campaign a Russian or two had lost his hide, I don't remember a single case of that happening in the Second. But many civilians died, including – disgracefully – children. When we saw those mines in the street we wouldn't hesitate to shoot them to make them explode, thus rendering them harmless. The idea of picking them up and trying to deactivate them, on the other hand, never occurred to any one of us.

The explorers' sniper had done everything alone. Besides making it all the way to our position, he had emerged from the sewers at several points to observe the enemy camp and had used a piece of hard lime to mark the areas of greatest danger on the walls. He had risked his life so he could tell us where and how the Arabs were positioned. To me he was a hero.

Now that I had a full stomach I went and carefully studied the map the sniper had drawn, trying to memorise all the points marked on the route, but there were so many I couldn't even count them. So I took out the map they'd given us at the beginning of the operation, and with a pencil I traced every single enemy post.

In the meantime, Nosov was talking with the major, discussing the possibility of launching an attack to free the trapped soldiers.

'Before we attack,' the major said, 'we have to wait for the planes to arrive, to bomb the perimeter, and . . .'

'But that means sentencing our men to death!' Nosov broke in. 'We have to try a passive attack. We push the Arabs back to their positions, and take back control of the perimeter. Then from there, we create a path for us to get to the area where the soldiers are stuck . . .' Nosov wasn't used to having to explain things to other people.

The major barked:

'Captain! You are an officer in charge of one unit. Do all of us a favour; devise strategies with your men however and whenever you see fit, but don't try to resolve something that goes beyond your capacities!'

Nosov, however, didn't want to listen. He went on with accusations, using the same old stories about Afghanistan, talking about how he had been abandoned by a bunch of 'officers with no balls' worried more about their medals than about the soldiers who were dying in the 'traps laid out for them by the generals in the

Kremlin', people who had sold out to those 'faggots at the Pentagon' . . .

At a certain point the major lost his patience and he went outside the tent, asking to be brought a field radio.

Three soldiers came running up. One carried the radio; the other two – Cossacks armed to the teeth, with vests, guns, Kalashnikovs and extra clips all over – went into a corner and started talking with the explorers' sniper.

The soldier with the radio fiddled with the equipment a little, then passed the handset to the major. They were calling the unit of trapped infantrymen, who had been holding out heroically for hours.

'Twelve thirty-two! Twelve thirty-two! Birch calling! Birch calling!'

They answered right away.

'Birch! Birch! This is twelve thirty-two!' You could hear the agitation in his voice, gunfire in the background.

The major took a deep breath, and said in a shaky voice:

'Soldier, what is your situation? Request confirmation of your situation!'

For a moment everything on the other side stopped, you could only hear some shooting and a couple of loud explosions. We all stared at the radio, holding our breath.

After a moment the voice returned, even more agitated than before:

'Birch, Birch! Confirming our situation! The unit is under siege. Lots of two-hundreds!* The three-hundreds

---

* Radio code for casualties.

are almost gone,* we have no more medi-kits! The unit
has run out of supplies, I don't know how much longer
we can last! We request air strike on our coordinates! Fire
on us!'

The soldier's voice seemed not to come from the radio,
but to come from somewhere beyond. It was more than
desperate — it was defeated. After a brief pause, he
concluded the conversation:

'Goodbye, brothers, remember us, and may God bless
you! The whole unit and I salute you . . .'

Afterwards, we heard a long whistle; that sound meant
the other side had ended communication. The major
ordered the radio to be turned off and sat down on one
of the crates, his face tired. He took an unfiltered cigarette
and started smoking it with fury. He looked Nosov in the
face, and then said quietly:

'Captain, unfortunately you heard for yourself how
badly off they are. Sending our units would be a futile
sacrifice, pure insanity . . . Independent of whatever action
we decide to take, command has already given the order,
and soon we'll have confirmation — they're going to bomb
the perimeter. All we can do is be ready for the attacks
from the surviving enemy groups, who will most certainly
try to flee the area.'

Nosov turned back to the map. The major got up and
ordered the soldier with the radio to return to his unit.
Only then did the two Cossacks approach the major. One
of them, the older one, gave him a military salute. The

---

* Radio code for wounded.

major stood up, and before responding, checked to make sure his hat was on* – you could see that he was tired and worn out too.

The Cossack said:

'I'm Osaul† Ustinov, Sixth Division of Free Kuban Cossacks . . . My son, Private Ustinov, is in the enemy-surrounded area. I ask your permission to join the attack group going to support our boys!'

The major looked at our captain for a second and then, lowering his eyes, began explaining the situation to the Cossack:

'I understand your request, but the boys have no hope. They requested fire on their position, I'm certain they won't make it to daybreak alive . . . I officially apologise for our total powerlessness in the face of a situation like this . . .' From his tone of voice, it was almost as if he were apologising for having personally killed the Cossack's son.

The Cossack's face went dark, like a cloud heavy with rain. I was standing beside him, and I had the impression he was going to burst at any moment.

'How much time do we have before the first air strike?' Nosov suddenly asked.

He was focused on the map and didn't notice the expression that came over the major's face. Naturally, the major didn't want to take on responsibility for any potential plans that came from Nosov's mind. Despite all that, he replied:

---

* According to Russian military code, you may only salute with your hat on.
† An officer in the Cossack army.

'About an hour and a half, Captain . . . But I don't understand – what does the time of the strike matter now? The situation is cut-and-dried, unfortunately . . .'

Nosov looked up from the map, took a piece of bread from the table and chewing it almost cruelly, said:

'Major, with all due respect . . . In an hour my strays and I can break through the enemy defence, check out their position, free the boys and come back home. We'll have time left over for breakfast . . .'

At these words my heart sank into my boots: Nosov was going to take us straight to hell.

The major took off his cap and sat down on the crate. He looked like he was about to have a heart attack; he was probably already picturing some superior stripping the stars from his uniform. He tried to object, without conviction, and raising his voice just a touch, he repeated:

'That's not within your competencies, Captain . . .'

But Nosov shot back arrogantly:

'Major! Let the beasts in the forest cry, we're soldiers and we must do our duty! My men and I will go into operation immediately. We'll go through the sewers, you prepare a group to cover us, because within an hour we'll come out at this exact point.' His finger pointed to the spot on the map.

Nosov traced a line marking a little street that went behind the trapped infantrymen's position and ended just opposite our units. Between those two points there was a kilometre and a half with enemy positions. Looking at it on the map, the route seemed short and simple, but to physically travel it, on the actual perimeter, definitely wasn't going to be a cakewalk.

The explorers' sniper came up, shook my hand and said:

'Good luck and may God protect you, do everything you can for our boys . . .'

I, at that moment, was thinking that if anything went wrong, there wouldn't be anybody to do everything they could for us. If we tarried even a little we would get bombed by our own planes. Nothing to be cheery about.

The major looked Nosov in the eyes and said:

'Captain, there's nothing I can do to stop this insane endeavour of yours, but remember that if anything happens behind the line, no one will be able to help you . . . As an officer of the Russian Army, all I can do is restrict myself to calling your actions dangerous for the lives of the soldiers under you. Personally, I'm against anarchy . . .' After these words, the major made a sly face, and whispered in a low voice, 'But, Captain, if you need anything in particular, all of our magazines are at your disposal . . .'

Nosov spoke seriously, as he would do whenever he could already taste victory:

'Prepare the support troops at the places I showed you on the map. In an hour we'll be there.' Without another word he exited the tent.

Before leaving, I paused to salute the major according to regulation. Looking at me squinty-eyed, he just waved his hand as if he were shooing away a fly.

*

Our captain was roaming around the yard looking for my comrades. The first one he found was Moscow. They spoke briefly, and right afterwards Moscow yelled:

'Saboteurs! Battle alarm!'

As our men came from various places, running, throwing on their jackets, putting their clips and everything in place, Nosov slung two grenade launchers and a couple of bags of extra ammo over his shoulders.

Once we were all there he spoke in a low voice, as he did whenever he wanted to explain something important:

'We'll go on foot, without using the car. We'll go through the sewers and then, following the map, we'll come out directly on the perimeter where our guys are trapped. When we get there, hopefully we'll find some of them still alive . . .'

We listened carefully. We too needed to know what sort of death awaited us.

Suddenly the Cossack came over with his young side-kick. The old man interrupted Nosov, his words full of desperation:

'Captain, I beg you, take us with you, my son is there, you understand? How could I go on living knowing that I could have done something to save him and I didn't?'

Nosov replied calmly, as if he had been expecting this question his whole life.

'I understand you, Osaul, and for me personally it's not a problem. But we saboteurs are a family, and we make decisions together. If even one of my boys doesn't agree to it . . . I'm very sorry, Osaul, but you'll be staying here . . .'

The Cossack turned towards us. He wore a moustache, and he looked dead tired. He seemed about fifty years old.

'My boys, help me at this difficult moment! One day, God bless you, you will be fathers too, and I hope you never experience what I'm going through now . . .' He gazed at us with sad eyes and stiff lips, as if a cramp had frozen the muscles in his face. You could tell he wanted to say something else, but couldn't manage to get it out.

Moscow was the first to speak:

'It's fine with me . . .'

We all gave our assent.

The expression in the old man's eyes changed instantly.

At that point Nosov said:

'We have about an hour, so let's try to hurry as much as possible, on the double, and no messing around . . .'

We quickly introduced ourselves. The old man was called Vasily, the young one – who was much less worried about the gravity of the situation – Yury. They were uncle and nephew, and they seemed like good people to me. I was glad that someone else was joining our group on such a dangerous operation – it was an unusual occurrence, and maybe it would bring a little more hope to all of us.

We checked our equipment one last time, while Moscow and Zenith explained to the Cossacks what they needed to remove and what they should keep on. The two immediately lightened their jackets, tossing their guns that would have made noise and restricted

their movement. The Cossacks were expert soldiers –
no one had any doubt as to their training – but
we didn't have time to explain saboteur rules and
conduct.

We had to cross the street, go through a yard and from
there go down into the sewers. In the darkness of the early
morning there was a cool wind that caressed our faces; you
could still see the stars up in the sky.

As we moved in silence, I noticed a cat, an old male
tabby, perched on a half-destroyed car. He observed us
attentively, while we prepared ourselves covertly for the
mission. The presence of cats, according to Siberian tradition, brings good luck. I hadn't forgotten that terrible
darkness I'd seen inside the vat of water, and the cat
seemed like a positive sign.

The yard shown on the map was full of empty cases
that had held the explosive charges for the cannons. There
in the middle was the entrance to the sewers, sealed with
a heavy slab of iron. So as not to get lost, we had to
follow the indications the explorer had drawn on the
sewer walls. Along the entire route, as the captain had
explained, we would find his unit number, 168, serving
as our guide.

One by one, we jumped underground. Nosov and
Moscow – the first and the last in line – had flashlights
with red bulbs so as not to arouse the enemy's suspicion.
The sewers were paved; they formed a very narrow tunnel

that forced us to walk with our heads down and bent almost halfway over.

I had only one thought in my head: the fact that the explorers' sniper hadn't blown up didn't mean there weren't any mines down there.

We ran behind Nosov, and it felt like we were mice. It was dark, it was dead hot, there was dust everywhere, and I felt like I was breathing sand. At multiple points we heard the Arabs' voices coming from above.

Suddenly Nosov froze, stiff as a rod. We stopped behind him, breathing hard. Moscow spat on the ground and cursed softly. Nosov studied the map with the flashlight, then pointed the light at the wall, looking for the sign. When he found the number with a little star drawn next to it, he didn't waste any time. He turned to us and said:

'Ready for action – let's go!'

We loaded the barrel, Zenith and Shoe put two charges in the grenade launcher.

'Kolima, you and Moscow go up on recon. If it's all clear, one of you come back down here to lead the way.'

I climbed up a narrow stepladder that went from the sewer tunnel to the exit. You couldn't see a thing, Moscow was climbing up after me with a flashlight, but that weak red light didn't help. I groped my way up.

After a while my head touched the ceiling. There was an iron cover, it must have been five metres wide. I tried to lift it but that thing didn't even budge a centimetre. I thought something heavy was blocking the exit; maybe a car was parked on top, or maybe there was a light cannon. I kept pushing, even using my shoulders, but I really couldn't lift it. My sweat was cold.

'What the fuck are you doing? Take off the bloody cover!' Moscow yelled at me.

'Holy Christ, they've put something on top, it won't open!'

'Bullshit!' Moscow came up and I moved aside, balancing myself on the ladder with one foot off the rung. 'Fucking hell, Kolima! You're not even capable of moving a bloody manhole cover?' He was raging now.

'They've put something on top, I'm telling you, it won't move!' Any more and I was going to cry.

'Stop saying that. Let's try together.' Moscow started pushing on one side and I on the other. The cover lifted a little.

Slowly inching it aside, we managed to clear an opening. The cool morning air came rushing in, and my lungs greedily took it in.

'They've put something on top . . .' Moscow made fun of me, in a simpering little voice. 'Eat more, otherwise you won't even have the strength to take a shit!'

I went out into the yard first. Outside it was brighter than when we had left. The sun wasn't out yet, but there was already that strange morning light that at times seems like a reflection in the distance.

There were open crates of equipment everywhere, all empty. There was absolute silence, no sound of gunfire. On one corner there was an armoured car like ours, a

BTR with one side burned out and the rear doors open. Someone had dismantled the machine gun from the turret – it was clear that, once they had realised the danger they were in, the infantrymen had tried to gather every weapon they could.

For a second I thought we had got there too late. Then I noticed movement in one of the windows of the third floor of the building. Someone was pulling a rope, lifting something. Moscow pointed towards the entrance; lying on the ground, there was a soldier. I couldn't see the details; I could only make out a dark spot. He moved slowly, crawling towards the door as if he were afraid to get up. He went a couple of metres, then stopped; I thought maybe he was wounded.

Moscow touched my arm and said:

'That's our guys, let's go!'

We hurried across the yard. Partly because we were used to the dark and partly because day was starting to break, we realised that the bodies of our soldiers were scattered here and there; none of them had his vest or gear. We could see that the living had pillaged the dead.

Sneaking along the walls, we peered in the windows. The building was square, with identical rooms and a wide, long hallway with high ceilings – it seemed to be a school or hospital. It was completely destroyed, and our soldiers' bodies were in piles on the floor.

Once we reached the corner, I saw one of our positions. Next to a ground-floor window a soldier sat on the inner side of the boundary wall smoking a cigarette butt concealed under his hand. We crawled over to him and he didn't notice a thing – he kept on sitting there, without moving, smoking calmly. Moscow approached from behind and immobilised him, like a spider clutches its victims. He put his hand over his mouth and whispered in his ear:

'Relax, little brother, don't worry. We're the saboteurs, we've come to get you out of here . . .'

The soldier hadn't had time to react; the cigarette fell to the ground and I covered it immediately. When Moscow let go he looked at us as if we were aliens.

'How did you do it, guys?' he said, incredulous.

'Your sniper, the explorer, went through the sewers and showed us the way,' Moscow summarised. 'We have to move now, while it's still not too light . . .'

The soldier grabbed an empty shell from the floor and threw it somewhere inside the building, into the darkness of one of the rooms. We heard a tired voice say:

'What is it, Mitya?'

Our new acquaintance replied:

'We have visitors – the saboteurs are here!'

From the other room the voice perked up instantly:

'Fucking whore of a war, finally!'

There were sixteen infantrymen left. They had occupied a wing of the building and resigned themselves to waiting for the last attack from the enemy, who would come back at dawn to exterminate them.

While Moscow went to alert our guys, who were waiting for an update down in the sewer, I started talking to the sergeant. He was a really competent guy; he'd taken over after their lieutenant fell, planning their defence in an attempt to stretch what little time they had as much as possible. His name was Lavrov.

'I'd been hoping that, when dawn came, some of our men would start to push onto the line of fire,' he confessed to me. 'That way maybe the Arabs' attention would have been taken from us to defending themselves . . .'

'Sergeant,' I preferred to tell him the truth right away, 'unfortunately, Command already approved an air strike . . .'

He looked at me in astonishment – he couldn't believe our command had been ready to sacrifice them without trying one last time.

I told him to gather the men from his unit right away, and within a few minutes all sixteen of the surviving soldiers were there in front of me. They were tired and worn out, but alive. Poor guys, they had only two boxes of rounds for the machine gun; if things went well that would have lasted them about five minutes of combat . . .

So as not to carry unnecessary weight, I decided we should leave the heavy machine gun behind, but first I plugged the barrel with a misshapen Kalashnikov shell and removed the lock to make the weapon completely unusable. I slipped it into my pocket; I'd throw it into the sewer later.

I picked up a few bulletproof vests, which could turn out to be useful during retreat, and passed them out to the guys. It was good to have a few extra – we could use them to cover the holes in the windows, to cover the radio and keep it from getting broken during transport, or to protect some other thing of value.

Moscow came back in a rush, all out of breath:

'Let's hurry, the Arabs are coming. I heard noises in the distance . . .'

We headed out. I led the group, Moscow closed the line. The infantry made noise; their uniforms had tons of latches and they had some useless stuff on their vests that we hadn't had time to tell them to take off. But we got through the yard without any problems, and at the entrance to the sewers, one by one they went down.

Moscow and I covered them from a possible enemy attack, but everything was calm – there wasn't the slightest sign of the Arabs. Finally, when everyone had got to safety, we jumped down too. We carefully replaced the cover and off we went.

Nosov was down below, preparing some booby traps to mine the sewer entrance. He climbed up, and with some bandages from the medi-kits he affixed three grenades to the second rung of the iron ladder. Then he threaded some wire through the pins, tied two bullet-proof vests to one end of the wire to act as a counter-weight, and slipped the other end of the wire under the cover, which kept it in place and kept the vests hanging in the air. If someone moved the cover, the wire would come loose and the vests would fall and trigger the bombs.

Besides obstructing the sewer entrance, the explosion would surely kill a few enemies as well. An F1 model hand grenade had a lot of explosive power, and could shoot metal fragments up to a distance of four hundred metres. It was a real bitch, that bomb.

Nosov came down and looked at the soldiers:

'So, you're the only ones left?'

Sergeant Lavrov replied:

'Yes, Comrade Captain, the others have fallen.'

It was dark and you couldn't see anything, but from our line the Cossack's voice emerged:

'Does anyone have word of Private Ustinov?'

A cry came from among the infantry:

'Papa!' A young soldier jumped out from the group and practically threw himself on the old man. The two men embraced, and then the cousin too. They were grinning, happy as children.

'Let's save the family reunions for later, Cossacks!' Our Nosov motioned for everyone to follow him.

We went fast. It really seemed like everything had gone smoothly, and I was almost happy that we had managed to conclude the operation without having to shoot a single bullet. As we passed under the grates, you could see the first rays of sunlight filtering down to the sewer floor. At those points we crept along against the wall so we couldn't be seen from above.

The infantrymen followed the saboteurs, and Nosov ordered me and Moscow to bring up the rear. Although the group had grown, although our heads were down and we were hunched over, we moved even faster than we did on the way there.

'I knew I was going to be okay,' Moscow said at one point, though almost under his breath.

'What?' I asked, without stopping. I wasn't sure I'd heard him right.

'My neighbour, the gypsy, she read my future on the cards . . .' He was smiling now. 'She said I would die an old man, in my sleep . . .'

He told this story every time he got through some serious trouble – that is, all the time. I was about to say something, when suddenly we heard such a strong explosion that for a few seconds our ears were plugged. It was our booby trap.

Nosov halted. We looked at one another, scared, half-deaf, feeling trapped. Our captain said:

'We have to get out fast, now, wherever we are . . . I'm sure they've already given the signal . . . Now those beasts'll be throwing bombs into every sewer in the area!'

Within a minute we found an exit, also closed by a cover. Without a word Nosov climbed up, moved the cover and went out. Then he peeked in and gestured for us to follow him.

We moved so fast that we looked like a group of navy soldiers used to going up and down the passageways of a submarine.

Coming out in broad daylight in some random place, however, would expose us to any possible attack.

We found ourselves at the end of an empty street facing a cement wall full of holes and rusty shards. Nearby there was a low building, a small power plant. There was one in every neighbourhood – they were good places for escaping heavy artillery attacks, because they had very thick walls, and sometimes even a tank had trouble knocking them down; they were kind of like little bunkers. The problem is that they were blind, without windows – they had a door and that was it. Many soldiers had lost their lives in those places, because in trying to take shelter they ended up getting trapped.

Behind us there was a half-destroyed, abandoned apartment building. Nosov headed there and we followed. Once inside, we all began trying to figure out an escape route.

Nosov pulled out the map and showed us our location. We had gone in the right direction, but we were about three hundred metres from where we were originally supposed to come out. According to the directions I had copied, we were right in the middle of the enemy's second line of fortifications.

While the others hid in the building, Nosov asked Moscow and me to come with him to explore the area. The silence was unsettling – it felt as if we were crossing a dead city. But as we went through the streets, we spotted several places where machine guns poked out from building windows. Evidently the Arabs felt safe, and that was why they had no ground cover. Still, it was a big stroke of luck that we hadn't come out in a place defended by the snipers, otherwise we'd have stepped into our own grave.

There was an armoured car, a BTR, inside one of the courtyards, where someone had written something in Arabic with white paint. We looked around, and not seeing anyone, we went in. The back doors of the car were open; inside there was an enemy, sleeping.

Nosov didn't stop to think. He drew his knife and jumped on him like a flash. Without the slightest whimper, the Arab died from a jab right in the heart.

Moscow entered the cabin and started the engine. I hung on the side with Nosov. Obviously when we came onto the street, everyone would notice the car. We had to make it look like we were them, but also had to be ready to get off in case they recognised us.

Moscow drove the car perfectly, nice and smooth. Nosov had put on the dead Arab's hat and was making a weird face – it almost made me laugh to look at him. I had torn the pom-pom off my hat and turned it inside out, so that from far away it would look at least a little like the ones the Arabs wore. We went through the streets and everything around was still – it really seemed like our trick had worked.

We entered the courtyard of the abandoned house where our men were waiting for us, backing up as close as possible to the door.

Nosov suggested to the soldiers a plan to get out of there: they would all squeeze inside the BTR; two would go to the driver's side, another inside the gun turret, while we saboteurs would stay on top, in plain view. His idea was to dress the dead Arab's body in one of our soldier's uniforms, and then attach him to the car (they really liked exhibiting our corpses – I had seen videos with the half-butchered bodies of Russians being taken around the city streets like trophies), pretending to be their comrades. It was a crazy plan, but it was the only plan possible.

One infantryman took his uniform off without hesitation and took the Arab's clothes. We put the jacket on the corpse, wrapped his head in a rag to cover the black beard and long hair, and tied him up. In the car we found one of their flags, which was entrusted to Zenith; his task would be to shout the only Arabic phrase he knew, 'Allah Akbar', and wave the flag around like a nut. The rest of us would confuse things a little by shooting into the air and letting out some whoops.

It was already daylight. We had just a few blocks to go. We would dump the car just before reaching the territory under our control; otherwise there was the risk of our soldiers killing us.

Without much ado, we set off. The car barrelled onto the street at full speed; in front, under the gun turret, we had placed the corpse. The head dangled from side to side – it really looked like one of our men. We hollered and shot in the air every now and then, we had all turned our hats inside out. Luckily the road was deserted.

We were almost at the end of the road when we heard some shouting from a nearby house, then fire from a machine gun and some Kalashnikovs and pistols. Some Arabs came out of the door, jumping for joy, shooting into the air and waving at us, raising their hands high in the air. We kept up the show. I was next to the turret; Zenith was yelling so loud it almost hurt my ears.

We came to a big crossroads where there were lots of Arabs bustling about with heavy cannons and tanks. Some of them fired in response to us, but one group gestured for us to stop the vehicle. Nosov took a hand grenade and threw it right at a cannon, which exploded. Moscow and I opened fire on the Arabs, to their surprise. We wiped them out in no time, and our BTR kept going down the street into the distance.

There were still two small streets of enemy fortifications to cross; then we would come onto a wide street, and after that would reach our men. We were so close; I could almost see our post.

From the roof of a three-storey house, the enemy started shooting at us with two machine guns. One of the infantry-men who were driving the car made an abrupt manoeuvre, zigzagging around; we couldn't shoot, all our effort was concentrated on not falling off.

At a certain point I felt a tremor going from the armour to the handle I was holding on to, like a little earthquake. It was the machine gun hitting the front of the car. The BTR swerved to the left and, slowing down, went up onto the pavement.

Nosov jumped off the vehicle and we followed him. I fell, did a somersault and jumped back up. I kept on running although my ankle hurt like hell. The car had broken down a gate, gone through a yard, and crashed into a building. We rushed over, trying to enter the building so we wouldn't be exposed to gunfire.

The rear doors of the car opened and the soldiers burst out. The one who had been sitting in the turret had blood all over his face – part of a shell had hit him, leaving a wide, deep gash from the middle of his forehead to the top of his head. The boys who had been driving the car, however, were both dead, having taken the blast straight on.

We could hear the machine guns approaching, and amidst all the chaos I could distinguish the sounds of a precision rifle. From the deep echo it left in the air, it had to be a Dragunov. Suddenly, one of our soldiers standing in the middle of the yard fell over. His vest exploded as if it were made of glass, leaving him a hole in the chest that went clear from one side to the other.

Only anti-tank shells had that kind of power. They were heavy, had a strong steel interior and were plated with a thin layer of very soft metal that allowed the bullet to slide nicely down the barrel and follow a precise trajectory. Some snipers, to make them even deadlier, sprayed them with Teflon, which made them slip through armour like melted butter. The sniper couldn't be too far away, two or three hundred metres at most.

Backing up against the wall, I yelled:

'Stay out of the yard, sniper in the area! Keep inside, walk by the walls . . .'

I didn't have time to finish my sentence before another infantryman was grazed in the back.

Meanwhile, our captain was helping a soldier who was limping; his leg had probably been hurt during the accident. He carried him to safety inside the building, going through a window, gripping the ledge with one hand and helping the boy to enter with the other.

Before disappearing inside he yelled:

'Kolima, get rid of that bloody sniper for me. Now!'

I ran along the wall and at the end I saw an entrance to the basements. I ran in, and with my rifle aimed I went through some of the rooms. They were completely empty, but on the bottom level there were some small windows that looked onto the courtyard. I chose one in the shadows.

Before shooting with a sniper rifle I would cover my left eye with a small piece of cardboard I always carried with me, kept in the fold of my hat. It was an old trick my grandpa Nikolay had taught me; when he shot, he would always cover his left eye with a piece of cardboard – it was simpler to concentrate on the target without straining to keep your eye closed, and above all it didn't damage your sight, because keeping one eye closed and the other open for a long time would throw off your eyes.

I pulled out my VSS precision rifle, took the cover off the scope and unfolded the stock. I took a round table and placed it under the window, knelt on top, and started observing the area outside.

Suddenly I heard somebody coming up behind me and I flipped around, ready to shoot. Then Moscow's voice assuaged me:

'Come on, brother, take him out and we can get out of here – we still have to get across that bloody yard!'

I was trying to remember how the soldiers' vests had blown up to reconstruct the trajectory of the shot. There's a way to figure out the so-called 'approximation level', the information that helps pinpoint a sniper's location; you calculate the distance of the shot, which can be determined by the type of wound it leaves on the victim's body, and then its path. This is why the most expert snipers often use modified bullets that become misshapen inside a body – to keep the enemy from making a precise calculation. They use various compensators that reduce the bullet's potency or they lighten the gunpowder charge, so that a shot going off nearby could seem to have come from further away.

About two hundred metres across from me, there were two five-storey buildings. Behind those there was another one, taller, with at least nine or ten floors – only the top two rows of windows were visible. I made a quick calculation; the fifth floor of the two closer buildings could be an ideal spot for a sniper.

I began inspecting the upper level of the two buildings with the scope. Almost immediately, right in the middle of one, inside a small shed that connected the roof with the stairs inside, I found my sniper.

He wasn't set up like a professional. He hadn't created any sort of dummy position – many would intentionally leave small objects sticking out that resembled the barrel of a rifle, or they would plant mirrors to attract attention. I even happened to catch him smoking, relaxed as if he were watching television. He was young and had short blond hair, probably a 'tourist' from the Baltic countries.

He had to be a mercenary, or an athlete. Even choosing the roof showed that he was no expert; the roof is the absolutely least protected place in a house, and putting yourself there usually meant suicide.

In short, my sniper was what we would call a 'water boiler', a novice marksman who thinks he's a pro just because he has good aim. He was too sure of himself – it must have been his first experience with war. But he didn't know that it would also be his last.

I calculated the distance; he was really close. I was about to shoot when I realised he was talking to someone. So I hesitated, and in my sight a young woman appeared, with long blonde hair tucked into a military cap. She seemed like one of those American porn stars photo-graphed half-naked stroking a pile of guns. I felt total disgust at seeing two young people who had come here to kill our boys for money. I waited for them to come closer. She said something to him, smiling; he stood up for a moment and touched her face before kissing her. That's when I took the first shot.

I aimed at the lower part of his head, right at the chin. When you do that, usually the bullet ends up hitting the temple.

The rifle did its job; the empty shell landed on the floor. Moscow, standing behind me, held his breath as I did. The sniper had disappeared. There was just a red stain on the wall behind where he had been.

The girl was still for a moment, then she stupidly went to close the window, but I already had her face in my sight. It was a second, half a breath, and I hit her too. After the shot I saw her lifeless body still standing for a few seconds; her hat had flown off, her head seemed puffy and huge, but half of her face was no longer there. She hung on to the window with one hand, and then she fell down.

I ran straight to the next room to observe the scene from another position. I always did that so I wouldn't be found. Moscow came behind me and asked:

'So, d'you get him?'

'Yep, there were two of them, they were even making out . . .'

Moscow whistled:

'What do you know, those nasty homos . . .'

I laughed:

'They were no homos, Moscow . . .'

He looked at me, shocked, leaning his head on his rifle, which he was holding behind his back.

'No? What, then?'

I thought for a moment, looking out of the window and through the scope, framing the point where just minutes earlier the two snipers had been talking.

I was completely beat, and a strange feeling of home-sickness had come over me. At that moment I wanted to be somewhere else, away from the war, in some other reality, with other people. I don't know why, but I had a strange desire to joke. And to laugh.

I slowly looked away from the scope, and pulling myself to my feet I carefully folded my rifle stock. Then I answered Moscow, almost singing:

'My noble lord, behold he who hath killed Romeo and Juliet . . .'

Moscow burst out laughing at my little scene.

'Romeo and Juliet? You're crazy, my friend! And what does that make me? The Prince of Denmark?'

Laughing together, we exited the basement.

Our men were waiting for us to cross the yard. From the other side of the street they had begun firing shots from the Kalashnikov at ground level; the Arabs were trying to figure out our situation, trying to provoke us so that they could then attack us.

The bodies of the dead soldiers were in the middle of the yard. Their comrades had removed their ammo and then fired their rifles to render them unusable.

Nosov had placed a hand grenade in the car. He activated it so that if anyone opened the door, the explosive would blow up in his face.

The infantrymen struggled to carry their dead; Zenith had sewn up the head of the guy who'd been in the turret as best he could, but it was a messy wound, it bled too much, and you could see that the guy needed a doctor, some antibiotics, and some rest too.

Half our group followed them, the rest of us – led by Nosov along with Deer and Spoon – headed for camp.

The Arabs were behind us. There wasn't that many of them, probably twenty or so, only armed with Kalashnikovs – but we weren't able to move very fast.

Moscow, Zenith, Shoe and I covered the rear, sometimes

stopping to keep the enemy away with direct gunfire so the infantry could break away and retreat.

At a certain point, however, we noticed that the enemies had entered a small building, a sort of cottage surrounded by a half-destroyed fence. From there, they fired two long blasts at us – I could hear the bullets hit the house next to me. So Moscow responded to the fire with the grenade launcher. Their shelter exploded and four or five were buried in the rubble. The rest of the group started to run off, but I was still able to land a bullet in one's back. I saw him fall to the ground lifeless.

We resumed running and joined our men quickly. We were passing a road when a sudden blast of heavy machine gun fire came from the top of a building. Two of the infantrymen fell, almost split in half by the powerful bullets. The others were covered in their blood, and the gun was still shooting.

Private Ustinov, the young Cossack, and one of our comrades were carrying the soldier with the head wound. A volley of bullets hit them straight on. The wounded one literally split open – his body exploded, making a loud pop like when a tyre blows. The other soldier had taken a bullet to the chest and kept on running for a bit, but then his head turned almost all the way round, and after a few metres he fell down, dead.

Ustinov was wounded in the leg, and bleeding. His father and cousin managed to take cover in a nearby building, going through the window; some of our men and other infantrymen went with them. The rest of the group and I ducked into the house across the way.

Ustinov was on the ground, right between our two positions; the bullet must have fractured the bone because he couldn't get to his feet. The Arab with the machine gun tried to hit him, but he was able to hide behind a row of cement poles. Then the gun went for the poles and they crumbled one by one, exposing our wounded man's position more and more.

His father, Vasily, was on the other side, watching the whole scene from the window in desperation. Private Ustinov tried to hide as best he could, but the poles around him were popping off like matches.

At some point Shoe said:

'I can't stand here and watch this anymore!'

He took off his vest, belt and side pouches, and was left with just his jumpsuit. His vest was in pretty bad shape – it was full of dents and had two big holes in the chest.

Shoe put it over his head, and backing down the hall, he said:

'Cover me, boys! And forgive me if something goes wrong!'

He leapt out the front door, sprinting like a tiger hunting its prey. The machine gun began shooting at him too late, by the time he had already reached the poles, and didn't hit him.

From the windows, meanwhile, we fired non-stop towards the building where the Arab with the machine gun was. Kalashnikov shots came at us from a different direction, so I signalled to my men, pulled out my precision rifle, and moved to the back room of the building.

Moscow came with me, to cover me in case anyone ambushed us.

From the house across the way, Nosov launched a grenade. It blew up just above the machine gun, and while the machine gunner's position was enveloped in dust and flame, Shoe stood up, threw Ustinov over his shoulder, and threw the open vest on top of him. Then he rushed towards us.

They were shooting at him from the bottom floors. I hit one guy in the head – he had made the mistake of looking up and staying at the window a few seconds too long. I got another one in the chest; he fell backwards and didn't get up again. One, however, wouldn't let me catch him. He was very agile; he went from one room to another, appearing at a window and disappearing immediately afterward. I began to shoot at all the windows on that floor and hit him by chance.

Shoe hurtled into the house and fell face down on the floor, along with the wounded man. We all thought they'd killed him. Often someone would get hit by a bullet, even in a vital organ, but still keep running for a few metres.

Zenith jumped on him and turned him over. He was fine, without a scratch, he was just breathing heavily and couldn't talk yet.

Ustinov was completely white – he'd really had a close call. Zenith and Moscow treated his wound, using two individual medi-kits. They wrapped it in an entire roll of bandages, and with another they applied some medication right below the knee so he wouldn't lose too much blood. But it was clear that if he didn't see a doctor soon, the dressing wouldn't be enough.

Nosov loaded another grenade but this time he aimed perfectly. He hit their position straight on, and the machine gun fell to the ground along with some of the Arabs, right in front of the windows of our building.

We joined the rest of the group, and quickly consulted the map with Captain Nosov. We had to get to the closest building, on the other side of the street; we would enter it and then exit through the back. There, according to the directions, there was a group of private houses with gardens, and behind them we would finally find our positions. A few Arabs continued shooting a Kalashnikov from the windows, trying to catch us.

We made a shield that would allow our men to cross the street. The Cossacks carried their wounded relative, the others tried to run as fast as possible. Inside the house there was a small enemy group, but the infantrymen confronted and eliminated them in no time; when we got there all the work had been taken care of.

There was a large block of cement in the middle of the yard − it looked like the foundations of a building that had never been finished. It was about twenty metres long and empty inside, a good place to hide in. One by one we jumped in.

We were exhausted, all breathing as if we were on the verge of one big heart attack.

Nosov said that he and Moscow were going to try to reach the line to ask for assistance from our troops to create a free corridor for us to pass through. The Arabs had stopped shooting, and Nosov wanted to make the most of that invaluable moment. He removed all his ammo, threw it at my feet, leaving just two clips attached to his rifle. Following my lead, Moscow did the same, then he took his Glock from under his vest and gave it to the wounded Cossack. Though he was in such a bad way that he couldn't even keep hold of his rifle, he took Moscow's pistol and held it to his chest.

'We'll be back with our men in fifteen minutes,' said Nosov. 'Wait here, stay out of sight, and do not provoke combat in any way.' Then he jumped to the other side and started running across the yard.

Moscow went after him, saying in his usual lighthearted tone:

'See ya later! Be good!'

We stayed inside that makeshift cement shelter, waiting for our boys.

Waiting is the hardest thing. When you're waiting for something that isn't within your control, every second that goes by is torture. I checked my watch every ten seconds, then I realised that it was just making me more nervous and I stopped looking. So I took a better look at my new comrades – we had been through quite an ordeal, and I still hadn't seen their faces.

Sergeant Lavrov had slightly pointy ears and wavy blond hair – he looked like an elf. Private Ustinov, on the other hand, was an exact replica of his father. All that was missing was the moustache; in every other way they were identical. One soldier had a scar on his face, perhaps he'd got it even before entering the army. Another pulled a little kitten out from his jacket; it was black and white, with a dark spot around the eyes that looked like a bandit's mask. It was scrawny and scared, trembling all over and looking around, meowing weakly.

The soldier started petting him and he purred right away.

'How old is he?' Zenith asked.

The soldier smiled. 'A month old. I took him from the mother cat in the artillery unit last week . . .'

Shoe broke out laughing:

'So young and already initiated into battle . . . He'll become cat general!'

I was looking at the kitten and I felt like him. At that moment it was clear that we were all exactly like that kitten; alive because of fate. And it wasn't over yet, neither for him nor for us, unfortunately . . .

Vasily, the old Cossack, was breathing heavily. His face was bright red, and he was bathed in sweat. He had removed his jacket and was just in his undershirt, over which he had put a bulletproof vest. I noticed a few dents in the vest, a sign that he had caught a bullet or two. His son was sitting in front of him, his head down, as if he were ashamed of something. He was still hugging Moscow's pistol to his chest.

My ankle hurt like hell from the sprain I'd got jumping off the car. My foot was all swollen. I noticed just then that I was still and was breathing more calmly. Examining my vest I saw that a bullet was lodged in one of the Kalashnikov clips I kept in my inside pocket – amidst all the gunfire I hadn't even felt the impact. Shoe was also tracing the cut a bullet had made on one side of the vest he had thrown on Private Ustinov earlier; the projectile had taken a miraculous path, skimming the surface without going inside the vest. In military slang an occurrence like that is called 'blessed', as if God had intervened at the last minute to save a soldier's life.

We were all incredulous that we'd made it through such a close call. I'm sure that each of us, more than once that day, had silently bid farewell to life . . .

At some point Vasily took an orthodox cross from his pocket, stood up and went over to Shoe. Then he leaned over him and put the cross around his neck. Shoe looked at him in astonishment, standing up too. The Cossack embraced him and kissed him on both cheeks:

'Today is a happy day . . . Our Lord sent me another son . . .' The old man almost had tears in his eyes; he was as proud as a father at his son's wedding. Shoe looked at the cross for a moment and then responded, scratching his head:

'Thanks, uh . . . The fact is that we tend not to leave our men in the lurch.'

The Cossack smiled without saying a word.

We had been waiting for over half an hour, but there was still no sign of Nosov and Moscow. Every so often we could hear a few shots in the distance, and all of us were secretly thinking the worst.

I had just decided to poke my head out to get a look at the situation outside, when suddenly I had to duck back down. There were two huge explosions, most certainly the cannons on the heavy tanks. Right after that, we heard a brief burst of gunfire – the shots seemed right behind us.

I inserted my last cartridge in my Kalashnikov and sent the round to the chamber. I placed the selector on the single shot and along with the others got ready to fight. Just then we heard our men's voices; a group of paras was rushing across the yard behind the enemy positions. The gunfight was right in the back of the yard. Suddenly a paratrooper lieutenant jumped into our shelter, landing right in between us. Astonished, he looked at us for all of a second and then said:

'What the hell are you guys doing here? Don't you know that this area is under enemy control?'

Shoe grabbed his vest from the ground and threw it at the paratrooper's feet. Looking at the bullet holes, he whistled in surprise.

Shoe shot back sarcastically:

'Under enemy control? We had no idea . . .'

We emerged from our refuge. The paras and infantry-men went ahead, breaking through the enemy defence. I could feel my head spinning, like I was drunk. At some point, we saw a BTR pop out from a narrow road, headed towards us; on top sat Nosov and Moscow, who signalled to us not to come out into the street. We stopped by a house and hid behind a wall. The car came right to us and Nosov shouted:

'Jump on, boys! Quick, there are still Arabs every-where . . .'

We got on the BTR and headed off to our territory.

We powered through the streets of the city, heading for camp, passing by the ruins of half-destroyed houses that looked like the giant skeletons of prehistoric animals. One of the things that made an impression on me from the very beginning was all the rubble from the buildings. Everything around you, in war, becomes a sort of magni-fied image of what's going on inside you. It was like we were drowned in an inhuman violence that changed people, annihilated them, even our souls were reduced to rubble . . . I looked at the gutted houses, the collapsed walls and the burnt furniture, the photographs of people I didn't know torched and torn up, thrown aside without remorse, without any respect for memory. Anyone who experiences a war, whether fighting it or fleeing from it – either way, trying to survive – no longer has anything of his own, not even his own history.

None of us thought of the past or the future – every day was today. We were immersed in a long, single day. That's how I was, too, and by that time I'd become used to occasionally seeing toys among the ruins of houses; I didn't give them any weight, I tried to maintain the same indifference with which I observed everything I encoun-tered along the road: burned-out cars, big cracks in the ground, broken pipes, disfigured bodies . . .

The car went on ahead, and I was lost in my thoughts. I was beginning to see the reality around me like a series of short film sequences which appeared in my mind and paused there for a moment before vanishing. We had already left the city behind; the worst was over. I felt sleep coming over me, it felt like I was falling through space, but I did everything I could not to crash. Nosov was sitting in front of us, his back against the turret of the heavy machine gun. He looked at us with a half smile on his face, he was pleased. A few armoured cars and three heavy tanks came up the road behind us: the paratroopers and explorers.

I was facing backwards, looking at the column of cars in the procession, when I heard an explosion. The ground started shaking so hard that we were all about to fall off the car – the BTR began oscillating like a sheet of paper in a gust of wind. It seemed as if everything were about to cave in.

After the first explosion, another one went off, and then another. An enormous dust cloud rose from the city, and tall flames stretched up to the sky. Soon we were hit by an unbearable wave of heat. These were the effects of the air strike. Our attack had begun.

For a second I tried to imagine what was happening back there where the cloud was: total destruction. The temperature would be so high that the armour plating on the cars would drip off, leaving only the bare chassis, as if it had been covered in liquid material. Human bodies would burn completely – afterwards, not even the bones would be left.

You couldn't even hear the airplanes, nor anything to indicate that the bombs were dropping from the sky, just a series of explosions of such force and power that all the ground around us wouldn't stop shaking. The paras counted each explosion, gleefully shouting in unison, like when people count a birthday boy's age by pulling on his ears. I felt very lucky, and it gave me goose bumps to think that we too had risked ending up beneath those bombs . . .

The car finally came to the yard of our camp, the same place we had left that morning. The sandbag-surrounded tent was still there, and the major of general command was outside, with a bulletproof vest on and a Kalashnikov in his hands. He had a lit cigarette in his teeth, and when he saw us, he rushed over to our car:

'So you did it! My God, you're lunatics!'

He walked around the BTR looking at us one by one, as if we were objects on display in a museum. The car came to a stop and we all got out.

The infantryman sergeant approached the major and saluted:

'Comrade Major, permission to report!'

The major stared as if he had a ghost standing in front of him:

'Permission granted, Comrade Sergeant!'

The soldier took a deep breath and began, with a tired but firm voice:

'I, Sergeant Lavrov, from the explorer unit of the 168th armoured infantry division, report that the unit was surrounded by enemy forces and pushed into the occupied zone. We took defence of the perimeter, but sixty-seven soldiers, thirteen lieutenant colonels and four officers fell in battle.' He spoke these words with his lips taut, almost like he was shooting them out with a machine gun. 'Thanks to the assistance of the saboteurs, the unit returned to the safe zone, but during the course of the operation seven soldiers fell and one was wounded. Numbering nine soldiers, the unit is now at your command.'

The major paid great attention to Lavrov's report. He looked as if he'd been listening to news about his own family. At the end he shook his hand:

'We honour your courage, Sergeant. The whole unit displayed real . . .'

He wasn't able to finish his sentence because, on the other side of the yard, three of our infantrymen jumped out from the entrance to the building, yelling. One of them had been hit in the neck, but from the way he was moving you could tell that it wasn't serious; even if blood was gushing out the bullet must only have grazed him. Their shouting had interrupted the major, who'd been about to venture into one of those touching military speeches usually given by those who never go anywhere near the front line and are impressed by everything, placing grotesque importance on every little banality of war.

'For fuck's sake!' the wounded man yelled. 'What the fuck are you doing there, they're pushing us hard! Everyone over here, now, or else we're screwed!' And with some more insults as well as a nice string of expletives the soldier went back into the building. A battle was underway. Some enemies had managed to escape the air strike and attack our line of defence. Although some had died immediately, others had pushed themselves all the way to our camp. Now, a group of Arabs – probably about fifty men – was trying desperately to get into the building under our infantry's control. They were armed with light weapons, shouting, while our explorers, with ten support tanks, exterminated everyone they encountered on their path.

The other two infantrymen went to a crate of ammo in the centre of the yard and began filling their pockets and side pouches with Kalashnikov clips. Without waiting for an official invite, we went to help them out. There was no time to tie all the clips together, so I took a few individual ones, throwing them in my trouser pockets, and I slid a couple under my jacket.

The hammer of heavy machine guns on our tanks could be heard everywhere. I saw a spray of bullets hit a small group of about fifteen men; in an instant, body parts, arms, legs flew off. Everything was soaked in blood. Our tanks continued to advance, pushing them against the building. Although the building was defended by three machine guns shooting from under the roof, a few Arabs had managed to break through the defence nonetheless, penetrating the left wing on the ground floor and landing in a large room. We all ran towards the building to give the infantry our support.

Smoke was coming out of the left wing, and long blasts of gunfire could be heard; one of our men was calling for help, others were shouting to be careful of the hallway, because some enemies had hidden in the rooms, waiting to shoot anyone who passed by.

It was total chaos. It was impossible to tell where our men were or where theirs were. These situations are absolutely the most dangerous, because you can catch a bullet even from your own, or get trapped in gunfire from both sides, not to mention the shrapnel from hand grenades flying everywhere . . . In military slang, a situation like this is called a 'hurricane in a box', and the likelihood of getting wounded amidst all the chaos is very high.

We went down the corridor; we had to cross it all the way to reach the room at the end. Moscow was running in front of us, with a hand grenade poised to throw. Nosov was behind him, then Zenith, with his vest unfastened, hanging off him like the armour of a medieval knight. I was running behind him. Suddenly I slipped on a piece of broken glass and fell, hitting the wall. I got up almost immediately, running again as if it were nothing, but my ankle kept getting worse.

Moscow was going past a doorway when gunfire came from the room. He fell to the ground, letting out a yell, and then the hand grenade exploded in the room. I threw myself down, hitting a wall again, while the shrapnel from the bomb flew over our heads. Usually an explosion from a hand grenade makes holes in the upper part of the walls, which are made out of brick or another light material; whereas the supporting parts, made out of cement, can better withstand the force of the explosion and repel the shards.

Moscow had a hole in his left leg. He was furious,

and from a sitting position kept shooting into the room, out of which billowed dust and smoke – you could hear cries coming from inside, a man desperately shouting something in Arabic. It was hard to listen to, it was like an animal bellowing at slaughter. Nosov went into the room; the man said something else and our captain shot him, point blank. We scrambled to get a closer look; the Arab was stretched out on the floor, still moving. His body went through one last tremor of pain, and then went still. His legs were in tatters from the shrapnel; his right arm had been blown off at the elbow. Nearby were the bodies of three more; one of them must have tried to save his friends by jumping into the bomb, and had been literally disintegrated by the explosion. Bits of his body were stuck to the walls and there was a lot of blood.

I went to the window and saw three more Arabs coming to jump inside. They were about five metres away; one of them was surprised to see me there but didn't have time to lift his rifle before I'd framed him in the sight of my Kalashnikov. Trying to bend down, he let out a howl, and right after that my bullets hit him head on; I could see bits of his flesh flying through the air. I kept shooting, I couldn't stop, and I knocked down the other two as well. I used up an entire magazine on them.

Nosov looked at me and said:

'It's going to be a long day, boys . . .'

We went out into the hall. Moscow had got up from the ground and had resumed leading the group. He was really agitated; his leg must have hurt like hell.

Nosov yelled at him:

'Keep up, otherwise today will be your last!'

Moscow just made a gesture of irritation, and when he got to the end of the hall he went into the room first. The situation was really bad – our infantry already had six losses. There were so many Arabs: they were shooting from the windows and then hiding, probably waiting for the right moment to burst out.

One of the infantrymen said that the enemies had reached the stairs, so we divided tasks: Zenith and I would go on reconnaissance on the upper floors while the others would fight in the room along with the infantry.

We rushed up the stairs. On the second floor, we found three soldiers dead and one seriously wounded; he was lying down and couldn't speak, blood gushed from his ears, his legs were filled with shards – a hand grenade must have exploded right next to him. As soon as we looked into the hallway to go up to the third floor, we were met by a short burst of gunfire at the top of the stairs. A round hit me in the vest and I fell to the floor. Zenith responded by firing the grenade launcher attached to his Kalashnikov. I got to my feet and moved towards the stairs, this time more carefully.

I had almost reached the stairs, when one of our soldiers opened fire with an RPG heavy grenade launcher from the opposite side of the hall. I was hit by a powerful blast of air, which lifted me up like a leaf and propelled me all the way down the hallway.

*

I was stunned, I couldn't see a thing, and everything had suddenly become mixed up in my head. Scenes that I had gone through that day and other events in the previous days were getting confused with one another. I couldn't tell which way was up − I had a whistling in my ears that kept getting louder and I could hear voices but they were very far away, as if they were behind a closed door.

When my sight returned I realised that I was lying against the wall. Five infantrymen were running towards me, while Zenith was above me, trying to lift me off the ground.

'Cease fire, cease fire! Saboteurs, 76th division!' he yelled.

Little by little it seemed like the vertigo was fading, and the ringing in my ears had become a little more bearable.

I managed to stand up.

The infantrymen were explaining to Zenith that more enemies had reached the building and were preparing to enter. Then they turned to me, checked that I was okay and asked me if I could set up a sniper position over the left wing. I said yes, but my head was still spinning. I started walking towards the exit. Zenith went with the infantrymen to the fourth floor, where they had placed another machine gun, to check the area outside.

That whole day I went around in the midst of the battle like a ghost. I don't remember exactly what I did, I just remember that at some point someone gave me a grenade launcher and told me to shoot outside. I couldn't swear whether it actually happened or I imagined it, but in my head I have a very clear image of lifting the grenade launcher to my shoulder, trying to find a good room to shoot from, as perhaps someone from command had ordered me to do.

I had just taken position at one of the windows and was aiming at an armoured car when Shoe arrived.

'What the fuck are you doing, Kolima!' he yelled, startled. 'That's one of ours!' and he pulled the grenade launcher out of my hands.

Only then did I notice that it was already dark outside – it must have been late. I'd wandered around the building all day under the effect of the concussion.

'Go down to the courtyard and sleep with the others!' Shoe said.

Obediently, I went to the exit.

I walked down the hallway of this building where people had once lived and now there was only destruction, while the shards of that ruined peace crunched under my feet: glass, pieces of paper, broken furniture, pipes, burned books, bricks . . . in some places the ceiling had caved in; a block of reinforced cement leaned against a wall, it was straight and whole as if it had been cut out precisely, with a chisel.

I was so exhausted I felt like a magnet was holding me to the ground. My body didn't hurt anymore, the blows I'd taken on that never-ending day had been completely absorbed by the emptiness that my tiredness had plunged me into. I was limping, dragging my swollen foot; I could see it bent in an unnatural way but I didn't feel any pain. My headache, too, had become almost pleasant. Reality had gone and hidden somewhere else; a cloud of fog had fallen before my eyes, and like a giant strip of gauze, had dressed all my wounds . . .

Around me ran our infantrymen, paratroopers, the *spetsnaz* – they were all agitated, shouting, repeating the commands they'd been given. Right as I was passing by a room with windows overlooking the street, a violent burst of fire came. The bullets crossed the room and lodged into the wall in front of me. A cloud of dust rose up, and small bits of cement and plaster hit me in the face. Instinctively, I closed my eyes, but without making too much of it, and I continued down the hall. About ten infantrymen came in and started shooting wildly from the windows.

The rhythmic sound of the bullets calmed me down. It was hypnotic, it made me feel the calm and comfort you feel when you climb into a bed with clean, warm sheets after a day of tiredness and cold . . . Everything around me was moving at maximum speed, the battle was going ahead even if we had already condemned the enemy to defeat . . .

These are the moments in war in which human strength goes beyond its absolute limit; a sort of second collective breath comes on and everyone becomes fast and synchronised, like machines. But I saw everything as if in slow-motion; I felt like I was outside that reality.

I went out to the courtyard, where there were four armoured cars and a tank. There weren't many lights around, but the clearing was full of our soldiers, bustling around like ants. Ten artillerymen were placing two heavy mortars right in the middle of the yard, and within seconds they were ready to fire. Everywhere there were open crates with cartridges for AKs, hand grenades, ammunition for grenade launchers, and coils for submachine guns.

To one side, our dead were laid out in a row. There were ten or so. One of them had the infantry insignia on his sleeve; someone had put a lit candle in his hands, which were folded on his chest. Another had lost an arm, which they had tied to his neck with a piece of fabric from his uniform. Some of the bodies were completely charred, but seemed tall as normal. They were covered with military tent fabric, but the cloth had shifted a little to the side, perhaps it had been the wind. One had the skin on his face burned off; he didn't have a nose or ears and his teeth stuck out, as if he were growling. Last, there was a body with just the left arm – he had lost both legs, and around him there was a pile of other arms, legs, pieces of ankles and hands. A piece of cardboard was attached on top with the date written in ballpoint – it was the day before our arrival, when the infantry had suffered a night attack from the enemy – and someone had added, in handwriting like a three-year-old child's: 'Boys, here are all the pieces of the 201st unit, there was nothing else left in the area.'

An infantry lieutenant was standing beside the armoured car. I went over to him, and saw that he had a hole in place of an eye – the wound had been plugged up with a rag. He grimaced with pain, but he still continued giving orders to three sergeants, one of whom had a bloody bandage around his left arm.

Moscow was sitting on our car, treating his wounded leg. When he saw me he called me over right away, asking for help. I climbed up onto the BTR like a zombie; I didn't want to do anything.

Everything around us was black; the only light came from the machine gun turret, which Moscow had turned towards his leg. He was holding surgical pliers and a scalpel – the hole was about ten centimetres above his knee, towards the outside of his leg. The good kind of blood, the kind that's not too thick, was coming out of the wound, but there was a lot of it.

'You were so lucky,' I said, looking at his leg. 'A few centimetres and it would have hit your artery . . .'

'What the fuck are you talking about!' He was irritated, but his voice didn't betray any trace of suffering. 'There's no way they're going to get me in this war. The gypsy told me . . .'

Without replying I took the scalpel from his hand and made two cuts around the wound a few centimetres wide. That way it would be easier to extract the bullet; pulling the skin down on both sides, I would try to pull the bullet as far out of the flesh as possible.

Moscow intently observed the way I cut the wound, disinfecting it as best I could with a dirty rag that smelled like gasoline.

As always, he found something to complain about:

'Is that what you call a cut? Come on, go deeper!'

'What, have you got a missile in there?' I responded. 'That's enough, don't be annoying . . . Just hand me the pliers.'

Moscow made a disgusted face and passed me the pliers. I noticed that my hand was trembling from tiredness. Trying to gather my last strength, I closed my eyes for a moment and took a deep breath. Behind my closed eyelids, instead of darkness, I saw flying stars, white circles and flashing lights – a clear sign of exhaustion.

'What are you waiting for, I'm tired too!' Moscow shouted at me, bringing me back to reality.

Then he took his leg with his hands and violently pulled the skin down. The wound widened immediately and blood started pouring out – the skin was almost turned inside out. The light was directly on his leg, but even with that I couldn't see much. I strained to put things into focus.

I stuck the pliers into the wound, and they went down, sliding around smoothly. I pushed slowly, until the point hit the end of the bullet. I opened the pliers slightly, closed the bullet in the grip and tried turning it a little to make sure I had a good hold. The bullet seemed pretty firm and stable, so I tightened the pliers until they went *clack*.

Moscow was still. After all the action he was still full of adrenaline; the shock caused by the trauma hadn't yet subsided. At that moment I could have taken his appendix out without anaesthesia and he wouldn't have felt a thing.

With my hand trembling, I very slowly extracted the bullet from my friend's leg. It was a 5.45-calibre, it had definitely come from a model of Kalashnikov that has a short barrel, which had not put much force on the bullet. If it had been shot from a long-barrelled rifle, that same bullet would have entered the body but wouldn't have stopped, it would have travelled, slicing through the flesh, leaving little hope . . . A bullet like that could go into your leg and come out of your neck, making a pâté of your internal organs. Moscow had been very lucky.

I cleaned the wound a little more, since it kept bleeding, then I took out one of my medi-kits. Moscow didn't have any more: he'd just given his last one to one of the infantry soldiers.

'Hang in there, boy, you're all grown up now,' I said, passing him a needle and thread. 'You should sew it up, my hands are shaky . . .' He took the kit without a word, but he gave me a friendly slap on the back, his way of saying thanks.

I jumped down from the car, and walking unsteadily as if drunk, I went over to the back where Shoe was already sleeping.

I set down my rifle and couldn't even get my vest off before a superhuman force pinned me to the ground.

The soil was hot, boiling almost − I could feel it vibrate with every explosion. Thus sleep came over me, and looking up at the starry sky I felt a piercing sense of fear and weakness. I could no longer tell whether the stars I saw up there were real, or if they were just fiery bullets that were going to rain down over me. I wondered what those lights could be, and in this state of uncertainty I fell asleep. I was too tired, so tired I would have let myself be killed by the stars which I confused with the flaming lead mercilessly falling all around me . . .

We slept for an entire day. One of the infantrymen had thrown a tent cloth over us, just like the one we used to cover the bodies of the fallen. Even the clean-up crew took us for dead. One of them gave me a kick in the chest, as they would do – and as I had done too – to drive the rats out of the bodies.

I moved, and he was startled. I pulled down the cloth and sat up, looking around me, confused. There was no trace of the infantrymen; they had gone ahead with the rest of the troops.

Our car was the only one left in the yard. Next to it there was just one tank, and behind that a small mobile kitchen, where there was something good boiling on the fire. Two tankers were sitting on the tank, eating hot food out of little individual pots.

Behind me, I could hear that Shoe had woken up too. He gave me such a hard slap on the shoulder that I almost fell over.

'Ahhh, damn, what a great nap . . .' he said. 'And now it's time to eat! Let's move, Kolima, before everything gets cold!'

I scratched my head without really understanding, and I responded:

'Let's go, yeah, I'm dying to eat . . .'

And along with him I went limping towards the kitchen.

We ate in silence. When we finished, Shoe came out with a statement that seemed to me like an absolute truth:

'I understood for the first time today how nice it is to be in the world.'

That's what he said, simply, and it felt like he was showing me his soul as a material thing, like an object there in his hands.

NO ONE WILL EVER KNOW...

The forest burned over the river
and along with it burned the dawn.
Out of eighteen boys
only three of us remain . . .

How many dear friends
have fallen in the dark,
near an unknown town,
in a place with no name . . .

From the song of the Russian veterans of WWII

Russia is a country whose citizens are the first to support
government corruption. This is why our society will never be
able to become democratic or liberal: the Russians can only
live properly under some form of dictatorship.

*A statement made by the history teacher at
Bender's top middle school*

Parade uniform collects dust on the shelf,
moths eat at the gold epaulettes.
And we have the tough and thankless lot
of defending this world without law.

Today ancient evil's not scared of the cross,
chaos is trying on the crown,
and he who still has a clean conscience
is destined to become an outlaw.

On a series of fronts generals stage
this new drama of the nation,
but because of this theatre season
an officer's dignity is against the law.

In the bought prattle of media hacks
and functionaries at every level
we deploy on a military mission,
where our every step is unlawful.

In this poor downtrodden nation
that so much resembles a prison,
someone might as well stay
in the civil war – the outlaw.

*Song by Sergei Trofimov dedicated to the officers and soldiers
who took part in the counter-terrorist operations in the
Chechen Republic*

It was late October in Chechnya when our team was given a temporary post. We were sent to the 46th motorized infantry unit base. The position was in the mountains, at a strategic point with a view of two very narrow valleys.

The word going around was that the explorers had sounded the alarm because the enemy was concentrating military forces in those mountains. There were two large armed groups equipped with Igla single-fire missiles, a surface-to-air missile system they had used to take down one of our transport helicopters.

A few units from the two paratrooper divisions had reached the base first, in tanks and armoured cars; you could sense that a big military operation was getting underway, with several units of the Russian Army involved.

No specific orders came for three days but lots of strange stories circulated among the soldiers about that helicopter explosion. Some said that an officer from command had been on board, so it had to do with the death of someone important; others just kept saying it was scandalous for the enemy to possess one of our most powerful weapons. The infantry officers had in fact explained that some Iglas, about ten, had been stolen during a battle when one of our columns transporting equipment had been attacked by the Arabs.

As usual, Captain Nosov derided all these theories, and would say it was about illegal trafficking, supported and run by the men in command. He cursed those double-crossing traitors, who according to him sold all our most cutting-edge, high-tech weapons to the Chechens and Arabs to help them to resist us as long as possible, because 'it's in their interest for this war not to end too quickly'. As the captain often said, 'The generals and politicians at the Kremlin eat our charred flesh and drink our rotten blood.' Sometimes his rants almost seemed poetic.

Even back during the First Chechen Campaign, it was very common for the enemy to have the same equipment as us, even the latest models produced in Russia – which, for our army, were still considered experimental prototypes and thus were barely in circulation – sometimes ended up in their hands.

The Russian politicians of the time – led by that 'stupid drunk Yeltsin', as Nosov always called him, 'who sold out to the United States of America' – needed, according to our Captain, a black hole, a place that swallowed money and spat it out clean, supporting their so-called 'democratic' regime, which was run the American way – that is, with wars, lies, illicit trade and total lack of respect for the people of the Russian Federation. That black hole was Chechnya.

'The Americans gave Yeltsin and his men a huge helping hand – they were able to control the whole orchestration of this disgusting war,' Nosov vented for the thousandth time while we were on our way to base in the helicopter. 'Who knows how much fun the strategists at the Pentagon had when they came up with this foul plan of local war right within the borders of their old enemy, the USSR . . . And through misinformation, political and ethnic agitation, they provoked us like a bunch of war dogs, straining at the leash.'

Essentially, their tactics were analogous to raping a dead body. It wasn't enough for them to kill the 'Soviet bloc' – they still wanted to satisfy their sick thirst for dominion somehow, and to our shame there wasn't anyone in Russia capable of stopping them . . .

Our first day on the 46th infantry base went by without anything in particular happening; we saboteurs stayed in our assigned barracks, waiting for something. Indeed, we knew that sooner or later command would give us our orders; they wouldn't have moved all those units from one post to another without a specific reason.

The paratroopers, on the other hand – as often happened in times of calm – caused a ruckus, got drunk, hassled the girls in the infirmary and the kitchen, and ribbed the other soldiers.

Based on our captain's experience and advice, we got some rest. Whenever we could, we slept, and the rest of the time we ate like cows. Nosov personally requested a double ration for each of us and a little something extra when possible, stuff from the food depot that was usually reserved for the officers, like sweet hot tea and a kind of cake that we really loved.

In addition, Moscow had made a deal with the helicopter pilot who'd taken us to the base: in exchange for an American pistol – a Colt, and we had quite a few – he gave us a bag of lemons, ten chocolate bars and five tins of red caviar. It was a great deal; usually for a pistol we could get two cartons of cigarettes and three bottles of whisky at most. All the drivers and pilots asked the guys in the active units to get them American or European guns, and since in war money doesn't mean the same as in civilian life – 'the closer you are to the line of fire, the less money is worth' – we calculated the value of everything in food.

I should say that on that occasion the technical quality of the gun helped us out – it was really nice, and often for Russian soldiers, especially the ones who didn't fight on the front lines, a Colt was a status symbol, an object to show friends and family when they returned home, and who knows how many stories they told to show off, to look like someone who had fought a tough battle and in the end had won. We also had a saying:

'All the girls go for the guy who brings back a Colt as a trophy.'

So, after going to the 'store', we were able to spend a few peaceful days on base. Our group went by the 'law of the camel': whenever you have the chance, eat everything you can and as much as you can.

On the second night, a friendly nurse who would visit the various units to chat a little and look for some 'male affection', told us that our comrades in the motorised paratrooper division, unlike us, would usually offer her vodka. And they were happy to do so, seeing her as a symbol of feminine virtue.

'Don't you guys drink?' she asked us out of the blue.

I've never been much of a drinker, but the idea of downing a little good vodka didn't sound too bad at all. And the rest of the guys seemed to agree.

Zenith was the most eager; he had a real weakness for booze.

'Well, I guess we could go for a sip or two . . .'

'I know the tankers have quite a reserve,' the nurse said.

We started to think up a plan. It was pointless hoping that the tankers would give us any; we had no choice but to steal a few bottles from them or somehow force them to share their precious cargo with us.

We knew that the tankmen, like many other units, had a mascot. It was a very common practice in war; soldiers would often bring dogs or cats with them, or even try to tame wild animals like squirrels or hedgehogs – some even had an ermine. Our tankers, however, were notorious because their favourite animals were sewer rats – probably because in military slang the tankers themselves were called 'rats', since during combat they had to stay inside the small cabin space inside the tank yet still be able to move with agility. As a matter of fact, each tank had its own rat – everyone would feed it and it would get fat like an old spoiled cat.

Soldiers follow lots of superstitions in war, and losing the mascot is considered very bad luck . . .

Maybe we'd found the way to have ourselves a nice big drink.

Nosov had gone out a few hours earlier to visit an old friend of his, a major who'd fought with him in Afghanistan and now commanded one of the assault units stationed at the same base. When Nosov went to see his friends nobody was to disturb him, go with him or follow him. Everyone who had fought in Afghanistan had a tradition of sorts — they only met amongst themselves and didn't allow us young people to come.

That same night we left the barracks and headed for the area where the tanks were. It was a wide, unpaved clearing in the middle of the base. Down from the sky fell a light sharp rain that drummed on us insistently.

Autumn is melancholy in those parts, and since we were obliged to wade through the mud, I almost felt like we were in the famous folk poem by Sergei Yesenin, the one where he talks about this season in a rather crude way. It goes like this:

> It is cold, it's come autumn,
> the birds have quit pecking at shit,
> some cow crapped in the pail of milk,
> That's just the weather, fuck it!

The tanks were side by side, half a metre apart. The cannons were lowered so that water couldn't get inside them. But if you looked carefully at the ends of the cannons, every now and then you'd see a rat's nose poking out. Our tankers often kept their mascots there, and the rats liked it. They didn't run away; sometimes they went out to get a little fresh air but they always went back inside where it was warm.

There were some tankers standing guard, but we avoided them without too much difficulty and quickly reached the nearest tank. We waited a little, quiet, until a rat's whiskered nose peeked out of the barrel.

Moscow signalled for us to keep an eye out, and we surrounded the tank. Then he put on a pair of thick leather gloves, the kind that machine gunners usually wear, because during a battle the gun gets so hot that if you reload it with your bare hands you risk getting burned. Moscow climbed onto the tank, then grabbed on to the cannon with one hand while with the other he made a quick swipe, clamping the rat by the head and pulling him out with a strong and firm sweep of his arm. As soon as Moscow jumped down, we ran back to our post.

Back in the barracks, we got to know the rat. He was a big, fat animal, with a long tail and very clean fur that shone as if he shampooed it every evening. He had a collar made from a piece of green tent fabric, with the rat's name and the number of the tank he belonged to sewn on with white thread. It was a boy; his name was Zeus.

Zeus never gave the impression he was scared of us,

even if he seemed annoyed by the kidnapping. We put him inside a zinc box where we usually kept bullets for the Kalashnikovs. Moscow was very attentive to him; he put a piece of bread in his box, and made a little water bowl by cutting a piece out of an empty tube of tomato paste. Then he made three holes in the top of the box so air could circulate.

After all that Moscow looked satisfied. He gave the rat's temporary prison a little tap with his knife and said:

'In here, my dear fellows, we have not only the key to getting the vodka . . . but also the key to winning the tankers' respect!'

We started laughing. He seemed as determined as Napoleon must have been before his Russian campaign.

A delegation composed of Moscow, Zenith and Shoe communicated to the tank's crew the means, time and conditions for payment of the ransom. The tankers accepted our offer on the spot: a case of vodka in exchange for Zeus. We were ecstatic.

Around four in the morning five of them came knocking at our door, carrying twenty-five bottles of vodka in an equipment crate. We gave them back their animal, they quickly verified Zeus's health, and then we all decided to drink together in celebration of our happy transaction.

We sat down at the table and lit a small portable stove that ran on kerosene. Moscow took a zinc case to use as a pan and poured in four tins of stewed meat and some potatoes we'd nabbed from the kitchen the day before. At that point one of the tankers went to their base and came back with a big piece of salted lard; its smell was so strong, intense and appealing I thought I was going to faint. We opened the first bottle of vodka, and after pouring it into a big iron canteen our party finally began.

The canteen was passed from hand to hand, and one by one the bottles were emptied. Amidst many stories of war, peace and life, we started to get a little drunk. The tankers were really nice guys – often the ones who have to be on the alert are more human than the others; knowing they're risking their lives every day gives certain people a kind of purity that's hard to explain. Their leader, a young lieutenant, was great company. He always had a joke at hand, and knew the right thing to say when the conversation went off track.

Around six in the morning – by then we'd emptied almost half the case and could hardly stand – Nosov came back.

Our captain was tired and looked like someone who had just finished a battle. He was sloshed and stank of garlic and fried potatoes. His Kalashnikov was slung over his shoulder and he seemed to be in a terrible mood. He greeted the tankers with a gesture that recalled Stalin saluting his Soviet comrades from the platform at Lenin's tomb. He took note of our little party, then took a piece of bread from the table and dipped it in the melted fat in the zinc pan, where a few potatoes and bits of stew remained.

As he finished his bite, Nosov started looking at each of our faces with such profound desperation in his eyes that despite the effect of the alcohol I had a premonition of danger, as if something tragic were about to happen

. . . Then he got up from the chair, shuffled across the barracks and fell into the first bunk he found. His Kalashnikov was still on him, and it poked out from the bed menacingly, right in our direction.

Shoe said to Zenith:

'Brother, go and disarm our captain. Better not to tempt the Lord's patience . . .'

Zenith turned to Spoon and repeated Shoe's request verbatim.

Spoon went to move, but it was clear that it was a struggle for him to get up, so without anyone saying anything Deer stepped up. He carefully lifted our captain, who was already snoring, and unceremoniously grabbed the rifle out of his hands with a forceful and determined tug. Nosov didn't resist, and with his eyes closed he mumbled:

'We're at altitude 216 southeast of Jalalabad . . . Everyone down, fucking whore of a war! Nobody goes on recon without my permission . . . Bastard helicopter, we're not leaving anyone . . .'

He went on giving orders for a few minutes, cursing at the helicopter and getting pissed off with who knows whom. Finally, mentioning some general whose surname was followed by a vulgar term (which in Russian indicates the female genital organs after sexual intercourse with an animal), he concluded:

'Everywhere we've been, there's no life left . . .'

Then he fell into a deep sleep. We remained in silence for a little while, then we drank to our captain's health as the tankers started retreating to their post.

It was morning, but outside it was very dark. It hadn't

stopped raining yet, and the smell of fried food in our barracks intermingled with the smell of the rain. The air was damp and icy; you could feel the cold coming from outside all the way down into your bones. One by one, we fell into our bunks too.

Deer took off his shoes and lifted his stinky socks up to my face, but I was so tired and drunk that I didn't even have the strength to turn the other way, and I fell asleep inhaling the smell of his feet. Even that was over-powered by the odour that we were already used to – in war, everything is rank and foul.

We slept all day long. Around four in the afternoon my hangover had subsided, but I was still lying in bed, wearing a heavy winter coat. I stared at the ceiling without thinking about anything in particular, like a sick man just waiting to get better. I felt as if I had found myself in a place where we were condemned to stay forever, everyone in the rain, surrounded by the autumn air, pierced by a sadness that went through our souls like the dampness that soaked through our clothes . . .

Moscow and Zenith were sitting at the table and preparing their jackets, sewing the places where the fabric was torn and fixing the side pouches. They were talking in hushed voices about a previous mission of ours where Moscow had risked catching a blast of heavy machine gun fire but had been saved because Nosov grabbed his leg, pulled him down and dragged him into a trench that had been made during the First Chechen Campaign after the explosion of an air bomb.

'It was a close call,' Moscow said.

'I realised too late that I had stood up right in front of the machine gun, but that bastard had hidden himself well . . . For a second I thought I was going to die . . . If it weren't for Nosov I wouldn't be here to tell the story.'

'You should go on making war, not love . . .' Zenith joked.

They both broke out in quiet laughter, so as not to wake the others.

I turned onto my side and put my hood over my head. I couldn't sleep but at the same time I didn't want to get out of bed. Deer was sitting in a corner, and he was eating a piece of dry bread, his teeth making a noise as if he were chewing on pebbles. I turned again, took a deep breath, then closed my eyes and tried to fall asleep, but sleep didn't want to come.

Eventually I decided to get up and go outside to relieve myself. I opened the barracks door and looked at the desert of dirt and mud in front of me. The rain was coming down so hard and heavy it seemed like I had a wall of water in front of me. Without giving it a second thought, I pissed directly from the doorway. Right at that moment an officer wearing a rain poncho appeared out of nowhere and gave me the dirtiest look. Indifferent, I went on emptying my bladder, pretending not to see him. He yelled at me:

'Soldier! Call Nosov over, now – they're expecting him at the colonel's office! All the camp officers are already there, he's the only one left!'

I went to wake up our captain, who was still sleeping in the same position we had left him in. I bumped him with my shoulder and told him that the colonel was waiting for him. Nosov asked what time it was, then with his eyes still half closed, groped around for his rifle. Deer had left it on the floor, at a safe distance from the bed, and I passed it to him.

Nosov stood up and pulled a bag out from under his bunk. He opened it, took out a rain poncho and put it on. He went up to the table and took the canteen with the vodka. He took three gulps, resolute, then he looked at me with seriousness and said:

'Enough with the drinking. Prepare for action. Check the ammo and weapons. There are rain ponchos for everyone in here, get them out. They'll be sending us into the mountains soon . . .'

After these words, he left with the officer, who had been standing by the front door the entire time.

We just looked at one another in silence for a while, as if it seemed impossible that they really were sending us on an operation after all.

Moscow, biting off the thread he was using to sew his jacket, took a deep breath and then said:

'Yep, looks like our vacation's over . . .'

About an hour later, someone knocked on our door. Deer went to open it and found a group of infantry explorers in front of him. Their lieutenant asked:

'Captain Nosov's saboteurs? 76th division?'

Moscow replied in a light, almost ironic tone:

'Yep, that's us . . . Something bad happen?'

The lieutenant looked confident. He smiled at Moscow, and, entering the barracks like an actor would take to the stage, he said:

'For the moment nothing particular has happened, Comrade Private . . . but I think that soon all hell's going to break loose . . .'

Each of us stopped doing whatever he was doing and went over to the lieutenant to hear his explanation. He signalled for his men to come in while Deer went to put the water on to make tea.

The explorers were already prepared for the mission; they were kitted out with vests, weapons, rain ponchos. In the week following our army helicopter's mysterious accident, they had combed every inch of the surrounding mountains, informing our troops about the enemy's presence and watching every move that appeared remotely suspect.

At Nosov's request, they had brought each of us a pair of tall boots, waxed so that water couldn't get through – in war, having dry feet is very important. Personally, one of the things I hated most was when my trainers became muddy and slipped off. Running often carried the risk of ending up barefoot – not the most comfortable thing.

The explorers were equipped like Afghanistan war soldiers; they didn't have canteens attached to their belts but had a few bottles of water in their belly bags;

their rifle ammo was inside the pockets of their jackets, shortened up to the waist just like ours. They carried their knives sideways, concealed behind their belts. They also had side pouches, handmade specially; they were all armed with double magazine paratrooper rifles, some with optic or dioptric scopes. One had a precision rifle just like mine, a VSS with an integrated silencer, wrapped in a piece of soft cloth so it wouldn't get damaged.

They didn't seem anxious. Their faces were the classic faces of people who live in war: tired eyes, deep wrinkles in dry skin, skin corroded by wind, rain, cold and hunger. But behind these men's eyes there was that mix of humility and wisdom that comes only to those accustomed to dying and coming back to life several times a day. These were people who could witness the death of a friend with the tenderness of a loving mother putting her children to bed at night knowing she'll be waking them up in the morning . . .

They sat down on the crates, which were scattered around the room. Someone lit a cigarette, enjoying big gulps of hot tea while their lieutenant unfolded a map on the table and started showing us our destination.

We would have to cross the valley, go up into the mountains and reach the point on the map circled in red.

'Command seems really keen for us to get to the area of the helicopter crash as soon as possible,' the lieutenant said. 'There must be something important there, something we have to find at all costs. Provided the Arabs haven't got there first . . .'

'What if we don't find anything?' Spoon asked, his mouth full with a hunk of tea-soaked bread.

'I have specific orders,' the lieutenant said, serious. 'If the Arabs have arrived before us, we'll have to return to base immediately. We'll give the go-ahead for a general operation, involving all the corps of the military, including the artillery and air force . . .'

Obviously, none of us knew why there was so much interest in a simple transport helicopter that was just like so many others shot down during the war. We immediately started thinking up a million reasons, trying to figure out what could have been on board the ill-fated aircraft that was so precious to command.

One of the explorers said jokingly:

'It was probably a load of rubber dicks for the generals' wives!'

Everyone howled with laughter.

So Moscow, who was standing in the middle of the room with a boot on one foot and a sneaker on the other, triumphantly announced:

'Brothers, before all of you, I officially give this operation code name Operation Where's The Dildo?'

We couldn't stop laughing.

'What a great operation! Now I feel really important!' one explorer shouted.

'Rubber dicks . . .' wailed Shoe, who was about to fall off his chair he was laughing so hard. 'As long as they don't screw us over with them!'

'Let's get going, boys! And if we really can't find the goods, we'll just have to satisfy our generals' dear wives with what nature has given us . . .' Deer proposed.

The explorers laughed along with us, but their lieutenant seemed the most amused.

'Are you kidding, brother? I wouldn't even want to see those washed-up whores . . .' Zenith tried to look serious. 'We must fulfil our mission, I accept no alternatives . . .'

When the fits of laughter died down, the lieutenant traced on the map the exact route we had to take to reach the helicopter. At various points his finger would stop and he'd say:

'We found traces of them here.'

We would have to go almost twenty kilometres into enemy territory. The strangest thing was that during their week of night reconnaissance the explorers hadn't encountered a single terrorist. There had to be camps or mine fields somewhere, and yet they had moved through the area undisturbed. I had a bad feeling, as I always do when something seems too simple . . .

Before an operation, command usually identified certain reference points that circumscribed the area, then they would leave us in a predetermined location and the rest − especially the particulars of our route − was up to us. Nosov had taught us something he called 'combat recon', which meant scouting the area as the operation was underway. This strategy gave us the possibility of acting immediately, in real time, planning our moves without having to follow a particular route, able to change plans at any time based on the unpredictable developments of battle.

I really didn't understand why we should take the route

command had chosen; it didn't seem very smart to me – what did these officers know about the best path to take? They'd never set foot on those mountains; they just used the general picture the explorers had given them, and any military expert could tell you that one can't trust the information acquired through reconnaissance alone, because things change very rapidly in war and enemy positions can change from one minute to the next.

The guys kept on talking around me. Everyone put in his two cents but I wasn't listening to them anymore. It was like I was hypnotised by the map. I was inside it, on those paths, between one point and another, and trying to find an answer to the thousand questions tormenting me – like when you find yourself staring at something without really looking at it, and try to figure out what's in your head, your thoughts . . .

At that moment the door to the barracks was flung open. The explorers sitting by the entrance jumped to their feet and saluted, making room for Nosov to pass. I came back to reality and looked at our captain. He was soaked from the rain and the expression on his face definitely seemed serious. I was sure that he had a good idea of what was going on.

Nosov stopped at the table; the infantry lieutenant rose and saluted him.

'Lieutenant Razumovsky, leader of the 34th infantry division explorer detachment! My team is ready for action, Comrade Captain!'

Nosov answered the salute with an apathetic lift of the hand:

'Nosov, captain of the saboteurs . . .'

Usually before an operation our captain tried to make a show of being resolved and positive, to assure us that he had everything under control, to — how should I put it — lighten our mood. But that time he looked at us one by one, and then taking a deep breath, with his eyes down, he said:

'Well, boys, I don't know any other way to explain to you what headquarters has cooked up for us . . . So, I'll just say it straight and clear, tell you the truth as I always have.' After a short pause, all in one breath he said: 'Some piece of shit among our generals wants us dead, and it's going to happen tonight.'

A dead silence fell in the barracks. The only thing that could be heard was the rain beating on the roof and the irritating sound of Moscow's joints cracking, as they did every time he got nervous or had to concentrate on something important.

We all expected Nosov to go on, but instead our captain stepped back from the table, sat down on a chair and pulled out from underneath his bunk a zinc case full of AK tracer bullets, the ones that leave a green trail in the air when you fire them.

Before putting normal cartridges into our rifles, we would also put a few tracer bullets in to alert us that the clip was almost empty — in the middle of battle, when we didn't have the chance to keep track of how many rounds we'd fired, we would immediately change the clip as soon as we saw the green trail, without reloading the carriage, so at least one round stayed in the chamber and we saved precious time.

Those bullets also helped us to identify distant targets with precision and to correct our fire. A group of soldiers, the spotters, would be near the enemy positions where they could best spot the weak points where we should concentrate our fire. They would shoot at the enemy with tracer bullets, and our men at the machine guns in the more protected (and therefore best from which to fire) positions would follow the green trails and fire at the target, creating a constant, solid wall of lead. Being a spotter was very dangerous, because in addition to being in close proximity to the enemy you had to be very quick and skilled in changing positions at the drop of a hat. Usually people who joined the spotter team had lots of war experience and weren't afraid of close combat.

Lastly, tracer bullets were very useful at night, when we needed to follow a precise line of fire, because during combat in the dark there was a serious danger of falling victim to friendly fire, especially when the unit was scattered across several positions and couldn't communicate. That's why each of us carried four magazines with tracer bullets.

While Nosov was taking care of the magazines, Lieutenant Razumovsky made a move as if he were about to speak, but instead he said nothing. He scratched his head and sighed, looking at us almost as if he expected some sort of explanation from us.

We saboteurs, however, just stood there observing our captain. Nosov, after filling two magazines with tracer rounds and binding them together with black electrical tape, turned to Moscow:

'Take over for me, prepare twenty of these . . .'

Moscow obeyed right away.

Nosov went over to the table, pulled his pistol, an Austrian Glock, out from his inside jacket pocket, and began to disassemble it.

Without anyone asking him, Spoon got the jar of oil we used to lubricate the weapons, which were often full of gunpowder residue, and set it in front of the captain. Nosov dismantled the carriage of the gun, removing the spring, then the barrel. He lifted the barrel to the light and examined it carefully, then blew inside. Only when he started cleaning it did he begin to speak, but he didn't take his eyes off his weapon, as if he were ashamed of something:

'One week ago, in the early evening, a cow* left from this camp. On board there was an inspector from the military prosecutor's office and an investigative team composed of five army officers who were looking into the case of a general accused of collaborating with terrorists . . . The investigators had found a connection between that piece of shit and some of the officers from this camp, and had come here to conduct an interrogation. When the inquiry was over, they left. They had been in the air for a few minutes when their helicopter exploded. Nobody

---

* This is what transport helicopters are called in military slang.

saw a damn thing, but a young lieutenant, who apparently isn't too fond of his superiors, revealed to me that the helicopter didn't explode in the mountains like they want us to believe, but in a field nearby . . .'

After thoroughly lubricating the pistol, Nosov wiped it with a rag, reassembled the carriage and loaded the magazine sending a cartridge into the chamber. Then he slid the pistol under his jacket and placed both hands on the table, as if he were at a restaurant waiting for someone to serve him dinner. Only then did he resume his story:

'Long story short, there are two things that don't add up in this story: first, it doesn't make sense that the helicopter would go through the mountains when the better route would have been over the fields; and second, there hasn't been terrorist activity in that area for at least six months. Everybody knows that the enemy is hiding deep in the mountains, waiting to gather the weapons and manpower they need to launch a real attack . . .'

Lieutenant Razumovsky listened, sitting with his head in his hands – despite his young age he probably knew very well what it meant to deal with corrupt officers. Often they would cover up these incidents by launching a big operation, one that usually cost a slew of human lives – in this case, ours.

I felt completely paralysed. Of all the horrible things in the world the one thing I was sure I didn't want to end up dealing with was this whole thing about dead investigators, helicopters that explode while flying over a field and mysteriously reappear in the mountains dozens of kilometres away, and especially a high-ranking officer in command who feels trapped and is willing to use all his power just to get rid of a few inconvenient witnesses . . .

'After the explosion, some parts of the helicopter were removed,' Nosov continued. 'The lieutenant I talked to swears that they made sure part of the wreck ended up with the terrorists deployed in the mountains in a place designated by command. The rest of the helicopter was buried to eliminate all the evidence. They want to send us up there to confirm the terrorist presence and make the lie about the helicopter seem more plausible . . . In order to save their skins those bastards didn't restrict themselves to blowing up the helicopter. They also staged attacks, faked assaults on the patrols in the area and blew up two of our cars on the mountain roads. Some of our boys died . . . Only then were they able to request help from the main troops . . . And nobody noticed a thing, for fuck's sake, while we've been waiting around for three days without firing a shot, getting drunk and waiting for Santa Claus . . . Now the officers need something more substantial − so they arranged with the terrorists to set a real trap for us; that's also why they've shown us what route to take . . .'

I wanted to leave the barracks, run over to command headquarters and take out every single person in there. I could already picture the bullets from my Kalashnikov felling all those old generals, their crisp uniforms riddled with bullets and their bodies tossed on the ground like sponges soaked with blood.

But our captain had his own ideas on how to resolve

the matter. He asked Spoon for a cup of tea, which he quickly brought over. Taking small sips, he closed his eyes like a cat lying in front of a warm wood-burning stove.

Spoon took our last lemon and sliced it, neatly arranging the pieces on a sheet of newspaper and sprinkling a little sugar on top. Our captain appreciated Spoon's care and thanked him, tossing three slices of sugared lemon into his mouth, one by one. Then he swore and started speaking in the same conspiratorial tone as before, this time looking us in the eyes:

'Long story short, boys, none of us has any desire to die for these sons of bitches. I hope that on this point we're all in agreement.'

The explorers' lieutenant responded with a nod.

'Good. Outside there are two transport cars waiting for us. They'll take us somewhere and drop us off. We have about five kilometres to do on foot, after which, here' – Nosov pointed to a small plain at the mouth of the valley on the map – 'the Czechs* will start shooting at us. They'll probably open fire once we're past the plain, so we won't have a chance to escape and they can slaughter us without any trouble.'

He took a sip of tea and ate another slice of lemon. Lieutenant Razumovsky took one as well, and then Nosov pushed the cup of tea over to him. He took a couple of sips and passed it to his men, as Spoon was already pouring

---

* The soldiers in the Russian army often called the Chechen soldiers 'Czechs' – *čechy*, the same term used to indicate the people of the Czech Republic – to distinguish them from civilians.

another cup. Meanwhile, we could hear Moscow − who hadn't stopped preparing the sets of tracer bullets for a second − loudly heaping insults on the officers, the army and the war.

Nosov went on:

'The young lieutenant told me that he and another group of officers gave the investigators a statement, requesting further clarification about the case. Then they were given protective escorts. But as long as these corrupt colonels are in charge no one can go against them, so we have to carry out our mission, otherwise we all risk prosecution. But we have the right to carry it out as we see fit . . .' He gave a half-smile. 'I've already come up with a plan, which will work one hundred per cent . . . Or at least, it'll give us a chance to come out of this shit alive.'

Nosov showed us a place on the map about five kilo-metres north of where they thought our skirmish with the enemy would take place.

'We'll get to the mountain here, go all the way across on one side without ever going down to the plain. We'll find the enemy positions and once we've found them we mine their exit points. Then we'll position ourselves nearby, and as the proverb goes, "If you've got the whip in your hand, you've got to whip the horse . . ." Command says we have to travel light − they stressed that we need to have the bare minimum on us, so we'll present ourselves to them as we are now. But the lieu-tenant has already offered us his unit's arsenal. We'll take more grenade launchers and lots of hand grenades.

And don't forget your tracers – tonight we're going to play target practice . . .'

The idea of target practice, risking becoming the targets ourselves, didn't sit well with me – I would rather have stayed in our warm, safe barracks, drinking tea and sleeping. But by now the situation was clear, we had to steel ourselves. We had a none too pleasant excursion ahead of us.

We got dressed, prepared our jackets, and put the rain ponchos on. We each checked our weapons. I took my VSS precision rifle and a good number of rounds. That rifle was an exceptional weapon; I could shoot so fast that no matter how much ammo I had it was never enough. Naturally I took my trusty Kalashnikov, but I preferred not to load it with tracer bullets. I'd always been obsessed with the idea that the enemy would be able to figure out my position by following the green trail, a fear that snipers often have, a sort of occupational phobia.

In just a few minutes both groups were ready. We had quite a few people to kill, and we realised it wasn't going to be simple. As my grandfather Nikolay used to say, 'Be careful when you decide to kill someone, because death is close by.'

We came out of the barracks and went over to the yard where two armoured cars were already running. The rain was heavy, like a curtain between me and the world. In accordance with regulation we lined up in front of the

officers' barracks, and shortly one of them came out, even
if you couldn't see his stripes since they were covered by
his rain poncho. His face had the typical grimace that all
command officers have. All it took was a glance at that
bastard and already I felt like throwing up.

As the highest ranking soldier, it was Nosov's duty to
report first. Nonchalantly, he began to yell, managing to
be heard over the pounding rain:

'Comrade Colonel! The sabotage and exploration group
of the 76th division is ready for orders! Group commander
Captain Nosov at your service!'

The colonel gave a listless salute, then gave us a quick
once-over and asked Nosov:

'Don't you have a radio?'

'We're saboteurs, Comrade Colonel; a radio is not part
of our equipment!' Nosov replied, like a perfect soldier.
Only to us was it clear that our captain was mocking
him.

That pig looked at us again and without even listening
to the explorers' lieutenant, who was supposed to report
second, he said:

'It's better that way, you can travel light — this is a walk
in the park. Come tomorrow evening and you'll already
be back on base having dinner!' Then he turned around
and went back into the barracks.

What a dick, I thought, reflecting on how many guys
like me he must have sent to their slaughter over the
course of his military career.

We ran over to the armoured cars, light tracked vehicles.
A man in civilian clothes was saying something to one of

the two drivers. The guy said hello to Nosov, and I reckoned
he was the young lieutenant who was saving our hides. Before
going off to talk to him privately, our captain turned to us and
said:

'Get in there nice and tight now; I don't want to see
anyone riding on the armour!'

We obeyed immediately, also because the idea of being
outside in that rain was not too appealing. As my comrades
were getting into the car, I peeked inside. It was immediately clear why Nosov had told us to 'get in tight'; it was
packed with weapons, grenade launchers, ammo – there
were three heavy machine guns, various cases full of bullets
and three boxes full of hand grenades. Thinking about
how tiring it was going to be carrying all that stuff while
we were walking up in the mountains, I got in too. In the
two cars, including the infantry explorers, there were
fourteen of us in total.

Nosov joined us and sat in his favourite spot, with his
back up against the door, which he had just closed with
a bang. Smiling at me, he said:

'Wake up, Kolima, we've been sleeping enough
lately . . .'

The cars advanced through the mud while we made
the final preparations. My job was to assemble the hand
grenades. I took the explosive parts from one box – the
ones with the characteristic lemon shape, except they're
green, and on the surface they're cut into little squares
like a tortoise shell – and the detonators from another
box, where they were kept separately for safety. I screwed
a detonator into each grenade. It was a strange device,

thin as a pencil, with a handle on one side and a ring in the middle. Once I had assembled the two components, the grenade could be used at any time, you just had to pull the pin and the mechanism would go off – in three to four seconds it would explode.

There were different types of detonators: the most common were the ones for throwing, with a delay mechanism that allowed the bomb to be launched in complete safety. There were some slower detonators, where the explosive is contained in three separate compartments, which allows almost a minute between activation of the mechanism to the actual explosion; these were very useful for retreating from positions, or for when you're being pursued. A group of soldiers at the end of the column would stay a little behind and throw these bombs, leaving a kind of improvised mine trail. Then there was the model with the direct detonator, which went off as soon as the pin was pulled, but perhaps the most famous and also the easiest to put together were the ones with the trip wire, which in military slang we simply called 'trips'. The enemy would trip on the wire tied to the ring and immediately be blown to bits.

We saboteurs had every kind, because the nature of our actions was so broad that we had to be ready to use any tactical solution. The important thing was not getting them mixed up in the chaos of battle – that's why we each carried certain types of bombs in certain places that everybody knew, so if one of us happened to get hurt or killed, the others could take his bombs without wasting time figuring out what colours they were marked with. And of course the marks were very subtle; they couldn't be seen very well during the day, let alone at night or in the middle of pandemonium – one mistake could prove fatal.

I was afraid of grenades, as I was of explosives in general. They gave me the sense of something unstable, extremely dangerous. In my jacket, in a pocket I'd sewn on the back, I always carried one, but I never wanted to take more than that – expert snipers would often aim right at grenades naively kept in the most visible parts of a jacket. Once during a battle, I saw a stray bullet hit a grenade hanging from the vest of a VMF soldier. That mistake cost the soldier his life, and some of his nearby comrades were seriously wounded by the shrapnel. Fate is terrible: a weapon can be dangerous even for the person carrying it.

After about forty-five minutes, the cars – which used night scopes for illumination, keeping the headlights off – stopped near a bridge that spanned a small river. From there on we would have to go on foot. The rain only seemed to fall harder, and as soon as we got out we sank into the mud.

It was completely dark, and this combined with the rain created an uncomfortable sense of disorientation. We couldn't see the horizon, neither the sky nor the earth; we couldn't tell if the sky was up or down, if the water was falling or rising. I felt like I was floating in mid-air; I had the impression of being surrounded by emptiness and of being more than empty myself.

I leaned on the vehicle and as soon as I put my hand on the armour I realised I was standing, that the ground was beneath me and that therefore the sky was up above, because that's how things in nature worked . . . From behind, Moscow gave me a shove:

'What's come over you, brother? You okay?'

'It's nothing . . . it's just that for a second I couldn't tell up from down with this rain . . .' I replied, a little out of it.

'What's there to tell? It's as simple as shit: water is falling, that means it's raining.' He nudged me with his shoulder and went to help the others pull the gear out of the cars.

It took just a few minutes to distribute the weapons and ammo. The drivers wished us luck and vanished into the dark in their vehicles, splattering more mud on us.

Nosov quickly explained our situation. Despite the torrents and the darkness, we had to trust him and follow his lead. We set off without a word, and the explorers followed behind.

We walked in the rain for almost two hours. Nosov used a compass to keep track of our orientation, stopping every so often to check the route with the infantry lieutenant, illuminating the map with a small red flashlight, just like the one each of us usually carried.

Our captain listened to Lieutenant Razumovsky's suggestions carefully, because after scouting the vicinity with his group for a whole week, he was the one among us who knew the area best.

The road was unpaved. The ground was a mixture of mud and rocks that weighed down our every step and slowed our progress. We kept close to the trees, whose branches bowed from the weight of the water, closing us in almost like a cage.

After a while we noticed the outline of the mountains appearing majestically in the distance. They were dark, darker than the night, and there was something very menacing about them.

Nosov ordered us to take a short break. My comrades took the opportunity to swap equipment in order to temporarily lighten some of our loads. I took Zenith's light machine gun, even though Nosov usually didn't want me to get too tired; he said that as the sniper in the group I always had to be more rested and alert than all the others, because I needed to be able to concentrate to do my job.

We sat down to rest. Nobody smoked or ate – in these instances it was forbidden. I was thirsty, despite all the water that kept falling from the sky. I took a few sips from the canteen and closed my eyes for a minute.

When I opened them again it wasn't raining so hard. The sky was slowly becoming free of the clouds and you could see a few stars in the distance. Of course, it was still completely dark, but it had become that kind of darkness that we called 'dear' – a friend, a partner you could trust – because in the dark we saboteurs felt at home.

Nosov gave the order to head out, in 'millipede' formation, and off we went.

When a big group moves through open territory, it often uses this formation, because it's an effective way to avoid mines and not leave too many tracks. The leader of the company observes the surrounding territory and then chooses the best route, guiding the column. All the others have to follow him about one metre apart, walking in exactly the same spots he did. That might seem difficult, but actually you learn fast and soon it becomes natural. You get used to walking without thinking too much about it. It must look funny from the outside, an entire group perfectly imitating the movements of the first person in the line, as if they were all mocking him. It's a good system for the soldiers' safety – the group moves compactly and it becomes difficult to see from far away because it's as if everyone were hiding behind one another. But it also has some negative aspects; besides forcing the soldiers to move slowly, if there's a sudden attack it takes a lot of time before you can take up proper defensive positions.

Usually our infantry units and paratroopers moved according to a formation called 'chess'; with at least three metres' distance between one soldier and the next, and each soldier moving quickly and independently, it was important to maintain the same direction. If they were attacked, the men had enough room to drop to the ground and set up a position. There were still disadvantages: the group was highly visible, and in unknown territory the risk of blowing up was higher. Often anti-personnel mines would be placed on the sides of the road, precisely to catch those moving in 'chess' formation.

Each military unit followed the tactic chosen by its

commander, but obviously each commander was different – each had his own war experiences behind him, and therefore used the solutions he considered the safest. Nosov said that the millipede formation was the most used in Afghanistan, especially on the mountain roads where there were many mines. We saboteurs all had complete faith in our captain, because his unit was the only one in which nobody had died since it had been formed. We felt protected, which was crucial in war because, as Nosov often said:

'The soldier who feels defenceless is already halfway dead.'

After another hour of marching we reached the valley.

A soft wind blew on our faces, and it was very pleasant. It had stopped raining almost entirely, and the horizon could be seen in the distance. We still had a few hours of darkness before the dawn.

We took another break, sitting in a circle under a split rock. Nobody spoke. We passed the canteen around in silence, trying to recover our strength.

The explorer lieutenant and Nosov were bent over the map. They spoke in low voices, discussing our route.

'It's dangerous to go down too low,' Lieutenant Razumovsky said, worried. 'We risk running right into the enemy . . .'

'That's true,' Nosov replied. 'But we can't go up either. We don't know the area and time is tight . . .'

In the end the two decided to send a small group on recon.

It was a pretty safe method, but often the soldiers who were in the recon group – who never carried heavy weapons in order to move more easily – took an enormous risk. If they ran into an enemy encampment they had to able to retreat quickly, and sometimes (especially during night battles) on the way back to their positions they would run into friendly fire. To avoid these sorts of accidents, usually when it came time to retreat, the soldiers communicated with flashlights from the distance. We didn't use a radio because it was a direct route to death: every frequency was monitored by the enemy.

The soldiers communicated by flashlight with a very specific code. To indicate that they were returning to base was three short flashes, at ten to twenty-second intervals, to which the rest of the company was supposed to respond with the same intermittent red light. Two short flashes meant that the group was staying in position for the moment; a single long flash meant that the enemy had been spotted; a short flash was used to tell the main group to join the others. Flashlights were used at short distances: fifty metres, two hundred at most. In open spaces, with few obstacles, like fields or areas near rivers, you could also go a little further, whereas in the city, the woods, or in underground tunnels, it was better to stay close by because the risk of losing visual contact was very high.

Communication in war is a strange thing. Lots of important decisions – the ones that can cost the lives of many people, including yours – are made on the basis of things

like a series of signals made with a flashlight. You have
to blindly trust whoever is sending those signals, because
at that moment he's the eyes and ears of the whole group.
Personally, I didn't really like the idea of depending on
someone else, but in situations like that you didn't have
many alternatives. Trust was the only thing that made
you and your comrades act as one big organism.

Nosov didn't really trust the skill levels of men in other
units, especially if he didn't know them very well or they'd
never been with him on an operation. And so that time
in the mountains, he decided that the group to go on
recon would be composed of three of us: Moscow, Deer
and Spoon. Zenith, Shoe, Nosov and I would stay with
the infantrymen. Some of them helped us, carrying the
heavy stuff our guys had been carrying until then – grenade
launchers, a few bags of hand grenades and various gear.

Leaving our refuge under the split rock, we headed off,
hugging the mountain, and then we entered a young forest.
The path was steep; you could feel your legs bending with
strain. The group ahead of us signalled for us to stop, so
we lay on the ground while the tireless Nosov sat and
waited for the next signal, which punctually arrived a few
minutes later. We proceeded very slowly, moving with the
utmost care. In the mountains it's as if every sound is
magnified; the human voice carries a greater distance than
normal, especially if there's a lot of moisture in the air.
For this reason it's also easier to make mistakes, and a
noise that seems far away can actually be close or vice
versa, according to how the echo ricochets off the rocks
and gets muffled or amplified by the trees or other external

factors. Even one's vision can be fooled by particular optical effects, and subjects can seem closer through a rifle scope. This type of operation requires total concentration, because the mountain is an unforgiving place.

We tried not to make any noise, not to stir the rocks, passing through the bushes in silence and carefully pushing aside tree branches. The dead leaves under our feet were soaked with water, in some places it was like a slide – all it would take was one of us to take a wrong step and we could all fall down like dominoes, going back to where we started from in two seconds. Here and there the path broke off completely, stopping at a wall of rocks and starting again higher up, a couple of metres from the ground. So we helped one another up, passing the load to the person who was already on top, but always without a word and with care as to where we stepped. Despite the cold mountain air, despite the humidity and a faint but constant wind, I felt hot, and my back was covered in sweat.

We went on like that for quite a while, moving through the thick of the forest. Time went by easily – it was always better to be moving than standing around waiting, at least to me.

We climbed for some time and then we suddenly reached a clearing with a narrow road that formed a kind of natural bridge between two mountains. It was a hundred metres long and curved in two places; the path was illuminated brightly by the stars.

We stopped, because the group who had gone ahead on recon was already on the other side of the mountain and had signalled for us to wait. So Nosov called me over. He was leaning on a tree and looking towards my comrades. Without taking his eyes off them, he said to me in a faint and feeble voice:

'We're almost there, be ready.'

I got the message. I instinctively reached for my precision rifle.

Our men didn't signal for a while. We waited in silence, though surrounded by the sounds of nature: the wind whistled between the trees, a bird chirped, some stones fell somewhere, in the distance, up high. I was so focused, I noticed a sound that was perhaps water on rocks – there was probably a small stream nearby. Just beyond the edge of the road there was a very steep slope covered in trees and bushes. I tried to look down, but from where I was I could hardly see anything.

Fighting in a place like that would be very difficult – how nice it would have been to spend that night and the following day exploring the area without ever seeing anyone, and then just go back to base . . . at which point the inspectors from the prosecutor's office, who were probably already on the scene, would cancel our operation. It would be so amazing to just coast through for once, without having to risk our hides in the middle of the mountains, I said to myself, daydreaming . . .

Suddenly Nosov pulled me away from my thoughts, giving me a little tap on the head, and when I looked towards our group I saw the red light, which stayed on for a long time. That could only mean one thing: they had found the enemy positions. A moment later, on the road between the two mountains, I saw some shadows moving towards us. They were moving very fast, sliding flat against the mountain. Nosov was still, concentrating. The shadows came closer. I recognised Moscow first, followed by the others. You couldn't even hear their steps, it almost seemed like they were flying instead of walking.

Resolute, Moscow entered the glen and sat down next to Nosov, as if he'd known where our captain was in advance. The others gathered round him.

'Right past the road there's a stream,' Moscow whispered, a slight tremor in his voice. 'They've planted four mines; we pulled out two, and we left the others where they were, but defused . . . The Czechs are about two hundred metres further down. The stream goes over their position; there, they have two guards. They're very calm, they're talking at normal volume, joking around . . . As I approached I caught a strong smell of hash. I went past them without any trouble and went down to their camp. There's about forty men. They lit a fire and covered it with a light tarp; I could see their barracks in the distance. Some of them were sleeping, others smoking, there were lots of Arabs, a few Czechs . . .' Moscow paused for a second, as if he were trying to remember something.

'What about the weapons?' Nosov asked him.

Moscow went off again like a spring:

'So . . . I saw four heavy machine guns, two with night scopes. One Arab was sleeping next to an RPG. They have bags everywhere with charges for grenade launchers. Some of the Arabs are very well equipped, I saw one soldier with an unusual oar,* definitely designer. That's all I could see . . .'

Nosov put a hand on his shoulder, as if to thank him. Then he stood up and went over to the infantry lieutenant. My comrades seemed excited; it was clear that the presence of the enemy electrified them. I asked Moscow what he thought of the situation. He looked at me:

'We could position ourselves above the stream – it's full of rocks, it seems like a good place. They're not waiting for us up there. I'm sure they have another group further down towards the valley, but if we can get rid of these ones, the others won't have any support . . . We can kill the guards without making a sound, plant mines around their camp and then bury them in lead; with the grenade launchers, hand grenades and our machine guns we should be able to take care of them in a flash. There aren't many of us, and so we'll be able to move faster than them . . .'

The idea of destroying them in a single strike was a very good one, but – as often happened in that war – anything that seemed easy became hard as soon as it was put into practice. There were only fourteen of us, very few compared to the number that were certainly hiding in those mountains . . . Attacking such a large group, without precise information on the location of their other units, was really very dangerous.

---

* Military slang for precision rifle.

I looked up. The forest was immersed in darkness, breathing loud. The trees seemed alive, like people — ruffled by the wind, the branches did a strange dance, a constant hypnotic motion. It was unquestionably a gorgeous, enchanting place. It's a shame we had to see it through war, which manages to make even the most beautiful and extraordinary things in this world horrific.

I never stopped being afraid in the war, not even for an instant, and I think this is actually the reason I stayed alive and didn't lose my mind. Every day I found myself facing situations that seemed to exceed my capacities; I had to make choices that forced me to surpass my physical and mental strength, and so I always tried to be very careful, precise and resolute . . . In war, the idea of death never leaves your thoughts. Everyone tries to exorcise it in his own way — some try to dispel it, others become obsessed with it and end up becoming its victims, still others act tough, trying to bring out the worst in themselves as if generating negative things in their minds deludes them into thinking they're deferring death's power . . . But the risk is turning into a stupid puppet, in the service of another.

With time, I learned that the fear of death had to be exploited, used as a resource that human nature offers to those who know what to do with it. All the things that make an individual what he or she is, attitudes related to conscience, morals, respect for others, elements that vary according to culture and upbringing – all this disappears when confronted with the instinct for survival. In extremely dangerous situations, it's instinct that guides you. That's how I was, often without really realising it. I made decisions based on the fact that the primary goal was to save my skin. Everything else came second.

I talked to Nosov about this a few times. On the whole he agreed with me, but he always stressed the fundamental difference between fear and terror:

'Fear will make you grow eyes even on your back, but terror makes you blind.'

That night in the mountains I had my eyes wide open, waiting to see what was going to happen.

Lieutenant Razumovsky came over to us, followed by Nosov. With all my lung power I took in the cool and pure mountain air, savouring every mouthful as if there soon wouldn't be any left.

As Moscow had predicted, our officers had decided to attack from above, thus making use of the surprise-effect. We broke up into two teams: the infantry explorers had to position the machine guns and grenade launchers at strategic points, and be ready to fire; my comrades and I, plus Nosov, had the task of taking out the guards and mining the territory around their base with explosives.

In truth, if there was one thing I hated it was planting mines, but you can't argue with orders, as soldiers would say, so I filled my pockets with explosives to put the 'trips' together. My comrades were nervous. Moscow started checking every bomb himself − he wanted to be sure that everything went right. Nosov and the infantry lieutenant repeated the plan one last time. Finally, after just a few minutes we were all ready to attack.

We came out of the woods and set off down the small path connecting the two mountains, running hunched over so we couldn't be seen. Moscow and the others who already knew the area led the ranks; Nosov brought up the rear and I was in front of him. We quickly reached the other side of the mountain, and then Moscow signalled for us to keep completely quiet and showed us the way. We had to go down along the brush, since the slope was steep and there was nothing to hold on to; thus we went, with our bottoms almost touching the rock.

The sound of the stream kept getting louder, and at a certain point past the trees' lush branches I saw the glittering water gliding between the rocks. We stopped near the stream. It must have been a metre and a half wide, and it wasn't very deep; you could see some big stones jutting out, polished by the water. We could hop across without any problem. It's always better to cross streams by jumping whenever possible, because walking on stones, however flat, isn't very safe; it's too easy to slip and fall.

Ten metres away from us sat two individuals. One with his back to the mountain was smoking a cigarette, covering

it with a cupped hand, and was chatting with the other
guy. You could tell they were relaxed. They were sure we
were going to come from below, where their other group
was probably waiting to ambush us.

Nosov signalled to Moscow, who understood immediately what our captain meant. He gave Deer the rifle and
pulled out his knife, holding it with the handle down and
the blade concealed under his wrist to keep the steel from
reflecting. Nosov handed me his rifle and took out his
knife as well. Without a word, the two went out from
behind the trees towards the guards. We observed everything in silence.

The one who had just finished smoking was stretched
out on a rock. His rifle was resting on his thigh and his
arms were straight at his sides; he looked tired. The other
one was sitting up, his back straight, holding the rifle
between his legs, every now and then lightly gripping the
barrel. Nosov and Moscow took over five minutes to
reach them. They moved slowly, creeping through the
bushes, almost hugging the ground.

There were no trees near the guards. The water gave off
so many gold shimmers we were able to see every detail.
The smoker was young, while the other one was older.

Now that our men were no longer visible, our eyes
were glued to the guards. We were waiting for something
to happen, but everything seemed calm. Suddenly there
was movement; the older one got up and went towards
the stream. He set his rifle down on a rock and bent over,
bringing his lips to the water and drinking on all fours,
like wild animals do. At that moment his comrade lifted

his hands upward a little and made a noise, a sort of whimper. An instant later a shadow popped out from behind him – Moscow. The Arab was no longer moving. Meanwhile, the one who had gone to drink some water already had his head dunked in the stream and a knife plunged into his neck. Nosov was holding him fast under the water, clutching him like a spider its prey. The Arab's right hand scraped at the stones in a hopeless attempt to grab his rifle, but Moscow was already holding his weapon, and then had a foot blocking his arm. After a moment he ceased struggling. Nosov slowly slackened his grip, then turned him onto his side, lifted his left arm and to be sure sank his knife between his ribs, where the heart is. It was like seeing how one should kill an animal, not a man.

We went closer. Together, we hid the bodies in the bushes nearby. Now we had to move along the edges of the camp, planting mines to avoid leaving any passageway free.

The forest sloped down, but the enemy's barracks rose in the middle of a nice wide clearing that was visible from a distance. We crept along like snakes; we were so close that we could hear the crackle of the wood burning in the fire in the centre of their camp. Once we got within about fifty metres of the barracks, we split up, with Deer placing the bombs in the trees on one side, Moscow planting the tripwire, and Shoe and Spoon covering, keeping an eye on the area; we were on the opposite side, doing the same task.

Nosov ordered me to plant the bombs in the trees. He

pulled the first one out of the bag and I wrapped the wire around the fuse; Nosov carefully tightened the wire, while Zenith kept an eye on our surroundings. The enemy was near – I could hear them talking, some were laughing. Nosov periodically showed me when the wire on the spool ran out, so I would pull another one out of the bag and hand it to him. We did everything fast – it was almost like decorating a Christmas tree. Within a few minutes I had completely emptied my bag. We'd already planted fifteen hand grenades, but that still wasn't enough. I signalled to Zenith and he immediately passed me another full bag.

We kept going more rapidly and efficiently – after a while my fear of explosives was almost gone. Our movements were precise, automatic and repetitive; while the body worked, the mind detached, as in yoga. I set up the bombs, thinking of my house in Bender, of the river where I used to go fishing, of the smooth, delicate water it was a pleasure to take a dip in . . . Often during the war, a projection came into my mind, like at the movies, a mental screen where the most comforting images from my past would roll by. Sometimes they were so real I could almost feel the warm summer wind on my face that blew on me as a boy when I would go sailing with my friends . . . In those moments I was really fine, I was able to relax, and even if everything around me was like an inferno, inside I was able to maintain great calm, an absolute peace. But immediately afterward, as soon as I realised that the pleasant sensation was fading, I would despair – it was like falling through an empty space.

We had almost finished mining our side of the camp, and backing up little by little we returned to the stream where the guards had been just before. There, we planted the last grenade. Zenith was looking in the direction from which our comrades were supposed to come, but we couldn't see anyone yet. We went back across the stream and hid behind the trees, waiting for the others to arrive. I had taken off my gloves to secure the bombs as well as possible and now my hands were freezing; I put them back on, trying to warm up.

A few minutes later the others finally arrived, almost in a rush – we were all afraid that some Arab would set off a mine early. As soon as the group rejoined us we went back up to our position where the infantrymen were waiting for us.

The explorers had already arranged everything as best they could. The machine guns were shielded by the biggest rocks, the grenade launchers were arranged on the side and in the centre, and there was a broad space for the rest of us.

Everyone took his place. Moscow and Zenith went to two machine guns, an infantryman was at the other. I prepared my Kalashnikov and placed it next to me, then I unslung my precision rifle, opened the stock, and loaded the cartridge in the barrel, trying to make as little noise as possible. I took the piece of cardboard from the fold in my hat, scrunched up my eyes three times – a little concentration exercise that helped me to aim better – then covered my left eye and started observing my targets.

I was in a comfortable position; the visual on the enemy

base in front of me was good. There were a few Arabs sitting, some were lying down. There was a fire in the middle, carefully concealed by the tent. It was clear that they had set up their camp so it couldn't be seen from below, but from my location – despite the dampness and the dawn that tarried to come – with the scope I was able to make out everything. First I noticed a group of five people – they were sitting on a log all in a row with their backs to me, warming up by the fire. I decided to start with them. They were awake, and when we attacked they would definitely be among the first to react. I aimed at the one on the far left. There was a big tree next to him, behind which he and his comrades could hide, whereas on the right was ten metres of open space; when the enemies realised that one of them had been shot down, they would instinctively jump to the right, and that's when I would have all the time I needed to kill them.

The Arab sitting on the left had long hair, wore an American jacket and was armed with a folding stock AKS that he had resting against his leg. Even if I was able to see only the back of his neck, he looked like a calm type. His movements were relaxed, and observing him made me feel calmer too – and I love calm, I can't stand chaos. Breathing slowly, I took aim; his neck was in my sight. Now I was just waiting for the 'blessing' of our captain, who in the meantime had come over to me.

'I'm ready,' I said, without taking my eye off the scope. Nosov made the sign to everyone to be on alert, then he whispered a very precise order into my ear:

'Fire!'

I filled my lungs with air and held my breath. When my body got as hard as a rock I pulled the trigger. As I've said, my rifle was a very quiet model. Once it had been released, the bullet travelled through the air like an arrow shot from a bow – in fact, among soldiers the VSS was known as the 'black arrow'. In an instant I had unloaded four more rounds, each time aiming at the neck. None of the enemies had even had the time to get up from the log they were sitting on. They slid to the ground one by one.

The bullets didn't have much force and therefore they simply *killed*, going through the men's heads without their bodies making the kind of violent spasms that would arouse the suspicions of those near them. It was a death poor in movement – seen from the scope, the target still seemed alive. If the bullet struck the head you could see the victim make a quick half gesture, as if he were tossing back a lock of hair that had fallen on his forehead. He would freeze for a second, and then immediately collapse like a marionette whose strings have been cut. If the bullet struck the heart, you couldn't see anything at all – the target would be still for a few seconds, and I would often shoot again until I saw him fall.

Once during a skirmish in the city, I found myself shooting at a guy who just wouldn't fall down. Although I had unloaded an entire clip into him he stayed on his feet. At some point I hit his head, but nothing doing . . . When the battle was over and I was able to get a closer look, I saw that the guy was completely propped against a wall, his feet shifted forward a little, which kept him standing although he had already been dead for some time. His arms were folded across his chest, plastered with bullet holes; his head dangled, revealing two deep holes in the back of his neck. That occurrence made a strange impression on me; it erased the border in my head separating images of the living from the dead, and from that moment on I haven't been able to distinguish between them. When I look at the living I can perceive signs of death, and vice versa . . .

Seeing people die when they don't expect it, killing them while they're immersed in total calm, is a privilege reserved exclusively to snipers. Soldiers normally see another death, one that's more physical, full of facial contortions and bodily struggle. In hand-to-hand combat, when the firing distance ranges from ten to a hundred metres, you often can't tell exactly where or who you're shooting at. You shoot while running, amidst enormous confusion, with your senses spinning, and it's impossible to see things from the right distance. I, on the other hand, had learned to do my job with patience, to watch scenes of death with great calm, to look at them the way one looks at a painting.

The other soldiers, when they found out that I was a sniper, would often ask me what was so great about my position that had me roaming around at night in the middle of enemy territory, going through mine fields, risking my life to find the best position and staying there motionless for hours watching the enemy, when most of the time things were resolved in a few seconds, or with a single explosion . . . I'd smile just slightly, but if I were sure that they wouldn't take it the wrong way, I would reply that I was motivated by a great love for death, the true pleasure that only hunting human beings can provide. A sick feeling.

I stood there in position waiting for the exact moment to shoot, and it seemed as if I was being cradled in the arms of death, that death appeared just for me; a shiver went through my body, like when someone you love touches you or breathes on your skin . . . I knew I was putting myself on the line for this one second, but in that moment death and I were the only ones left on Earth, and she did her terrible dance for me, the one that's always the same but different every time, charged with emotion, with grace and a lethal beauty that made me feel good. In those moments I felt like I was part of an eternal mechanism, an entity that surpassed human understanding. It was without a doubt the madness of an assassin – me – but it gave me certain sensations that can't be compared to anything else.

When the war was over and I was back home, I talked about this experience a lot with my grandfather, telling him how killing human beings had made me feel differently than hunting animals in the forest. In his way, he consoled me:

'Every man carries both God and the Devil within himself. In some situations it's right for one to prevail over the other; that's the only way man can survive.'

The war in Chechnya was a true hell, and my personal devil had to be at the height of his strength: that was his place and his time.

Once I unloaded the round in the last guy's head I immediately glanced at the others; they were all lying on the ground except for one. He was on his knees, one hand gripping his throat and the other making strange motions in the air as if he were swimming. I'd hit him in the neck, and even though the wound was fatal he still had a few seconds to live before leaving this world. Often, during battles – especially if there was more than one target, as in this case – I had no way to observe that macabre spectacle I found so captivating, and so death did its dance alone, without sharing it with me.

I immediately shot another round and hit him right in the head. His body fell beside his comrades'.

Just then we heard shouting coming from the enemy camp. I didn't have enough time to look up before our men had already opened fire, using all the firepower we had prepared.

With the grenade launcher my comrades hit the bags where the Arabs kept their ammo. Two powerful explosions lit up the sky. Someone shot a volley of bullets at us from a nearby bush. I tried to take aim and shoot him, but the enemy immediately stepped on one of our mines and blew up. Then there was a series of more shouting, shooting, explosions, tracer bullets whizzing through the air – they were trying to get rid of us, but our fire was so heavy they couldn't. One by one the enemies began to emerge from the camp, and, running towards us, they set off the mines we had planted all around. Everything was on fire; within moments there were bodies in flames everywhere, on the ground, in the trees – the enemy camp looked like one big bonfire with the Arabs running around disorientated, shooting in every direction.

I hit one in the chest and he fell right away; then he put his palms on the ground and tried to get back up. I got him in my crosshairs and shot again; the second bullet demolished his nose and maybe also his eyes. His head dangled, but he was still alive – he held a hand up to his disfigured face as if afraid to touch it, or as if he wanted to free himself from a sticky substance. I aimed again and this time the bullet lodged right in the back of his neck. Through the scope, I saw his raised arm slowly droop down.

Nosov shouted something to me, but with all that racket I couldn't make sense of anything. Then he motioned for me to look to my left. One of the infantrymen was placing the machine gun right next to me, in order to strike the enemy from a closer distance. As soon as I realised, I covered my ears with my hat the best I could, but within seconds the infantryman had already used up the first magazine. Hearing a machine gun from close up is like getting pounded in the head, I hated it. I grabbed my Kalashnikov and crawled a few metres over to Nosov. Our captain was firing single shots, using a dioptric scope.

'That bastard has a grenade launcher, take him out before he can fire!' he ordered me.

I immediately started looking for the target, but I couldn't see it.

'Right behind the tent, between those two trees!' the captain yelled.

I looked in the direction Nosov indicated. I couldn't see anyone, just an RPG grenade launcher peeking out from behind a tree. I shot at the RPG but didn't hit it right away; I only got it after two tries. When it exploded, a man fell dead from behind the tree. Another man popped out from the same place – he was clutching his belly, bent over so far he seemed hunchbacked – clearly he'd been hit by the shrapnel. Anyone who has been in war knows that it's better to take five bullets than a single fragment from a grenade. I took him out too, firing a round right at his head. He fell, his hands still on his stomach. A part of his skull flew off; once he was on the ground, his head looked like a half moon with a huge crater.

The enemy was no longer responding to our fire. We were only firing single shots, at most a few short blasts from the machine gun. The entire forest in front of us was on fire, and now and then, when the flames reached the bodies, you could hear the rounds exploding directly inside the enemies' guns, or in the magazines hooked to their bulletproof vests.

The flames were very high; nothing of their camp was left. Perhaps in addition to the ammo for the grenade launchers, the Arabs had had some gas-powered devices. When they explode, they can create a fire that can reach a temperature of ten thousand degrees for a few seconds over a ten-metre circumference. The burst of flame they produce can incinerate armoured cars instantly and leaves little trace of the human body. You only know that there was a person there at the time of the explosion from the oil stains you find on the metal or the cement.

In an instant, it was all over. I had observed that terrible spectacle through the scope of my rifle, while Nosov watched the enemy camp go up in flames through his small pair of binoculars. The fire was strong, blinding; ammo continued to explode, you could see sparks flying everywhere, but around the clearing everything seemed calm. Our captain was satisfied, making a quiet noise that sounded like a purr – he always did that when he was happy with the outcome of an operation.

Suddenly, about five kilometres further down, at the opening of the valley, a green signal flare went up in the sky. It lingered in the air for about ten seconds, and then started to fall. It was another enemy group, maybe the ones who were originally supposed to attack us – they had probably intended to block the exit from the valley, push us into the mountains and make us fight the group we had just eliminated. A plan like that revealed their fear of direct combat. They had surely planted mines on the path that they'd wanted to force us to take. All these elements proved that it had all been planned down to the last detail – undoubtedly with the support of our command.

Unfortunately for them, they weren't very well trained. Word was that the Arabs had a makeshift field hospital in those mountains, where in addition to caring for the wounded they sent the younger soldiers to learn something from those with more experience. Our blazing victory and the panic that had spread among our adversaries (although the attack had been unexpected) were proof that these weren't expert soldiers – otherwise the whole thing wouldn't have been so easy.

Nosov put down the binoculars and smiled at me:

'Kolima, son, you know what that flare means?'

'I don't have a clue, Ivanisch,' I replied, though in reality I had some idea.

He gave me a light tap on the head, like adults do with children when they've made a mistake.

'That flare, soldier, means that today we're going to ram it up their arses so far they'll get sore throats!'

Hearing him talk that way was a good sign. Nosov only said things like that when he was certain of victory. So I smiled too.

The captain rose to his feet and ordered the others to pick up the ammo scattered all over the ground. Everyone got to work. An infantryman snapped a twig off a tree and swept the shells away, hiding them under the bushes. Soon the terrain was clear.

The infantry sniper came up to me:

'Hey, brother, where'd you learn to shoot?'

'In Siberia, I used to go hunting with my grandfather

. . .' I showed him the piece of cardboard I used to cover my eye. 'See this? It helps.'

He was young. He seemed fascinated and intimidated. It was clear that he had found himself with a precision rifle in his hands just because someone in his command needed to assign the role of sniper to a draft soldier.

Often with infantry snipers, nobody explained anything to them. They learned to shoot in combat. When I had the chance, I showed them what were, in my opinion, the essentials for getting through this gig.

There's a whole science behind using a precision rifle. To ensure that your shots make the maximum impact, you have to calculate every detail. A person who's a good shot at a non-professional level can learn during war – over the course of six months – all the little tricks and secrets to turn him into a master sniper. The important thing is to get a lot of practice and be careful of everything, obviously first training yourself how to avoid getting shot. Many soldiers, since they'd never had any instruction, developed instinctive personal techniques, some of which were actually interesting, and so sometimes I also learned something from them.

I met quite a few snipers who came from highly specialised schools – people who knew everything about the theory – and used excellent, extremely accurate weapons, with which (thanks to very sophisticated electronics) they could cover great distances. Yet they came to a bad end the moment they came face to face with an enemy armed with even just a regular assault rifle, a weapon that couldn't shoot more than six hundred metres away.

That happened because they came to war without field training. Nobody had told them that the sniper's primary talent depends on his capability to kill without thinking. You have to be calm, relaxed, and – as the old Siberians used to say – 'have a frozen heart and a cold hand'.

Nosov, without losing any time, called three from our group and three infantrymen to scour the enemy encampment:

'Don't pick up grenade launcher rounds, explosives or undetonated hand grenades – take only the ammo we can use. If you find usable weapons, collect them, put them together and blow them up. If you find anyone still breathing, use your knives, use fire only if necessary. If you find any documents, maps, electronic devices, means of communication, bring them here immediately . . .'

Moscow, Deer, Zenith and three explorers went right down. I took position to keep an eye on them, and the young explorers' sniper accompanied me. A little way from us, Nosov surveyed the scene with his binoculars.

For a while there was no sign of our group, and then Moscow came into view. He led the others, keeping his rifle levelled, and Deer and Zenith followed, covering him on both sides. The explorers brought up the rear, the last one walking slowly, backwards, looking around. They stopped in the middle of the camp, illuminated by the light of the fire. Moscow signalled for Deer and Zenith to lower their rifles. They pulled out their knives and went off in opposite directions, each followed by an infantryman with his rifle up, ready to shoot if necessary.

Moscow went over to an Arab who was lying face down. He turned him over and cut his bulletproof vest laterally; he quickly checked the pockets, emptied a bullet case, putting the cartridges into his backpack, and moved right on to the next, while the infantryman followed him like his shadow. At one point, Moscow came across a man who was wounded; he slid his knife into his heart and the man died without batting an eye.

Within ten minutes the entire camp was cleaned out. Deer and Zenith had backpacks full of ammo; Zenith had found a heavy machine gun with a night scope. He dragged it along with a set of magazines looped together with a belt.

After emptying the chambers, they threw all the weapons they had found into a ditch in the middle of the camp, and then set them on fire. Zenith and Deer took two big heavy logs, placed them over the hole to stifle the explosion a little, then they left with the infantrymen, running towards us. They jumped over the stream and clambered up the steep little road, and in a second they were back with us again.

Moscow was alone in the middle of the camp. He

looked around for a moment and then tossed a hand grenade in the ditch. Then he threw himself somewhere in the dark, under cover. The explosion was very loud and we instinctively ducked down. Fragments of weapons went flying everywhere, scattering around the camp and surrounding woods; they were almost all from AKs, which were now completely unrecoverable. Moscow's figure emerged from the dark. He went over to the ditch for a second, toed what was left of a rifle and then ran back over to us.

'Excellent work, boys,' Nosov commented.

Zenith went to the captain and showed him the machine gun that, against orders, he had kept:

'Ivanisch, don't be angry,' he implored, 'but I couldn't leave it there. It'll be useful to us – look how many clips it has, and it even has a night scope . . . I'll carry it myself, I swear . . .'

Zenith was physically very strong – none of us had any doubt that he could carry the weapon without any trouble – but we knew very well how important respecting orders was to Nosov.

The captain seemed lost in thought, and then all of a sudden he turned to me, pointing to the machine gun:

'Kolima, make sure the scope works and that it's calibrated right. If everything's okay, Zenith can keep it. It could prove useful to us in our next battle . . .'

I took the machine gun and examined it. The scope had a cloth cover, very crudely hand-sewn; I took it off and switched on the night scope. I waited a second for it to come on and when I saw the shine of the phosphorescent reticule, I brought my eye to the lens. The view was very good, the scale clear. I set the weapon on its stand and after pointing it at the field I loaded the chamber. The release was smooth, making an even duller sound than a Kalashnikov. I aimed the crosshairs at a dead Arab lying on the ground, arms outstretched, in the middle of the camp. I couldn't see the surrounding area too well because of the flames – the camp, the body, the trees, everything was bathed in a hazy green light. So I removed the night scope's battery and the light scale went off; then it had the faint light of a regular scope.

Every scope has an indicator – a 'fixed point', 'single point' or 'pattern' – that signals the distance from the weapon to the objective. Usually on precision rifles this point corresponds to about two hundred metres. At that distance there's no need for correction; once the target has been pinpointed you can fire.

If the target is at a distance of more than two hundred metres you have to correct the sight a point lower on the scale, while if the target is closer than that you have to go a point higher. You also have to take into consideration certain external factors: wind, rain or the specifics of a given place – if there's a river nearby, for example, the air will be more humid – will vary the correction. This goes for the precision rifle scope. A machine gun, however, is a little simpler. Its fire capacity is higher than a rifle's, but it's much less precise; besides single rounds – which aren't its forte – it can cover a very broad area with a single volley of bullets.

*

'Is it any good?' Zenith asked, impatient. He was pacing more nervously than a father waiting to find out whether his newborn child was okay.

'Just one second, brother,' I replied, moving the selector to single shot.

I took my mouth guard out of my pocket – I carried it with me for shooting a Kalashnikov. It prevented my jaw from getting hit too much and the headache that would ensue. I framed the head of the corpse lying in the middle of the camp in the sight. The trigger was hard to pull, unlike the one on my rifle, which was nice and smooth.

I fired a round, and the head of the corpse came apart. Although I had a good hold on the weapon and was in a comfortable position the recoil was so strong that I felt it smack me in the shoulder. There was an annoying whistling in my ears, though I thought I'd compensated the force of the shot better than that . . . It was very strange. I switched the regulator onto blast and, clenching my teeth, I aimed at the Arab's vest. It literally burst into pieces, as if it had exploded from inside.

My comrades were speechless, and I couldn't believe my eyes either. Machine gun bullets could make holes in bulletproof vests, but usually they didn't destroy them in such a violent and devastating manner.

I had a hunch. I took a flashlight and pointed it at the chamber, opened it up and examined the cartridges. The shell was grey instead of brass.

'Fuck,' I said out loud.

'What? What?' Zenith asked, all excited.

I stood up and reported my discovery to Nosov:

'Ivanisch, there are amazing bullets in this little toy,' I said, my voice serious.

The captain took the gun and examined it carefully.

The bullets were polished to a mirror shine, the tips painted black. These were very expensive special cartridges, definitely not stuff meant for the army. The body was steel, covered with a light coat of varnish, and the tip was metal so it could go through kevlar or iron the same as air. The matrix was liquid mercury, which made its trajectory extra precise; most importantly, the gunpowder charge was stronger than normal, because it had to create enough force to propel the bullets, which were much heavier than normal ones.

We didn't have ammunition like that in our possession, only the Arabs did. It came from the black market, through ties with America. People said that a special company in Texas manufactured them, and that they cost five dollars each. This type of projectile was famous and feared among the soldiers, because there was no bulletproof vest that could withstand their force. In military slang they were called 'bye-bye mommas' – if a round like that hit you were done for.

Nosov passed Zenith the gun.

'Nice surprise. Use it wisely, son . . .'

My comrade's eyes shone like two polished buttons on a general's uniform.

*

In the meantime, Moscow and Deer opened their back-packs and began passing out the ammo they found in the camp – many were clips for AKs.

Moscow came over and held out two clips:

'See if they work on yours, they won't fit in mine . . .'

I took them, but even though they were the right calibre they didn't work in my pistol either. But so as not to throw away useful stuff I put them in my side pouch anyway, under the medi-kit. We weren't short on ammo, but it was always better to have a little extra.

We put all our weapons in place, making sure everything was in order. I pissed in the bushes and had a big drink of water.

Nosov and Lieutenant Razumovsky had spread out the map on a rock and were trying to decide the best way to circumvent the other enemy group. We had to keep hugging the mountain, then at some point the road would open out onto the valley. There, we had to go down and cross the valley, and then we would be on the way home.

Nosov set off down the path with a fast and determined stride, and the rest of the group followed behind. The explorers joked amongst themselves, a sign that after our victory morale was high. One of them passed me a piece of bread; I thanked him and started chewing on it slowly. Only then did I realise that I was hungry. Despite my days of rest and the spreads on base, I devoured it in seconds. As my elders often said:

'It doesn't take long to get used to the good things . . .'

We walked quickly in the cold morning air. The moon in the sky was a thin crescent and soon would disappear with the dawn. Nosov was watching the road and we were trying to keep up. The road was flat; once in a while there would be some bushes and then our captain would send one of us on recon. I took advantage of those moments to close my eyes and try to get at least a few minutes of rest.

Thus we continued for a while, until we reached a spot with a view over another mountain. It seemed close by. The sky was dotted with little clouds, riddled with holes as if someone had shot at it with a machine gun.

Nosov and the infantryman lieutenant stopped, ordered us to go to the side of the road and take a break. We didn't make them say it twice. We sat right down, leaning against the huge rocks that must have slid down there who knows how many years ago. We were all really tired. Some drank, others ate, and one infantryman took off his backpack, put his rifle down, lay out on a flat rock and closed his eyes. He stayed like that for about a minute, and then got up, stretching and yawning, as if he had just got out of bed.

Nosov gave me a piece of hardtack, and rubbing his neck, sat down beside me. For a while he didn't say anything, and then he explained:

'The next leg will be almost all in the open, near the boulders. It's a three-kilometre route.' He pointed to the space between the two mountains. 'At the point where these mountains are at their absolute closest they're probably about three hundred metres apart. That mountain leads to the north, and it's completely treeless, whereas this one has some very dense areas of forest . . . If I were in the Arabs' place I'd hurry across the valley, then I'd go up by the trees to set an ambush, that would be the only safe place. They're afraid of direct combat – I'm sure they'll station themselves there. Just as long as they can get there in time . . .'

I chewed on the biscuit as if hypnotised. When I listened to my captain's voice the rest of the world turned off, there was only room in my mind for whatever he was saying. He put his hand on my head, as if giving me a blessing, and continued:

'Get ready – in five minutes you'll go with Moscow and Zenith to survey the hill. You'll go on "detachment".* We won't be there to cover your arses, so be quick and keep your eyes peeled . . . Stop every ten metres and observe the terrain carefully. If you see any strange movement, if there's something that makes you suspicious, come back immediately . . . We'll be twenty minutes behind you, don't forget. And be careful – I don't want anyone losing his hide.'

In short, it was clear that the whole operation had reached the crucial moment, the turning point that could determine our future (or non-) existence.

When I went on recon I became another person. I

---

* This was what we called a small group that went on reconnaissance and had no contact with the rest of the unit.

was much less confident than when I just had to be a sniper. I worried about making mistakes, not being able to observe the terrain well, not noticing important details ...

Reconnaissance, in war, is a very difficult task. It doesn't only mean penetrating the enemy's territory unseen and watching them, it's a matter of assessing various factors, in order to reach a conclusion and deliver it as quickly and precisely as possible to your captain. Each operation is different. You have to spot the things that seem invisible to the normal eye, predict the enemy's moves, think like him. It's like hunting in the woods, following animal tracks. The difference is that in war both sides have weapons, the hunter and the hunted.

Your senses must always be on alert, especially if you don't know the area. You have to memorise every detail, even the most insignificant. Each individual stone and ditch, every tree and possible path. If something unexpected happens, it's crucial to have already figured out a quick escape route different from the one you took there. And to give a precise report, you have to remember all the places where firing positions can be set up, probing every bit of land to find the most appropriate plan.

Even today, I often find myself observing open spaces and thinking how perfect they would be for a military operation. Where a normal person sees a landscape and contemplates the beauty of nature, I realise that, against my will, I am figuring out where the machine gun should go.

I was sitting and chewing on the biscuit the captain had given me and trying to gather whatever strength I had left to carry out my job. Meanwhile, Nosov had gone first to Moscow and then to Zenith to give them the same little speech he had given me.

We had to cover two kilometres through a small forest, after which, according to Nosov, we would come to the clearing. This was the point from which we would go and explore the other mountain.

My comrades and I started filling our pockets with ammo. Zenith pulled an individual medi-kit out of his side pouch and put two clips in its place. When we went on recon we had to travel light but carry as many clips as possible. Getting into fire combat without anyone covering you was usually the fastest way to reach the great beyond.

We did our usual jumping on the spot to make sure nothing we had on us would make too much noise when we moved. I asked a soldier drinking some water from a plastic bottle if he would let me have some. I drank slowly, leisurely, letting the water slide down my throat. My head was light, I felt as if I'd got a second wind. In a certain sense, it was as if our adventure had only just begun.

Moscow came over and smiled at me:

'It's up to us once again, little brother . . .'

'May Jesus help us this time too, as always,' I replied.

We saluted and headed out.

Zenith walked behind us. With the machine gun he'd found and all the clips on his jacket he looked like some kind of robot.

At a certain stretch, when we were already almost past the first curve, Nosov came running up. For a second I thought he wanted to join us, but that wouldn't have made any sense.

He gave Moscow two hand grenades and, looking at us almost affectionately, he said:

'Be careful, boys, this isn't a walk in the park . . .'

We went through the woods. A few times we dropped to the ground, alarmed at noises that seemed like footsteps very close by, but that were actually stones falling down somewhere else.

Trees became more and more sparse, and after a very tight curve we saw a wide, bare rocky area ahead. Crossing that entire stretch in our two groups without being discovered − if there was anyone hiding out waiting to kill us − would be no easy endeavour.

'I'll go first,' I said, trying to muster my courage. After a long breath, I went onto the path, flattening myself against the wall of the mountain. I realised that there was a small ditch at my feet, almost half a metre deep, perhaps created by the rainwater, so I tried walking inside it. It was easy going, and it gave me a sense of protection from possible bullets, but the path was irregular; in some places the ditch slanted up and almost reached the level of the main trail. I went on like that for about ten metres, then I stopped and signalled to my comrades that I was going to come back onto the path.

I lay down on my belly. I could really smell the wet grass, the air was still completely moist, but there was no fog. I went on my hands and knees across the trail until I got to the other side. The ground was soft, swollen with rain, and the water went right through my clothes, right to my skin. We had taken off our rain ponchos because they limited our range of motion significantly, and besides that they made enough noise to reveal our presence immediately.

I turned on my rifle's night scope and looked at the mountain. The first area I decided to scout was about thirty metres wide and half a kilometre long; it was covered with small trees, but they weren't very close together. I looked slowly, moving the scope from high to low, right to left and then back. To scout a place it has to be divided into sections, so first you give the entire area a quick once-over. At this stage, it's helpful to identify some features of the landscape that you can use later as points of reference, like a stream, a fallen tree, a big or unusually shaped rock . . . Each of these elements serves to create an imaginary network in your head that you can go back over later through the scope for more careful inspection. An expert eye can notice a human presence even with peripheral vision. The important thing is never taking your eye off the scope, not changing position or allowing yourself to be distracted by anything outside your field of vision.

I didn't notice any Arabs; I crawled back across. I signalled for Zenith and Moscow to join me, and together we walked through the ditch. We stopped several more times – every ten metres, as the captain had said – taking turns observing all the details of the mountain, but there didn't seem to be anything suspicious.

We were almost finished; it was my turn to explore again. All I could think about was when we would be back on base. Maybe Nosov's worries were exaggerated; our enemy wouldn't be able to move through the mountains fast enough to catch up with us and ambush us.

I went to the edge of the trail and began observing. Suddenly something appeared in my scope. It was a man, walking uphill, and he was carrying lots of ammo. I felt like someone had poured a bucket of ice water on me. The man was moving slowly and his phosphorescent figure, as I saw it through the night scope, gave the impression that he wasn't afraid of being discovered. I lowered my scope straight down a little. Below him, about ten metres away, other armed figures were climbing up the same path. In total there were thirty-four, and they had two transport animals, mules perhaps.

When I saw the mules I grew really scared. It could only mean one thing: those bastards were carrying something heavy. For an instant I looked away, and I inwardly cursed Nosov, him and his eternal knack for always being right. Then I went back to observing.

After a bit Moscow came over. He crawled slowly, and when his face got near mine, he whispered:

'So did you see something?'

I probably hadn't moved for a while, and my comrades must have grown suspicious. I'd taken more time than usual to scout the area, wanting to be sure of the enemy's exact numbers. I set my rifle on the ground, put my hand over my mouth to avoid an echo, and as softly as possible I said:

'Thirty-four 'spirits',* lots of ammo . . .' And then I couldn't go on. If I didn't say it, maybe what I had seen would be less true.

Only after a moment did I find the courage to finish:

'. . . and two mules.'

Moscow put his hand over his eyes.

'Fucking Christ . . .' he said. 'Mortars . . .'

A mule could transport a light 85-calibre mortar and some ammunition. Usually a grenade launcher was enough to attack a column of soldiers – you only used mortars when you really wanted to create a living hell. If the enemy was able to position them and use them against us, our endeavour would be over within minutes. Those were deadly weapons, with an extremely powerful charge, capable of completely razing a trail such as the one we were on right now . . .

*

---

* The Afghani authorities called the Taliban *dushman*, or 'enemies'; the Russian military abbreviate the word to *duch* ('spirit' in Russian), probably because they appear and disappear so quickly.

Once I saw an entire column of vehicles taken out by mortars.

After the explosion, all that remained was a hodgepodge of various mechanical parts, completely misshapen, mixed with ammo, remnants of human bodies, weapons, food, mud . . . You couldn't make sense of anything, it was complete chaos. It was as if a giant had taken all those cars filled with people, put them in a huge washing machine and then, after putting them on spin fast enough to send every single bolt and bone flying, had tossed them into the street. The idea of ending up in a situation like that took my breath away.

A tactic often used by the Arabs was occupying each end of a road with a mortar. They would fire and keep moving little by little towards the middle of the road, progressively reducing the distance and thus sowing total destruction. This tactic had been used against our ranks in Afghanistan – it was crude but very effective. Soldiers had nowhere to run, because after an explosion the shrapnel would fly everywhere and was more devastating than bullets, mercilessly tearing the human body to shreds.

In the mountains a mortar was even more dangerous, because there was nowhere to hide. Even if the person firing didn't have good aim, the shells still hit the rock, and the pieces would come off the mountain and fall down like rain. For a small group like ours, with only fourteen men and no heavy artillery (if you excluded an RPG grenade launcher), it was certain death . . .

Moscow and I were lying on the edge of the road, with our cheeks sinking into the damp soil, both thinking the same thing: if we let the Arabs get through the mountains with those mules now, then nobody would be able to cross that road. There was no time to turn back and report to the captain — before long the enemy would pass the visible part of the hill and would be hidden deep in the forest.

When I spoke to Moscow my mouth was dry; my tongue stuck to my teeth, as if glued on. I was anxious. I never would have thought I'd have to make a decision like this.

'You're a corporal. It's up to you to give the orders, but I want to tell you my opinion anyway: we need to act now . . . If any of their men are waiting for them higher up, if the ones we saw weren't the main group but were just heading to a position . . . Well, in five minutes we'll be a trio of corpses . . .'

'You're right,' he replied. 'We can't let them get to the woods. I give the orders, that's true, but there are three of us and more than thirty of them . . . you know what'll happen if we open fire? We can get rid of the mortars, and we three risk dying. We can go back, and all fourteen die together. What if Nosov has an alternative route?'

I was too tired and nervous to think. The only thing to do was act. I felt like a machine, a tiny piece of a mechanism that does things without making decisions, and does them that way because it was only programmed to do that specific action. My reply came out of my mouth before I'd thought it through:

'Nosov's not here now, and we don't know shit about the roads on this stupid mountain. All I know is that when I look through the telescope I see a group of Arabs transporting two fucking mortars. If they have any snipers positioned anywhere we're screwed, but we have to take out those mules at all costs . . .'

Moscow nodded, and went over to get Zenith. I pointed the rifle towards the enemy and began studying the column. The mules were moving slowly, only a few metres apart. Usually the Arabs would tie them together so that if one animal stopped the other would pull it forward. If those mules were tied together, the best thing would be to unload a blast of gunfire on the first so it would drag the other one down when it fell, and the enemy wouldn't have time to react.

Moscow and Zenith joined me.

'Take this, Kolima,' Zenith said, handing me the machine gun he'd taken from the camp. 'You use it, you're much more precise than me.'

The gun was already loaded with its killer bullets. I took my Kalashnikov off my back and gave it to Zenith along with four clips. I looked at my comrades:

'When I start shooting, you guys look where they respond from and aim directly there . . . Don't stop – even if they kill us, their mortars will still be at the bottom of the valley . . .'

Zenith gave me a wink:

'Don't shit yourself, brother, we'll have lots more drinks together . . .'

'And Moscow will take you to another nurse . . .' I replied.

This was our way of boosting one another's spirits.

For months Zenith had been going on and on about this thing he had for his neighbour Larisa, who he would always spy on through the window when he was a little boy. She had, he said, such beautiful soft hair between her legs it was like a priceless rug. He wanted to touch it, he wanted to survive the bloodbath of the war and make love to her, that's what. It was a nice story, but the fact that Zenith had never been with a woman made us sad, so one day Moscow took him to a nurse who finally freed him from the slavery of virginity.

Talking about alcohol and women fired us up at the time. It's weird to think back on it now, but the possibility of ending my days on that mountain didn't have any particular effect on me. At that moment all I wanted was to get rid of those damned mules.

I took a deep breath, then I pushed out the air and held my breath, trying to become completely still and hard like a rock. I put my eye to the scope, and as soon as I pinpointed the first mule I fired. The first blast was very short, but I had to correct my aim immediately, since, as I had already experienced, that machine gun had a strong recoil, and it was hard to keep a good grip on it. I unloaded another blast and then another, whereas the other side hadn't fired a single round. The mules fell down, along with a few men. We could hear their shouts, the animals' cries, and then there was a loud explosion. I aimed the gun at the column and emptied the rest of the clip without stopping for a second, almost euphoric. I felt every round on my skin – it was as if with each explosion the air pressed on a different part of my head.

I was so absorbed that I didn't notice when the Arabs began responding to the fire, but I felt the pieces of rock hitting my back. Zenith and Moscow had already moved away, shooting wildly like I was. The enemy was running in every direction, but luckily there didn't seem to be any snipers in hiding; maybe they felt safe in their mountains and hadn't bothered to set up a position.

'Zenith, another clip!' I shouted. My ears were ringing – the noise the gun made was incredible – and it felt like I was being pounded on the head with a great big hammer. Zenith pulled two clips off his jacket and threw them to me. The machine gun was smoking, and when I opened it I burned my fingers. The clips were heavy; I inserted one and in a few seconds I was shooting again. A few Arabs tried to climb up, others ran down; amidst all the chaos, I was able to knock down about ten of them. The mountain was steep, and they didn't have enough space to set up a firing position. I could see their rifle ammo exploding upon contact with the bullets, and then the enemies' bodies falling off the mountain like stones swept up in an avalanche.

Suddenly we saw a bright light that illuminated the sky like daylight. Moscow barely made it in time to shout:

'RPG!'

Suddenly everything I could see with my right eye turned blinding white, like when you look at the sun for a long time with dark sunglasses on and then quickly turn away and try to look somewhere else. There was a violent explosion on the wall behind us, and our backs were pummelled with boiling stones. The impact was so strong that for a second I felt like my whole body was made of cotton – I had become light and soft, I couldn't even manage to keep my hand on the trigger . . . Moscow had a small flaming rock on his shoulder; seeing such solid material catch fire was impressive. Zenith had his head down, his hands over his ears, his mouth open and his eyes wide. The Arabs started shooting a few tracer bullets, trying to correct their aim in order to send over another grenade.

So I pointed the machine gun at the mountain and without ever taking my eye off the scope I unloaded the rest of the magazine, following every human figure that came into my sight. I couldn't remember with any precision where the RPG blast had come from, nor did I know what my comrades were doing at that moment. I was in a state of complete confusion . . . My head hurt like hell, every little noise irritated me, but I kept shooting anyway, changing my clip again, working like a robot. We could hear some people shouting and others sobbing, desperate . . . The cries of the wounded seemed so close that if you closed your eyes you could imagine them next to you. I looked through the scope, searching for movement, but nobody had been responding to the fire for some time. So I began shooting at the bodies strewn along the path until there was an explosion – I must have hit the RPG rounds or the mortar shells.

I stopped and closed my eyes. I was thirsty. My mouth was so dry that when I opened it to take in some air, my lips cracked; running my tongue over them, I could taste blood. That brought me back to reality. All three of us were lying flat next to one another, breathing hard.

Zenith, who was on my right, was covered in shells from the machine gun. He got up and made the sign of the cross, then he looked at me with a smile and a crazed look in his eyes.

Moscow, as if he had just woken up from a nightmare, leapt to his feet, gave me a kick on the side and yelled:

'Let's move! Come on, we have to tell the guys!'

Then he hurried off to reach our group. I pulled myself up too and followed. Zenith came last; he hadn't hooked the machine gun stand very well, so it had opened and was making a lot of noise, bumping against the barrel.

I wasn't thinking about anything. I felt good, like I had freed myself from something that had been tormenting me for a long time. Our captain often said that was what winning felt like. Running back to the rest of the unit, though, I felt less and less protected, as if at any moment a bullet could hit me in the back.

At some point, Moscow turned around and yelled to me:

'Fucking whore of a war, we did it!'

We saw them from afar, running towards us; after hearing the gunfire, they had decided to come and help us. It was Nosov and Shoe, with their rifles levelled.

'Saboteurs here! Identify yourselves!'

'Ivanisch, it's us!' Moscow yelled.

'We heard an explosion, what was it?' Shoe asked, lowering his gun.

Moscow was all excited, like a happy child:

'Thirty-four Czechs with two mules and two mortars! Fuck, we took them all out!'

'Move, move, let's go!' Nosov ordered the rest of the group. He didn't want us to stop; we had to get out of those mountains as quickly as possible.

It was good for me to see my comrades' faces. As always, after getting through danger, it was like seeing family; I wanted to hug them all, greet each one, ask how they were . . . After an especially stressful action, I got too sentimental.

Nosov continued questioning us:

'Did you make sure there weren't any others? Are you sure you killed them all?'

Moscow repeated his version like a broken record:

'We took them all out, every single one of them . . .'

And then, short of breath from running, he started recounting every detail of our action. I asked for something to drink and an explorer gave me his water bottle. I took big gulps and found the water so good I almost felt inebriated. After a few minutes we came to the spot where we had been shooting earlier. The ground was covered in shells, and that particular point on the road, now that our group was all together, seemed much smaller than when there were only three of us just minutes before. On the side of the mountain above us was the huge hole made by the RPG. Looking at it, I thought how lucky we'd been − if the round had hit just a few metres lower the falling rock would have killed us . . . I felt strangely relieved, as if all the bad things that still awaited us were contained within that hole in the rock.

We kept on running. The sky was clear, everything was preparing for the coming of the light. The air was cool and damp – if I closed my eyes for a moment it felt like I was back home on my boat, on the river, out in the morning air, on my way back from a night of fishing . . .

Suddenly I felt a shove and I fell forward onto my left side. Tracer bullets were coming from the mountain in front of us, I don't know how, but we were in the middle of gunfire. I'd been saved thanks to the soldier who had pushed me down. He and I rolled into a nearby ditch and took cover, and I realised that my comrades were already there. The fire was so heavy that we couldn't raise our heads at all. The soldier next to me started shooting with his assault rifle, but I stopped him right away:

'You have to cover the flash supressor; otherwise they'll keep shooting at us!'

The infantrymen's Kalashnikovs didn't have modified compensators or flash suppressors; the rifle's burst of flame could easily be seen.

None of us responded to the fire. We all hid in the ditch, our heads down, listening to the bullets exploding all around us. In all that pandemonium it was hard to work out the one thing that mattered to me most: whether or not they had a sniper.

At some point something strange happened – the enemy stopped shooting volleys. Only single shots came, and we couldn't quite make out where they hit; perhaps the enemy couldn't tell where we were. Then we heard the unmistakable sound of a battle in the distance. From the way the echo reverberated off the rocks, these new rounds were coming from the opposite side of the valley − in fact, right from where we were headed ourselves.

There must have been a very violent battle going on. We could hear every sound of the fight perfectly, as if we were at the cinema instead of in a ditch. I recognised the pounding of a heavy machine gun, every now and then the roar of an RPG, and in the background the incessant bursts of the Kalashnikovs − the assault rifles shrieked so loudly it seemed as if they were going to drown out their own voices.

The captain said:

'Shit, those are our men. They're pushing them to the other side of the mountain . . .'

A few Kalashnikov shells came near us, but they seemed to be aimed at a point much higher than where we were. Nosov ordered everyone to identify himself, reporting his status. As soon as he was able to get in touch with our superiors, he would communicate precisely who was wounded and who was not. My comrades identified themselves, stating their role and unit, and then added the most important thing: 'in rank'. The expression 'in rank' meant they had not been hurt and could continue to fulfil their tasks. When it was my turn I said: 'Sniper, saboteurs, in rank!' Luckily, nobody had been hurt or killed; all of us had been able to take cover from the unexpected fire.

Cautiously, I raised my head above the ditch and through the scope of my precision rifle I began observing the mountain opposite us. I saw the first enemies about two hundred metres away. There were three of them, slowly moving towards the valley. I reported to the captain:

'Ivanisch, I see three subjects coming down . . .'

'Liquidate them immediately!' he ordered.

I hit the first two with four rounds but the last one responded to the fire, shooting at us, but without good aim. Then he started running higher. I decided to follow him with the scope; I wanted to see where he would lead me.

He was climbing the mountain very quickly, first running in a zigzag pattern; then when he noticed I wasn't shooting anymore, he slackened his pace and started following the path. After about fifty metres he came to a flat area by a forest, and there he sat down on a rock to catch his breath for a moment. I fired, but I wasn't able to hit him – he stood right up, so I shot at his legs, and this time he fell down, letting out a long, pained howl, which faded in the damp mountain air like a gust of wind. Just after that, another man came out from behind the trees. I got him straight in the chest. The guy who was already on the ground suddenly turned and shot another blast in our direction, but it too was imprecise. I aimed carefully and this time I took him out, blasting two rounds into his chest.

'Those bastards are hiding in the woods . . .' Moscow said. I hadn't even realised he had come up to me.

'Our men should have defeated them,' I replied. 'They're abandoning their defence and coming towards us . . .'

The situation was troubling. Our men would follow them, and we – who, without a radio, couldn't send any kind of communication – risked getting caught in friendly fire. Paradoxically, our men could be more dangerous to us than the enemy, especially if the infantry units were among them, or worse, the Internal Ministry's Special Rapid Response Unit. The soldiers in the rapid response unit didn't listen to anyone, they shot at anything that moved. It was best to avoid them, to quickly come up with a plan to make sure we weren't spotted.

We had been in a similar situation before, when, because of a misunderstanding, we saboteurs had a very close call . . .

On that occasion, we had been stuck in a building for three long hours, besieged by constant fire from our own infantry.

What had happened was, as we approached their position, we had shot two red signal flares to identify ourselves, as we had determined before the operation. But their officers didn't see them – one was seriously wounded and in the infirmary, while their lieutenant, recovering from a long battle in another part of the city, was sleeping in an armoured vehicle.

The lieutenant colonels, sergeants and soldiers hadn't heard a thing about the red flares. After shooting them in the air, we headed for their position, crossing the yard with complete ease. From the third floor of another building about five hundred metres away, two heavy machine guns and a Kalashnikov started going to work on us. Deer took a volley of bullets right in the chest, but luckily his vest saved his life. We hid inside the adjacent building, with nothing to do but wait, hoping they would soon run out of ammo. They even threw a couple of grenades inside our refuge, to burn the house and force us outside where they could kill us. We were able to hide in the cellar, but if the infantrymen decided to enter we would really be trapped.

Their lieutenant only woke up three hours later. When they told him they were shooting at an enemy group who had fired two red signal flares before approaching, he ordered them to cease fire immediately. He sent over a group of explorers — by a sheer miracle we didn't shoot at one another. The explorers then escorted us to our positions, communicating their status via radio.

Having too many soldiers in a military operation isn't always such a great thing.

About ten enemies began going down the path; some running hard, trying to escape faster, others stopping and trying to set up a cover. Further up, a group of our men continued shooting unceasingly; we could hear them shouting orders in the distance.

Deer squeezed in between Moscow and me:

'Christ, the guys are really pushing – in a few minutes they'll be taking us out too . . .'

The battle went by fast, almost in a flash, and at some point our men loaded a grenade launcher. After a few seconds the first bomb hit the enemy, then another, and another . . . The trees and bushes caught fire immediately, and the Arabs started yelling. Through my rifle scope, the whole tremendous spectacle looked like a puppet show: the enemies' burned bodies, reduced to bits, fell through the air into the valley.

Two rounds had landed very close to the place where I had taken down the last enemies – *too* close . . . I checked the path and saw three enemies hiding in a bush; one started going down, trying to flee our soldiers' attack. I shot and killed him, then I tried to pinpoint the other two. I shot a few rounds, wounding one of them; then our men threw a hand grenade at them, leaving no trace of the enemies' bodies.

Nosov took control of the situation:

'Join up for immediate retreat! Saboteurs go first, infantry follows a hundred metres behind. In case of enemy fire, do not shoot without my permission; our men are in the area . . .'

We jumped to our feet and began running down the road after Nosov. We had to scram before our men noticed us . . .

We ran like men with nothing to lose, until we came to a point where the road became very narrow.

'Once we're past the bend,' the captain said, 'we'll leave this fucking mountain behind us . . .'

Passing through the bottleneck between the rocks we reached the other side of the mountain. A wide plain appeared before our eyes.

We could finally see the light of day. The sun was rising, but we had to be sure we were in the clear before we could stop running.

After half an hour, Nosov let us take a break.

'Two minutes!' he yelled.

We were exhausted, panting. I took the canteen from my side pouch and drank greedily. Just then I heard a blast of gunfire coming from the top of the mountain on our left. I dropped the canteen and threw myself under a rock. Seconds later we were all belly down.

'Shit, it's not over yet . . .' said Spoon.

The bullets lodged one after the other in the ground in front of us. We couldn't see anything, just a sea of sand, clay and pebbles that rose and kept moving through the air, like a whirlwind. Keeping your eyes open was impossible and painful, they instantly filled up with sand and dust. I felt trapped. Everything had happened so fast, I didn't even know exactly where the shooting was coming from; they seemed to be firing from every direction.

We stuck to the mountain as closely as possible. We had about fifty centimetres of room where the bullets couldn't reach. Our infantrymen, on the other hand, had taken cover behind a row of big boulders. From there, they began shooting over our heads – they must have spotted the enemy. So the Arabs stopped shooting at us and responded to the infantry. The dust in front of us faded little by little.

One of the enemies let out a loud yell – he had probably been hit; another fell in front of us. He had a fatal wound in his neck, but he was still moving. Moscow finished him off with a couple of shots.

While the infantrymen distracted the enemy, we tried to change positions, dragging ourselves to the opposite side of the road. I was last and I couldn't see where we were going, but any other hiding spot would be better. The Arabs threw a grenade somewhere close to us. The explosion was deafening, and everything filled up with dust again. I had sand in my eyes, my nose, my mouth . . . It was as if I had dived into a pool of sand, and then my ears started to ring . . . Someone grabbed me by the jacket and started dragging me, scraping me against the ground. I couldn't tell if it was someone in my group who wanted to save me or an enemy who wanted to capture me, all I could do was hold the rifle tight in my hands while I kept repeating:

'I can't hear! I can't hear!'

It was an ugly moment. My eyes hurt like hell. My back came up against something hard, and then gradually I could hear voices. It seemed like my comrades, but I still couldn't completely make them out. Someone splashed my eyes with water, and I was able to wipe away some of the sand.

'More . . .' I said. 'More . . .'

More water splashed onto my face, and the figure of Nosov slowly came into focus. He was standing over me and staring.

'Were you hit by shrapnel?' he asked me, alarmed.

I looked around, a little stunned. We had all moved behind a rock, and my comrades were trying to set up a position, responding to the enemy fire from this new shelter.

'No . . . I don't think so . . .' I replied. 'I don't feel any pain, I don't think . . .'

'Well, Kolima, you have Deer to thank – that bomb almost blew up on top of you, and if he hadn't taken you out of there . . .' Then he went to see how the rest of the group was doing.

The situation was clear. We had to arrange our cover so that the infantrymen could get through – now they were the ones who were trapped. Even if we had the enemy under fire, even if they were busy responding, it appeared that they had no intention of letting up on our infantry.

'Stand back,' Nosov said as he loaded the RPG.

He placed the mouth of the grenade launcher into an opening between the stones and shot a round towards the Arabs. As soon as the bomb exploded, the infantrymen took advantage, coming out from their cover and running over to us.

Moscow and I started shooting in order to create a wall of fire and keep the enemy from hitting our soldiers. The Arabs, from above, started throwing more hand grenades.

The skirmish was violent. Neither we nor the enemies had a decent position; we were all behind rocks, fifty metres apart. The bullets whizzed over our heads and there were constant explosions all around us.

Moscow took a round in the chest. The bullet was stopped by the vest but it still managed to send my friend's body flying as if he were a doll. He fell at my feet.

'Everything okay, brother?' I asked, still shooting.

He gestured that he was okay; he just had to recover from the blow.

A bomb hit the bottom of the valley, exploding in the distance. Another ricocheted off a rock without hitting the road; it blew up, bringing lots of stones down on the soldiers' heads and forcing them to slow their retreat. The last bomb fell right behind them, and after the explosion we saw an infantryman hit the ground. His comrades picked him up right away and rushed over to our shelter.

The guy who had been hit had some nasty cuts on his legs and his jacket was full of shards. Some infantrymen joined us to increase our firepower, while others treated their comrade as best they could. The infantry lieutenant, along with one of his men, made an improvised stretcher out of the wounded man's vest.

'We have to get out of this hellhole, now,' Lieutenant Razumovsky said. His face was very pale – you could see that he was concerned about his man's fate.

'Moscow, Deer,' Nosov said lucidly, 'you go with the infantry.'

Then he turned to the lieutenant:

'Relax, we'll be here to cover you . . .'

We had to continue keeping the enemy occupied, and about twenty minutes after the infantry group had left we would start to make our retreat.

I was still stunned by the bomb explosion. I was

shooting along with the others but I was slow, I didn't really know what was going on. Nosov must have noticed:

'Kolima,' he said, 'take cover. I'll take your place.'

I moved to the side of the path, in between the boulders.

The infantrymen were able to retreat without any losses. I could hear the gunfire continue, but now our men were limiting themselves to firing single rounds. The enemy fire had become a little less intense – they probably wanted to retreat too; maybe there were few of them left or maybe some of them were wounded.

Often, in firefights between small groups, the following phenomenon would occur: a series of blasts, even violent ones, would be exchanged for a few minutes, and then suddenly, both sides, as if by unspoken accord, would withdraw. It was a kind of pact of mutual trust between the two groups taking part in the conflict, a chance, time-restricted choice of non-violence against the enemy.

There were various reasons for doing this. One unit might be in a hurry to reach another target and didn't want to lose time or risk their lives on an unplanned battle, so they tried to evade it, to 'slip out', as we would say, or leave without provoking the enemy at all. In many cases, however, this tactic would be used when a group had reached the limit of their capacities – if they didn't have much ammunition, if there were any wounded, or if they couldn't establish a decent stable defence.

Sometimes, obviously, this tactic could be a good way

to trick the enemy. A small group of soldiers would detach from the unit, approach the enemy positions and pretend to have wound up there by accident. They would put on a real show, making the enemy think they were completely confused. They would pass themselves off as soldiers who were lost and trying to find a way out of the area. One of them would yell things like 'Where are we? Who has the map?' that sort of nonsense, acting like idiots. At that point, if they'd been loud enough, the enemy would open fire, thereby revealing all their positions. The others would respond, while within a short time the larger group – alerted via radio by their 'decoys' – would come to back them up.

It was a strategy that the Russian army was really fond of, and one used often in both Chechen campaigns, especially in the city, where the streets were usually occupied by various units, everything was chaotic and nobody could figure out exactly what was going on. The Chechens quickly learned this tactic, and on occasion used it to lead the Russian troops into traps in the woods or the mountains.

Sheltered behind that rock I sat with my eyes closed for a moment, but my head started spinning straight away. It was like being on a merry-go-round, I felt nauseous . . . So as not to fall into the trap of exhaustion – which in war can cost you your life – I decided to take part in the battle anyway. I took my precision rifle and began inspecting the area where the enemies were. As far as I could tell they didn't have any snipers; they must have hit Moscow purely by accident – when a sniper shoots at someone from fifty metres away, that person doesn't stand a chance . . .

A few rounds were exchanged, but we were all pretty weak. It was obvious that the enemy was also trying to find a way to pull out of the skirmish.

I had to do something to get rid of the headache that was eating away at me, keeping me from thinking. I could feel exhaustion creeping over my entire body, my knees and back ached . . . I felt weaker and weaker . . .

Thinking back on it now, I feel horrible and ashamed, yet in those moments, when I thought that if I closed my eyes I was going to go mad, I would repeat to myself, like a prayer, the phrase 'I have to kill an Arab', until I was able to regain control of myself . . . I don't know exactly how the subconscious works, but at those times it was as if my body were running on automatic pilot, as if a part of me had gone to sleep, surrendering to my hunting instincts.

As I was looking through the scope, I heard a loud explosion. I immediately hid behind the rock, and there was a series of powerful explosions just like the first. From the sound, it seemed like they were coming from an AGS, a kind of automatic weapon that shoots grenades instead of bullets. Our men had arrived! We all pressed ourselves to the ground – the rocks falling on us were so scorching hot we could feel the heat through our uniforms.

The AGS was a very efficient weapon; it could clear out an area in a very short time. Soon we would smell burnt flesh – we just all hoped that it would be the enemy's and not ours . . .

When the AGSs stopped shooting, Nosov shouted:

'Withdraw immediately!'

We started running in the direction the infantrymen had gone. I had a brutal headache, but I just put one leg in front of the other. I remember asking God to put a stop to all this chaos around me, because I wasn't at all sure I could make it with the little strength I had left. I ran without feeling anything, only fear and confusion.

Often, especially after a long and arduous mission (when I had a ringing in my ears that wouldn't stop, and everything around me looked like a surrealist painting seen from a speeding train), I would get overwhelmed by strange emotions . . .

At certain times I would suddenly think I had forgotten something, but I couldn't work out what. I felt like I didn't have my rifle, whereas I actually had it in my hands; or I was convinced I was wounded – sometimes all it took was the *idea* of a wound, and immediately I'd have a phantom pain in some part of my body, which didn't subside until I was able to make sure that I really was okay.

One time, right in the middle of a battle, for some inexplicable reason I couldn't find a pair of trainers that I was sure I'd just taken off an enemy's fresh corpse. I looked for them everywhere. I blamed Deer, insulting him and accusing him of having taken my shoes. 'You have them on, you dick,' he said to me. When I looked down and saw them on my feet I was shaken – I really didn't remember putting them on at all . . .

Following my comrades, I felt the cold on my face. I couldn't tell whether my mouth was closed or open, I couldn't control my muscles too well, it was as if I'd been given partial anaesthesia . . . It was one of the effects of concussion: your hands start trembling, your eyes start twitching; you need to rest, avoid making sudden movements . . . but you have to follow through with the rest of the unit all the way to the end of the mission.

Behind us we could hear the sounds of the battle that was still going on as we walked down a very narrow path. The rocks jutted out over our heads; the sunlight hadn't completely reached us yet. I was last in line, and I felt like I was in one of those dreams where you're trying to reach a point, but the further you go the more distant it becomes. Soon this will all be over, I kept telling myself in order to keep calm.

We were almost at the end of the path where there was an opening with a thin ray of light coming through. We could feel the cool air coming from the other side. Nosov said that we were to go through the opening and would find a steep slope overlooking a densely wooded area. We just had to go down the slope and we would finally reach the plain.

Zenith and Spoon went first. Then it was Nosov's turn.

After him went Shoe, and last was me. When our captain entered that sort of vortex of light, I thought I saw something strange. For a moment his figure completely blocked the current of damp mountain air, and the rays of sunlight seemed to erase the features of his face, making him look like a kind of luminous ghost . . . I was about to ask Shoe if he saw the same thing, when a spray of bullets came right through the opening.

I saw Nosov fall on his back, his arms outstretched like Christ on the cross. It was so unexpected that for a few seconds I was paralysed.

Shoe, on the other hand, responded to the fire immediately, shooting madly into the light.

Spoon and Zenith could have been anywhere. Wounded, dead, or in the clear.

'Get him, take him to shelter!' Shoe yelled at me while still shooting.

I grabbed the captain by the jacket and dragged him over to a small cave in the mountain that we had passed earlier.

I tried to determine whether he was seriously wounded. I looked on the ground to see if there was a trail of blood, but as I was moving him I didn't see anything out of the ordinary.

I remember fearing Nosov's death almost more than my own. The loss of our captain, for me, would be tantamount to the end of our entire unit. Up to that moment he had been the truest, strongest thing we had encountered in that war. We all knew very well that we risked our lives carrying out his orders, but no one had ever thought that he could be the one to die. Of course, we had been given instructions on how to lead the unit in the event of losing our commander, and maybe we could have got by on our own, but Nosov was the very incarnation of our faith as soldiers, our security, a talisman that we always had with us through the chaos. As long as he was there, nothing could really scare us, nothing could defeat us. The idea that he too, like the rest of us, could lose his life during an operation, was so terrible that none of us had ever dared bring it up. To us Nosov was sacred.

And at that moment I was dragging that sacred person, who was giving no signs of life, away from the battle . . . We reached the cave; I sat down and caught my breath. In my head, everything was frozen at the instant when that blast came, like when you pause a movie. I couldn't think or make decisions. I looked at Nosov's body, dazed, trying to work out what to do. My hand shaking, I put my finger under his nose and felt a light puff of air; I touched his neck and realised that I could feel his pulse. His heart was pumping hard.

'Thank heavens,' I said to myself. He had only passed out; his eyes were closed and the muscles on his face were relaxed, like when a person is resting or having a good dream.

I rapidly inspected his vest – it had a pretty big dent in the middle and the central plate was broken in half.

I propped him up against the wall of the cave and then stepped outside. I could hear the bullets coming from both sides – we were caught between two sources of fire.

I rushed over to Shoe, who was still swearing and cursing the entire Islamic community.

'Is he alive?' he asked me.

'He took a blast in the chest . . . He doesn't seem hurt. He's breathing, but he's still unconscious . . .'

'We have to get him out of here, this is a bad spot,' he said, changing his rifle clip.

'But where?' I asked, shooting a couple of times into the opening myself, even though nobody was responding to our fire. 'If we turn back they'll kill us for sure. It's better to try to go this way. Maybe there aren't that many of them . . .'

Shoe looked at me without saying a word. I stopped shooting, and for a second we fell silent, trying to guess what the situation beyond that opening was. Everything seemed still; there was just a faint gust of wind, making the same sound as a conch shell when you put it up to your ear.

'I wonder where those two ended up,' Shoe said suddenly.

There was no need for him to name them. I too had tried to imagine what happened to Zenith and Spoon after they went through there . . . Then my thoughts went back to our captain, who was propped up nearby, unconscious, thrown in a corner like a broken toy.

I was desperate. I felt far too close to the 'end of the line', as we call the point of no return in war, the moment when a soldier can't take it anymore and becomes cata-tonic or goes mad with fear and desperation.

Amongst all the confused thoughts spinning around in my head, there was one that seemed stronger than the others until it became a cement wall that was about to bury me. It was a phrase, simple and definitive, one that could paralyse me completely. It went:

'This is the end.'

And then I felt a great lightness go through my body, and I thought I had died for real . . . I didn't notice that my rifle had slipped out of my hand, nor did I realise that I was lying on my back on the ground, like a real corpse. Even if I was seeing things as a living person for the last time, I wasn't sad at all − the sensation was like being a body carried away by the current. I could feel everything, the air passing over me, the ground beneath me, but it was as if it had lost all value, had suddenly become invisible, unimportant . . .

Shoe was shouting at me, but his voice didn't really reach me; it seemed distant − it was much better to stay down, motionless, dead. I don't think this episode lasted very long, but I felt as though I had fallen into eternity. I don't know what that scene looked like from outside; I remember that I wasn't anxious or worried − on the contrary, I was very calm, if only because by that point I was sure I no longer existed . . .

Suddenly I felt a strong jolt, like someone was shooting at me, and then a loud, booming voice *filled* my head − I don't know how else to put it. The voice went through every molecule of my organism, and now it was bringing me back to life.

'Soldier! On your feet, you stupid bastard! Take up your weapon!' Captain Nosov, furious as a beast, was standing over me and shouting right in my ear.

I was on my feet in a heartbeat, my rifle in my hands. I looked at Nosov like Mary must have looked at the sepulchre of the resurrected Christ. On the captain's face there was a horrible grimace of pain, and he had a nasty black bruise on his neck that he must have got from the broken plate of his vest hitting him.

From the distance we could hear Spoon's voice, which seemed to come from the sky, like a messenger angel:

'What the fuck are you doing in there? Come on!'

We went through the opening, one at a time, almost joyfully. In an instant we had that damned mountain behind us, and we were running down the hill. At the bottom, near the edge of the woods, Zenith showed us the place where the enemies had been shooting at us moments before. I was running so hard I was almost out of breath.

When we went into the woods, Spoon came up to me, nudging me with his shoulder:

'What was that? We thought you were a goner! We saw that blast you took . . .'

Gasping as if drowning, I replied:

'That wasn't me, it was the captain . . .'

Spoon whistled, and then looked at Nosov. At that moment he was resting with one hand against a tree and the other on his chest.

'What, soldier,' he said to Spoon, 'you think your captain would abandon you and let you go fuck around? Certainly not . . .' He spoke with a joking tone, even though the blow he had taken must still have really hurt.

'Shit, that's some luck . . .' Zenith remarked, his machine gun levelled to cover our retreat.

'Come on, boys,' Nosov said, 'our men will already be down there waiting for us.'

We could hear the battle continuing behind us – it was definitely our men who had succeeded in pushing the enemy somewhere and were smashing them to bits.

We walked through the damp morning air that rose from the wet soil and shimmered in the sunlight; the warm sunbeams shone through the tangle of branches, forming a mosaic of long, twisted shadows at our feet. There, in that fantastic theatre of nature that unfolded before our eyes, suddenly replacing the scenes of war, I was absurdly gripped by a thought; just as we were killing each other like maniacs, the world went on. While we were fighting, pushing ourselves to madness and brutality, nature went on existing. There it was.

I knew perfectly well that such philosophical thoughts usually came to me when my psycho-physiological state had reached total exhaustion. I began to worry. So as not to get lost in that mental spider web, I tried to remember the details of the events that had just happened . . . I thought it was important for me to make sure what had happened to me didn't happen again. Only then did I comprehend the gravity of my actions – I had abandoned my weapon and lain on the ground, putting my comrades in danger. *I was a disgrace walking through the woods with a rifle.* I could feel my cheeks burn. I thought about the lecture the captain was going to give me, and with good reason . . .

Nosov had picked up the pace – the shots were closer now, maybe an enemy detachment had entered the woods. Soon they would catch up with us . . . The exit onto the plain had already come into view. It was a straight, wide road; there was lots of mud and few trees. In the distance we could make out the hills and some uncultivated fields, abandoned for who knows how long.

I saw an armoured car about a hundred metres from the road, but then a blast of gunfire came towards us. We all dropped to the ground.

'Don't shoot! It's our men!' the captain told us. Nosov and Shoe began moving to the side, to get to them without being seen and tell them who we were. They quickly crossed the road and disappeared behind the trees. A few moments later we heard the armoured car start up – it was crossing the muddy plain to take us to safety. The bullets whistled over us, lodging into the bark of the trees.

Then we heard Nosov's voice:

'Saboteurs, on the armour!'

We got up and rushed over to the car. It wasn't ours – it had a red symbol on the side, the insignia of some infantry unit I didn't recognise. Nosov sat on top and next to him, thank God, were Moscow and the explorer lieutenant. I smiled and grabbed Moscow's hand, and he helped me up.

'Where's Deer?' I asked, a little anxious.

'He's inside, safe with the others,' Moscow said, patting the car's belly.

The car backed up about twenty metres and then,

turning in the mud with its ultra-powerful wheels, went forward, heading for base.

I watched the woods fade into the distance. I could hear the sounds of the battle and it was as if I was still there, amidst all the trees . . . A cold shudder went down my spine. A grenade exploded somewhere – I could see the smoke rising from the forest, spreading over the trees like a cloud and rising towards the outline of the mountains, where it dissolved in the air and faded into nothing.

After a while we were joined by the four other cars that had been waiting for us to form a convoy. They belonged to an elite unit of the 'internal troops', as they called the military police, a force that focused on special operations such as investigating corruption cases or assisting the arrest of terrorists, arms dealers or the various bands who tried to cross the Chechen borders.

Once we were back on base, we were met by the young lieutenant who had told our captain the true story about the blown-up helicopter, the same one who had helped us out by supplying us with weapons and ammunition.

As we found out from him, a few hours after we had left for the mountains, soldiers from the internal troops, officers from the military prosecutor, and even some agents from the FSB, the Russian state security organization that had replaced the KGB, had arrived on base.

They arrested six officers, about ten lieutenant colonels and all the authorities in command. One lieutenant colonel had managed to lock himself in a trailer that doubled as a kitchen, and at the legal officers' pleas to come out and turn himself in to the military police, had shot himself in the head with his own gun.

They wanted to send someone to try and stop us, but our armoured cars were already on their way back, and since we didn't have a radio it was impossible to get in touch with us. Meanwhile, in the other part of the mountains, a motorised infantry unit and a *spetsnaz* unit were in the middle of an anti-terrorist operation . . . That night in the mountains by pure chance we had crossed the line dividing the area controlled by our units and the area occupied by the terrorists. The two groups we had eliminated, the young lieutenant explained to us, were wounded and exhausted men who had been wandering around the mountains for days, pursued by our relentless infantry. This was confirmed by the helicopter pilot who took the *spetsnaz* to the other side of the mountains – they were supposed to go across, block the enemy group in the valley and exterminate them.

That night, in short, we had risked getting killed by our own men much more than by the enemy.

They let us sleep on base for a whole day and night. They gave us a ton of good stuff to eat; there was even hot soup, with potatoes and meat – a very rare thing, especially in the big units, where provisions were often scarce.

Even after resting and with a full belly, the shame over

what had happened to me in the mountains hadn't left me – on the contrary, it had become even more oppressive and wouldn't leave me in peace.

I went walking to and fro around the base. I was restless. At some point I ran into Deer, and I thanked him for saving me when the hand grenade had almost exploded on me in the mountains.

'Don't mention it, brother,' he replied, a smile behind his kind eyes.

But I still wasn't calm.

I went to the captain to vent my feelings. He was sitting at the table, taking apart his gun in order to clean it. He listened to me attentively, without interrupting at all. When I finished my sob story, he smiled at me and said:

'Rest easy, soldier. No one will ever know. I already talked to Shoe about it. I told him to forget the whole thing . . .'

I was happy. I felt as if an enormous weight had been taken off my chest. I gasped with joy.

Nosov went back to cleaning his gun. But suddenly he paused, as if thinking back on my words. He looked up and asked:

'Are you sure you felt yourself die? Maybe you were just tired, don't you think?'

Before answering I thought about it for a minute. I wanted to remember that exact sensation one more time. Once I did, I felt a strength awaken inside of me and take hold of my heart. A feeling that had no explanation.

'Yes, I really thought it was death. I did. But I didn't feel horrible, it wasn't so bad . . .'

He spoke without looking me in the face, setting the spring inside the shaft:

'Well, now you know what it's like to be dead. It's a good thing.'

CONSTITUTIONAL ORDER

The Russian soldier has three types of enemies. The first, the most dangerous, is in Moscow, the Russian capital: it's the government, which is afraid of its army and thus desires its death. The second is the air troops, because they often make a mistake and bomb their own units. The third enemy is the least dangerous: the one in the war against the Russian soldier.

Proverb of the Russian army veterans of WWII

Orders must be communicated promptly and without hesitation to the officers of the unit charged with their execution. After an order has been communicated, it may be submitted to appraisal by command, the request supported with valid reasons in conformance with army regulations. If the order were found to conflict with the Constitution of the Russian Federation, the officer in charge may not carry out the order and may immediately obtain a second assessment of the order.

From old Russian army regulations*

There is no Heaven or Hell – anyone who does wrong and commits serious sins is simply reincarnated as Russian.

Proverb often quoted by my grandfather

---

* Regulations were hastily modified during the First Chechen campaign, since many officers refused to follow orders due to their content, which they considered unconstitutional.

When the unit entered the city
it was a time of human kindness.
The people have gone on holiday,
flowers wilt in the squares.

It all seemed too peaceful,
like in the movies when a trap awaits.
Long ago the clock tower struck noon
of some day now far in the past.

Captain Voronin chewed on a blade of grass
and thoughtful he looked around.
He knew that everyone watched him in the glass,
and could hear his steps from afar.

But men trusted in him like a father,
they knew he would make a choice.
He was known as one who was never in a hurry,
especially when there was nothing to lose . . .

From 'Captain Voronin' by Boris Grebenshchikov, a Russian
musician in the pacifist anti-communist movement

One night our unit had to cross a series of fields alongside a river to reach a small town where several bloody battles had been going on for days.

There was complete darkness, and a thick cloud of fog had come down from the nearby mountains and spread over the whole town and its environs, transforming the landscape into something like the kingdom of heaven. All that was missing were the angels and saints.

A few hours earlier, when the fog hadn't yet shrouded everything, Moscow and I had gone on recon to establish where the enemy was positioned. We hid on the grassy riverbank; I inspected one side of the village.

Everything seemed very quiet – in war, silence like that usually meant a storm was coming. I observed the facades of the buildings through my rifle scope, searching the windows and the most remote corners for a human figure, or something that might indicate a sniper's position. Chickens pecked in the streets, pigeons and other wild birds skittered across the roofs – I felt like I was looking at a postcard of peacetime. I was almost intimidated by that melancholy world, I felt a strange nostalgia stir within me, as if someone had pulled a live string that tied me to my memories of home, of everything my past had been . . . But I had a bitter taste in my mouth, as I did every time I was about to tempt fate.

After a few minutes of observation I noticed that there were some oddly parked cars – they had been put one after another in front of the houses, like shields to protect against a possible attack. Some of the backyards had fences that were broken in specific places – they connected to the trenches, through which the terrorists could easily flee. All that had probably been ready for days – the trenches were well concealed, there was no suspicious activity, the enemies had decided on their plan of defence and were ready at their positions, waiting for us.

At some point, while observing the roads, I saw the fog arrive. It suddenly appeared amidst the houses, enveloping them in a thick white embrace. It covered the courtyards, the streets, the gardens, and hung there; after a while you could only see the roofs of the houses, or the electric poles that poked out from the white cloud. The dogs began to bark, and I could also hear the cries of a few farm animals, cows and sheep frightened by the atmospheric phenomenon.

When Moscow and I withdrew, the whole town was completely wrapped in fog and darkness, and the dampness went all the way to the bone. After crawling two kilometres through the fields on the edge of the little stream, once we were at a safe distance, Moscow said to me, with his usual sarcasm:

'Looks like we're going to be playing blind man's bluff tonight . . .'

I didn't answer. When I was little I hated blind man's bluff, where one kid would be blindfolded and have to try to catch the others, who would run away and push around whoever was 'it'. The idea of getting into a situation like that, facing the enemy in a town wrapped in fog and the darkness of the night, did not sound appealing in the least.

When we got back to base Nosov was in the tent talking into the handset of the field radio. He was explaining to someone in command that it made more sense to mobilise the artillery first, have our cannons and missile fire system go to work on the enemy positions, and only afterwards bring in the assault troops.

Moscow and I couldn't hear what command was saying, but from Nosov's face – which grew increasingly tense and sombre – it was clear that the person on the other end didn't agree with our captain's strategy at all. Next to Nosov sat a colonel who led a team of tankers in a paratrooper unit. He looked sad; he had an unfiltered cigarette clenched between his teeth, and from his lungs billowed a layer of smoke so thick and solid it hung in the air, filling the tent like in one of those Seventies discos so often depicted in movies from the West.

Nosov said goodbye to the person he was talking to on the radio, calling him 'Colonel', and then replaced the handset. The tankers' colonel took the cigarette out of his mouth and looked at our captain with a glimmer of hope in his eyes. Nosov placed both his hands on his bulletproof vest and then stared at his belly, as if he were gauging how much it had grown. Sounding exhausted, he said:

'The operation is set to begin today at twenty-three hundred hours. All active units will move in accordance with the orders received this morning. Confirmation of operational orders in thirty minutes . . .'

The tankers' colonel extinguished his cigarette in a dish, leaned against the crate of cannon shells, looked up at something only he could see, and began to speak very slowly:

'If we go that way, as directed in the orders, they'll wipe all of us out . . . What'll we do with the burned tanks left in the middle of the road? The Arabs will use them as shields, and we'll end up repeating the same mistakes we've made in the past . . . Those Muscovite pieces of shit at general command don't give a shit what happens here. Since this operation began I've lost sixty men and twenty-three tanks. We have to come up with something . . .'

'Orders have to be respected, Colonel . . . Tanks can't break through a city defence alone, we all know that, they have to follow the soldiers and support them in the attack.' Nosov spoke in a conspiratorial tone. 'But the place is small, and if we coordinate with the assault units, I'm sure we'll only need four or five tanks to keep the positions the soldiers have liberated . . . We'll use the other tanks for transport beyond the perimeter, outside town, to guarantee our boys protection from fire . . .'

I listened attentively to what our captain was saying. It was no surprise that a higher ranking officer took Nosov's tactical advice into consideration. Everyone knew that he was always able to find a strategic solution (often it differed from the original plan but still led to the desired result) that would save human lives and conserve resources while also carrying out command's orders. Experience was everything in war – rank meant almost nothing.

The colonel seemed like a humble guy. As Nosov spoke he kept nodding.

'All right,' he said, rising to his feet. 'I'll go rally the assault unit commanders. We'll try to help each other, as always . . . Nosov, are you sure you can get by with just one support unit?'

Our captain lowered his eyes, resting them on the make-shift table, where the town map was spread out.

'The less we are, the better it is. Now, they don't know what side we're going to attack from, and when our assault begins they'll move most of their men to the hottest point . . .' He pointed to a spot on the map and the colonel moved closer to see. 'We saboteurs will enter from the other side and go in deep. Once we've found a safe position, like for example this path here . . .' He ran his finger along a line traced in pencil. 'We'll shoot three red signal flares – at that sign your tanks and infantrymen can proceed. The important thing is for them to take this route and not take secondary roads; otherwise we'll end up killing each other . . .'

The colonel looked at the map, absorbed:

'With the dark and this damn fog we'll have to be pretty careful . . .'

'It's not the first time – actually, it could even be useful to us . . .'

Nosov seemed very sure of himself, but I wasn't so convinced. In the fog you can't see a thing, and even the softest sound seems amplified. The captain knew very well that it was a risky mission, but he didn't let it show.

The colonel suddenly noticed we were there and gave us a questioning look. Nosov introduced us right away:

'The sergeant and sniper of my group, they just inspected the western side . . . What's the situation, strays?'

According to military code it was Moscow's responsibility to speak, but since I was usually the one who gave reports, I went ahead.

I gave a hint of a military salute, and the colonel invited me to sit at the table with them.

'Show me what you saw, son . . .' He was nice and casual; we could act with him as we did with Nosov.

I set my rifle on the table, sat down and took a look at the map. There were already several marks; I limited myself to indicating the points where I had seen the trenches and the cars that the Arabs had arranged to block the roads.

When I finished, Nosov said that we could go.

'We start in a few hours . . . Eat something and get a good nap, and check my weapons and clips, get my vest and get everything in order – I still have quite a bit to take care of here . . .'

We left the tent.

Our boys were in an armoured car. Some were already sleeping; others were eating or preparing ammo for the operation. After a while we were joined by the infantry night explorer group that was supposed to come with us. I noticed how well equipped they were; the butts of American and European guns poked out from their jacket pockets. Their sniper had a rifle like mine, but his night scope was foreign, a model I'd never seen before. They seemed relaxed – they must have been through lots of battles – and this put us somewhat at ease.

I prepared my things and filled four magazines for Nosov. I tore off a piece of bread, wolfed it down, and went to sleep.

Shoe woke me up with a light tap on the chest. I opened my eyes and realised that I hadn't dreamed anything, as often happened in war.

Nosov was already mobilising the unit:

'Everyone get up, listen to the operational orders!'

We formed a circle by the car. Some sat on the wheels, others on crates or right on the ground. I was next to the explorer sergeant, a guy as big as a mountain; he was holding a light machine gun, which, against his belly, seemed little more than a toy.

Nosov and the explorers' lieutenant major – a young man already ravaged by war, his face marked by a long scar that went across his right cheek down to his neck – sat down in our circle.

They unfolded a battered, crumpled map on a crate. Nosov gave a brief introduction, showing us the areas where enemy defences were likely to be, explaining our moves and predicting the enemies'. He was very skilled at this – all he needed was a little information and he could construct the dynamics of an operation with precision.

'Snipers, listen up . . . We have to take the heavy machine guns down first. Logically, they should be here.' He pointed to two crossroads on the way into the town. 'Follow the sound and the flash of the fire. If you see a light go on and off in the middle of the fog, keep your eyes there and you can't go wrong . . .'

He went on, improvising a mini-lesson on the tactics of war in the fog, insisting on the fact that the most important thing was not to be afraid and not to lose control. Since he didn't know them very well, he seemed to be addressing the explorers in particular. To us, the ones in his unit, it was clear by then that we were going to spend the rest of the night shooting at each other in the fog.

Then our captain rose to his feet. We knew what was going to happen – in fact, we sat back to enjoy the show, as we usually did on these occasions.

The explorers, on the other hand, were looking around at one another, a little embarrassed. Their lieutenant gestured for them to stay seated and listen.

Nosov pulled a document out of his pocket, the executive order that was supposed to be read before every mission:

'Comrade soldiers! The Nation thanks for your indispensable service and cannot conceal the pride it feels in knowing that you will liberate it from the parasitic presence of Islamic terrorists hiding in the city of N–, which, for the sake of simplicity and military ignorance, we'll call by a name dear to every one of us: "objective!"' He read a little and made up a little, accompanying his performance with a series of gestures and facial expressions that kept us doubled over with laughter. 'At twenty-three hundred hours and fifteen minutes, Moscow time – Moscow, the incomparable capital of our magnificent Country – we received the highly anticipated confirmation of our absolutely invaluable order . . .'

The guy next to me sniggered, his machine gun bouncing rhythmically on his belly.

'Thus, the Nation orders you to go forth in two independent units directed towards the "objective", enter by combating within the "objective", breaking through the enemy defence, physically eliminating all the terrorists, Islamists, Muslims, dogs, cats and every living thing you find, until you reach the main street of the "objective", where the nexus of communication of enemy trenches is concentrated . . . Upon arrival, fire three red signal flares to signal your position to the tankers and support units, take your defensive positions and wait for them to reach you . . . Ah, the Nation also reminds you that dying, getting hit or hurt in any way is strictly prohibited . . .'

At that last sentence, the sergeant started laughing so hard he lost his balance, falling off the tyre he'd been sitting on.

We had to hold our bellies from laughing, and Nosov concluded:

'As the ranking officer of this company, I confirm receipt

of the order and wish you good luck, my dear comrade soldiers!'

After a few minutes we jumped onto the armour, and in good spirits – thanks to the captain's comic interlude – we left for our mission, even if we knew that really there was nothing to laugh about . . .

The car went down the dirt road, jolting up and down at every bump; so as not to fall off we hung on to anything sticking out on the armour. We could barely see a few metres ahead; everything around us was as white as milk. The car carrying the explorers followed us. The cars were equipped with an electronic navigation system that could follow the road even in the complete absence of visual points of reference, and they took us to the exact location indicated by our captain, right in the middle of the fields.

'Get off!' Nosov ordered when the tracks stopped. 'From here on we're walking.'

The car following us nearly bumped into ours. Braking hard, it stopped suddenly, and an explorer fell on the ground. Some of his men helped him up; he was fine.

Nosov ordered all of us to move in line, following him. He had calculated the exact number of steps it would take to get to the village. All we had to do was stay alert and follow him.

Walking through the dark and the fog gave me the sensation of being totally defenceless; even if I couldn't see anyone, I was sure that everyone could see me. We went down a path in the middle of the fields. Somewhere out there in the fog were the first houses in town.

Nosov stopped all of a sudden:

'Everyone get down and don't move!' he whispered to Moscow, who was behind him.

As opposed to many non-professional officers, who hide behind the backs of their own soldiers in the event of danger, our captain exposed himself without a second thought. He was like a tiger on the prowl; he perceived and processed every sound and every movement, and if something obstructed our route, while we were still trying to figure out what was going on, he was the first to aim his rifle and shoot, if that's what was needed.

Moscow turned to inform the others, and we passed the message to everyone in the line, forming a human chain. After a moment we were still, plunged into the most total silence imaginable. I squinted, trying to make out a shape in the fog, but I couldn't see anything other than the cold, damp substance that surrounded us like an endless white wall.

After a while we heard a series of loud explosions in the distance, from the other side of the town. Our attack had begun. Just after that the Kalashnikovs came out, and we heard the sound of glass rattling very close to us – someone must have slammed a front door. Shouts in Arabic and Chechen came from all around, and then there was a series of footsteps quickly moving away from the shots and blending in with the sound of the battle.

Our tanks had entered the town with the assault units
– we counted at least ten cannon blasts. Someone near
us kept shouting . . .

Nosov got up.

'Follow me, there's a house nearby: their first reinforced
position. We have to take it fast . . .'

Jumping over an old, half-destroyed wooden fence, we
entered one of the yards. In the pitch dark, completely
enveloped in fog, the house seemed very small, but that
was just an impression.

Part of the explorers' unit was to stay in the yard and
cover the access routes to the house. Nosov pointed out
a long wire running to our left: a tripwire to a mine.

Zenith broke down the door – that was his speciality.
In fact, Nosov called him the 'poet of the busted door'
– with minimal effort, he was able to break down almost
any door without making much noise. He would push on
them with his foot, swift and steady, and they would
obediently open.

'Moscow, Zenith and I are going first,' Nosov said.
'You guys break up into groups.'

Once we were inside we noticed that the hallway was
long and wide – there had to be lots of rooms, so we split
them up. With me there was Shoe, the explorers' sergeant,
and two of their soldiers.

The enemies had arranged a row of speakers against
the walls. So as not to attract attention, the windows had

been obscured with tarpaulins, the kind usually used to cover tanks. Placed on the ground, in the blind corners away from the windows, were lamps that gave off a dim light. All this gave the place a macabre aspect . . . The electric plant in town hadn't been functioning for ages; the light came from a combustion generator. Lots of houses had generators – usually they were kept in the cellar or on the patio, with a pipe system built to carry away the exhaust.

We entered one of the rooms. There were just a few mattresses and some sleeping bags; the floor was covered with clothes, Turkish toiletries, boxes of vacuum-packed food (some still half-full with spoons inside) and a pot with some tea. Next to one of the mattresses there was an unopened pack of single-use syringes; in a corner there was a pile of used syringes with brown spots on them, most likely heroin. On the mattress there was a brick-sized block: a nice fat chunk of hashish. One side of it was burnt and crumbled, and beside it was a box of filters and a bag with some tobacco. This was where our enemies prepared their 'vitamins' so that they could get through the attacks without fear and exhaustion.

Suddenly we heard gunshots. We looked into the hall and saw Nosov, Zenith and Moscow rushing past chasing someone.

We broke down a door that opened onto a large room. A few enemies were waiting for us inside. They fired a spray of bullets at us, but we were able to dodge it. After throwing three hand grenades, we entered the cloud of dust, which smelled of burnt flesh. We kicked the bodies a few times – everyone was dead. One was literally disintegrated – only his shoes were left, and his ankle bones protruded from them; his clothes were smeared on the walls, mixed with blood and flesh. The F1 is a very powerful fragmentation grenade, and it could chop you up mercilessly. If you're lucky you're just left an invalid, but three F1s in one room definitely won't spare anyone. The others must have thrown that poor wretch at the grenades trying to save themselves. They were blood-sucking junkies, with no honour or soul.

In the room there were lots of weapons and some crates of RPG-7 grenade launcher ammo, which had remained undamaged. A pair of grenade launchers was leaning against the wall. One was fine, whereas the other had been damaged by the explosion. I took the intact one and loaded a round in it, then passed it to an explorer. The RPG was a very useful weapon; if you knew how to use it well it could change the course of a battle. We only had one single-shot RPG at our disposal, which we called the 'fly' or 'hornet'. But whenever we came across a trophy as valuable as the RPG-7, we took it without a second thought, and after using it we would get rid of it.

We were coming out of the room when the sergeant said:

'Hear that?'

He turned back, and reaching out his gigantic hand he went over to a sofa where there was a blanket that, in fact, was shaking. With an indifferent face and pointed weapon, he tore off the sheet as if he were doing a magic trick. On the sofa lay a woman dressed in a military uniform, with the insignia of a group of Islamic fundamentalists sewn on the sleeve. The sergeant lowered his weapon and we moved closer.

She stared at us wide-eyed and mumbled something in an accent similar to that of the Chechens, Georgians and everyone who we disdainfully called *chernozhopiy* – 'black arses', or members of the Asian races of the Caucasus. She was speaking Russian, but what she was saying was completely incomprehensible. She was afraid to die, that much was clear.

The explorer sergeant extracted a huge knife from his right boot. It looked like something a butcher would use, very thick and with a wide blade. The woman went even paler, if that was possible, and without trying to get up from the sofa kept spitting out bursts of words that didn't make any sense.

'She must be their medic,' the sergeant said, for no particular reason.

None of us was able to say a word. We were all curious to find out how this romantic little encounter was going to end.

Shoe was behind me, and with a voice weakened by the cold he said:

'Come on, brother, shove the blade between this Muslim bitch's legs. Now we'll show you how real operations are done, we'll teach you what surgery is . . .'

Shoe was scaring me, but I was frightened of myself too. All of us were worked up, yet at the same time disgusted at what was happening.

The explorer sergeant grabbed the woman's neck with one of his huge hands, and held her still. She tried to scratch his face, she struggled, but he was smiling, as if she were his daughter and they were play-wrestling on their couch at home. Without any sudden movements he stuck the knife into her chest, at the left breast. The blade went in easily, and he pushed it in slowly. It seemed like he was enjoying every moment.

With his other hand he kept hold of her neck. She tried to free herself while foam started to trickle out of her mouth, and it quickly turned red. The woman's face was purple, swollen; she made a sort of deep, guttural moan, kicking and shaking as if she were having an epileptic fit.

When the handle of the knife hit the woman's uniform, I tried to picture the blade sunk all the way through her flesh; the knife was so long that it must have impaled her, its tip touching the fabric of the sofa. The sergeant lifted her and sat her down. She looked like a broken doll. Her eyes were empty, her arms hung limp, blood oozed from her slightly open mouth, but it was light – perhaps she had bitten her tongue as she was dying. She had the typical face of women from the Caucasus: small, barely pronounced eyes, a long and dispropor-tionate nose. She was young, she couldn't have been over thirty.

The sergeant, in a calm and almost affectionate tone, as if he were addressing a lover, said to her:

'There, good girl . . . See, it was all fast, no suffering . . .'

Shoe laughed behind me.

The sergeant pulled the knife out of the woman's body and wiped the blade on her uniform. Then he tore the insignia off her sleeve and put it in his pocket.

We all left the room without saying a word.

Nosov and the others were in the hall. They had captured an Arab. Zenith was holding him down on his knees, on the floor. Moscow kept hitting him on the head with the handle of his combat knife. His entire face was covered in blood. Nosov asked him something in Arabic, repeated the same thing a few times, then turned to Moscow:

'Sergeant, this warrior of Islam is clearly suffering from a concussion, give him first aid!'

Moscow responded by slitting the Arab's throat, blood spraying on the opposite wall, then he pressed the prisoner's head against the floor with his boot, bent down and drove his knife into his left side several times. He was dead; all you could hear was the air, pushed by the blood, coming out of the holes in his lungs.

We went out of the house. Nosov was pleased.

'We took an important position in their defence, they almost ran out of ammo,' he said, looking at us seriously. 'Whoever was here before must have gone to help the others against our assault units . . .'

'And what now, Ivanisch?' I asked. The fog around us had not dispersed.

'We have to cross the main street, get rid of the other

reinforced positions and signal to our tanks where to meet us . . .'

'Let's take this fucking town apart,' Shoe said, striking his chest with his fist.

We left. The houses were empty. We found a mine here and there, but from the way they had been planted it was clear that they hadn't had time to lay the traps carefully. We moved slowly through the fog; the real battle was on the other side of the city – no one would notice us.

We ran into a group of five Arabs in the yard of a house. Two of them were wounded; one had lost an arm. We took them out with a few blasts of gunfire; they hadn't been expecting it, they didn't even have time to lay a finger on their weapons. We inspected the bodies – they had some nice pistols on them. There was an American clone of the Colt 1911 with a few clips.

'I'll take this one,' the explorers' lieutenant major said, his eyes sparkling in that scar-ravaged face.

Nosov agreed. We divided up the Kalashnikov clips, and hid the weapons in an old kennel. The bodies, on the other hand, we laid along the walls of the house, so as not to leave them in the middle of the street.

The fog had become translucent and we could see much better now; we could make out human figures from a distance of about twenty metres. We went through the yards, one after another, until we reached the main street. The road was wide, with a long row of trees, many of which were broken or uprooted. There was almost no asphalt left; everywhere there were holes caused by bomb explosions. In the middle of several crossroads they had put the wrecked civilian cars, a few carcasses of burned-out armoured vehicles and some old tractors – tall piles of big truck tyres, like mountains, poked out from every angle. Everything had been arranged to keep our units from travelling quickly through the streets, even if a couple of tanks could have cleared the way in a couple of minutes.

We started to move along the walls of the houses, hunched over and not making a sound. By one crossroads there was a house with another enemy position. We were heading there from the opposite side, because as Nosov always said, before throwing yourself onto the enemy, you have to get a head start in order to make a good jump. This metaphor meant that he knew the way the Arabs prepared their defences and positioned their guards, thus he always tried to plan our strategy based on the enemy's habits. Even though in that conflict everything was so chaotic that the enemy often didn't follow a pattern, he just acted however seemed best at the time.

Having come within twenty metres of the crossroads, we went across the way and hid behind a wrecked armoured vehicle riddled with bullet holes. In the air was the strong scent of burnt, rusted metal, which came from inside the cars. It made an impression on me whenever I smelled it, because it reminded me that inside that car there had been soldiers my age who had died like mice in a trap.

It's a smell that anyone who has never smelled it can't understand, a smell that hits you like a bullet in the heart.

*

The only things those soldiers must have known were mud, filth, cold, a few scraps of disgusting food, military disorder and injustice, battles, blood, disfigured human bodies, souls devoured and emptied, and then death. Maybe after that, death might even be a blessing, but of course that wasn't enough to justify it . . . When I had a moment to stop and really look at what was left of our fallen boys, the sadness of their lifeless bodies, I thought about how no one would worry about them anymore – they were dead, full stop. The military operations would go on, and soon someone else would come and take their place, their bodies would be put into coffins, then in zinc cases and finally sent home, where their parents could bury them with the money generously offered to them by the government. At the funeral a handful of soldiers, on loan from the nearest recruitment office, would fire three blank rounds next to the fresh grave and the story would end there.

Every time I smelled that odour I would think of all that, and I told myself that I would rather have ended up with the 'missing'. At least that way they could spare themselves those empty shots, flags and the whole song and dance at my grave.

We were hiding behind that vehicle, while Nosov and Moscow inspected the area. The house was big, two-storey, and before becoming the private residence of some local big shot it must have been a nursery school, built during the Soviet era. The roof had been turned into a big terrace, upon which we spotted an anti-aircraft gun; we called it a 'Shilka'. It has four powerful cannons that fire so fast they can disintegrate an armoured car in seconds. It had to be destroyed; it posed too big a danger for our units.

In order to avoid killing one another, Nosov proposed the so-called 'closed' assault system: one team (the assault team) comes into the residence from one entrance, a second blocks the other exit (but doesn't shoot, just keeps anyone from going out), and finally a third covers the first two.

I was on the assault team with Nosov. Jumping over the nursery school fence, we entered the yard. We immediately noticed a group of Arabs. They hadn't seen us; they were sitting on some chairs by the stone staircase that led up to the front door of the house. They had their guns in their hands and were talking. Nosov signalled for me to strike.

While he and I shot at the Arabs sitting outside, three of our men jumped onto the stair, flung the door open and launched three hand grenades inside. They waited for them to explode, then to be on the safe side opened up again and threw in another two. The explosions were strong – the glass in the windows went halfway into the garden. The captain and I went inside while the other group went to block the exits. I opened a door, then Nosov and I shot two volleys crossways, making a big X in bullets, and then we jumped inside, into the dust. They responded with a long blast, we threw a grenade, then we moved to the next room. Three Arabs lay on the floor. One was trying to get up, but his legs were full of shrapnel.

I finished him off with a bullet to the head. Without waiting, we rushed off to the second floor . . .

An assault on a building, watched by someone who doesn't know the procedure, might look insane: people running through rooms, throwing hand grenades everywhere and shooting everything that moves. But in that chaos there is also a harmony; all the participants are perfectly synchronised, and they don't need to utter a word, because each of them knows his job. While one breaks down a door, another throws a grenade and yet another already has the next one ready; then the first shoots a spray of bullets from top to bottom, right to left; behind him a comrade does the same in the opposite direction, then they jump in, and so on and so forth . . . Speed and the proper use of hand grenades is very important, since if they don't injure the enemy at least they stun him. Being able to seize those seconds to kill him is fundamental, not stopping no matter what, just keeping pushing and pushing . . . Getting into a fire fight with the enemy is pointless and dangerous, because then he has the time to organise himself, make a retreat and exploit his knowledge of the place. If anyone gets hurt, he's left where he is; nobody is allowed to stop.

Jumping over a wall, running, or generally moving with any agility is very difficult if you're wearing a bulletproof vest and carrying weapons. It's not like it is in the movies, where soldiers break windows with their heads, start kicking at doors and jump around everywhere.

Well executed assaults don't last long. An expert squad can 'clear out' a five-storey building in less than ten minutes.

I was breathing hard; I could feel my nose was full of dust. The smell of burnt human flesh intermingled with that of fresh blood, explosives and gunpowder. I ran behind Nosov, pulling pin after pin from the hand grenades, throwing one into every room. I would shoot and jump in, passing the enemies' disembowelled bodies lying on the floor, hitting them with a few extra bullets to make sure they were dead . . .

We finally managed to reach the door to the roof, but we didn't have time to break it down before it was blasted apart from the other side when a powerful grenade hit it with a burst of flaming air. Luckily we were at each side of the door, and we immediately flung ourselves to safety into opposite corners. The room filled with black smoke; where the door used to be was now a burning hole in the wall. My ears were ringing unbearably and my eyes seemed determined to abandon me once and for all. I watched the scene as if I were outside my body; it didn't seem as if I was really there . . .

To keep the enemy from reloading the grenade launcher, Nosov threw a series of hand grenades into the newly-formed gap.

'Out!' he yelled.

Shooting madly we leapt onto the roof and into the

fog. We hit three Arabs. One of them tried to flee by jumping down onto the street, but our explorers were waiting below to finish him off. We put a hand grenade on the anti-aircraft gun then rushed back into the building. The explosion was impressive – the flaming fragments scattered widely, like so many fireworks.

We went down the stairs, being careful to avoid any surprises at every turn. But the enemy had been totally eliminated.

Only once we were outside the house did we start inspecting one another, to see if we were all in one piece. As I mentioned, many times someone would get some kind of wound but not realise it amidst the chaos of the battle. At the end of an assault, everyone inspected everyone else's vests. A little dazed, covered in dust and debris, we were otherwise fine. Shoe had a cut on his hand. It wasn't deep but a lot of blood was coming out; we wrapped a bandage around it to stop the bleeding.

'We can't let our guard down now,' Nosov said. 'Let's defend the perimeter of the building and prepare ourselves for a possible counterattack.'

We had to keep that house under surveillance at all costs, waiting for our units to arrive. Moscow rushed back onto the roof and shot the three signal flares in a row. There was the risk that in the middle of the fog they wouldn't be very visible, but a few minutes later we received a green flare in response from the other side of town – that meant that our column of men would begin marching towards us.

At that point our artillery units, who were positioned

a few kilometres away, shot some illumination flares. Everything was as bright as day, yet the shadows fell to the ground strangely – the flares came from several directions, and each of us had a row of faint shadows at his feet. It was unnatural, it gave me the creeps.

The time it would take to get to our position should be a quarter of an hour at most – the problem was that we could no longer count on the surprise-effect. Now our enemies could easily spot us.

Suddenly, an RPG shell came at us from the street. No one had expected such a rapid attack. The grenade hit the facade of the building, and two of the explorers fell to the ground, killed by the shards.

'Take positions!' Nosov shouted immediately. He too was shaken by the enemy's speed.

Moscow, Shoe and I left the school, looking for a good position from which to hit the approaching enemies. We quickly crossed a couple of yards, then settled beside a building opposite. From the noises we heard, the Arabs had only assault rifles and no machine guns. Amidst the pandemonium of the gunfire, despite the fog, I was able to pinpoint my targets and strike them by surprise. Even if what I was really looking for were their snipers. I knew they had to be somewhere around there, because I knew the enemy's tactics well – we often did the same things.

If a group wasn't strong enough or big enough, they would try to 'provoke' the enemy by keeping a building under surveillance with a few somewhat random blasts of gunfire. Thus, when the defenders responded to the fire, they revealed their positions, and the sniper, by observing the fired rounds' burst of flame, could pick them out and begin to work on them one by one.

Snipers could also work in teams of two or three. There was no exact rule; the Arabs often worked in pairs. Anyone who had trained in the military camps of Saudi Arabia, Afghanistan or other Asian countries under NATO control was used to working in groups composed of as many as six people – three pairs of snipers who communicated by radio.

These enemy groups were fought by the elusive anti-sniper squads of the FSB – high-ranking professionals, armed with foreign-made rifles, who showed up at the right place at the right time, completed their mission, and were picked up by the support units immediately.

The individual snipers were usually poorly prepared, often mercenaries, former athletes, hunters . . . hopeless men who had learned to shoot on their own. For the FSB teams, paradoxically, it was harder to spot the amateur individual than a pair of professionals, because the sniper who acted alone followed different tactics from those who were taught in military schools, and was, therefore, much more unpredictable.

I was lying on the ground, between blocks of cement that in their previous life must have been the pavement kerbs. You couldn't see much in the fog. Through the telescope, everything looked hazy, like the picture on a television with no aerial. Moscow and Shoe stood beside me, covering my position. I shot twice at the spots where I saw the bursts of rifle fire appear until the flares disappeared, and I continued observing the situation.

Our men responded to the enemy with a few short machine gun blasts and periodical rounds from the grenade launcher, which was positioned under the rifle barrels. Through the telescope I saw a guy with an RPG-7 pop out from a corner, run down the street and get on his knees, poised to shoot. I aimed at his head. He fell immediately, as if he'd been pushed from behind. His weapon slid out of his hands, the round fired, skidding on the tarmac, hitting the chassis of an armoured car.

Someone threw a grenade in our direction. It exploded about twenty metres away; fortunately there was a stack of old tyres and a wrecked car that blocked the shards. Without waiting I stood up and signalled to Moscow that we should move; by that point our position no longer served any purpose. He loaded a grenade in the Kalashnikov and fired at the enemy, then ran over to us and along with Shoe we did a loop around the building, reaching the space where at one time the garden must have been.

From the road we could hear the sound of our tanks, but we didn't have time to identify ourselves before they immediately fired a long volley of bullets at us. Moscow quickly pushed us to the entrance to the house; the bullets flew over our heads.

'Don't shoot, we're saboteurs!' Shoe yelled like a madman from inside the house.

'What the fuck are you doing here? Weren't you supposed to be at the end of the street, down at the crossroads?' they replied.

We came out. Our men were standing with their rifles pointed at us. There were ten of them; part of the infantry operation units, they were explorers and privates.

On the road, meanwhile, the tanks went over the tyre barricades and burned-out cars, freeing access to the position and blowing up the explosives the Arabs had placed between the carcasses, in case anyone were crazy enough to try to move them without taking cover inside a tank.

'There are three of us,' Moscow said. 'We set up a lateral position, the rest of the guys are in the old nursery school . . .'

We quickly joined them. The infantry, in a lightning attack, blocked the enemy groups in the middle of the road. Some tried to escape into the fog, and our men shot them in the back. A couple of Arabs tried to launch some more grenades, but they were immediately overpowered by our numerous assault units. There were probably a hundred men, and with four tanks and five light infantry tanks they surrounded the school.

We all went inside the building and took in the massacre that had happened there. Amongst the bodies of enemies and infantrymen I also recognised their lieutenant major; his head was crushed, shrapnel from a mortar round had killed him.

One infantryman had taken a blast right in the vest, and a bullet had gone into his side; he lay next to the dead lieutenant on an old dirty rug soaked in blood, while a medic stitched his wound with no anaesthesia. He didn't seem bothered by the pain; he was talking to a comrade who was observing the street from the window to keep up with how the battle was going.

In the meantime, more infantry arrived on board a BTR just like ours. They were equipped with a radio, and they set up an operation command post inside the building. Along with them there was a major and a lieutenant colonel, who started talking with Nosov, assessing the losses they had suffered and which strategies they should employ.

Our order, for us and for the explorers, was to join the assault units – we had to seize that town, and we wouldn't be finished any time soon. They gave us a radio and replenished our supplies. We were able to eat a quick bite; the tankers also offered us some hot coffee, a real rarity. Then we left the school with a precise objective: breaking through enemy lines.

We were immersed in the chaos of battle all night. Our units had made remarkable progress – by four in the morning they had managed to liberate almost half the town. We saw the people fleeing and tried to guide them to a predetermined area, in order to tighten the ring even more.

Our armoured cars moved down the streets looking for smaller groups of fleeing residents, while the clean-up teams passed by to check the liberated territory, blowing up the cellars and shooting grenades at suspicious places.

At seven, with the arrival of daylight, the fog disappeared

completely. The town was all ours – only one neighbourhood still resisted.

We found ourselves on the border of the area defended by the enemy; their fortified positions were fifty metres ahead. Our snipers had been trying to neutralise theirs since early that morning, receiving the same treatment in return. We were waiting for air support; the helicopters were supposed to 'comb' the area with surface-to-air missiles, and then we would come in. But, knowing our air units' tendency to always enlarge the range of action, we shifted back a block, moving one house at a time to avoid giving the enemy the impression that we were retreating and thus letting them get away.

The helicopters arrived at the arranged hour, and, as we feared, started to drop missiles on the position we had just abandoned. We prayed that none of the missiles would fall on us . . . There were maybe five helicopters in constant motion. They swooped over the area to drop their charges, which blew everything up the moment they touched the ground, transforming the streets and the houses into one big endless fire.

When the helicopters had finished their job, we heard a weak signal on the radio. It was operations command calling us.

'Birch, Birch, 102 here! How's the field? When is the joust set to begin?'

These spy movie codes they used in radio messages were ridiculous, and they only made communication more compli-cated. We knew that the enemy monitored our radio conver-sations as we did theirs. But command insisted on speaking in code, and so the units would respond with simple words, often embroidering them with lots of swearing.

Nosov approached the soldier with the radio and replied personally:

'102, 102, Birch here! Tell the air patrol to fuck off, and if those bastards shoot at us again, I'll take them down with the RPG!'

'Birch, answer the question, forget the rest!'

'I won't forget shit. Thank God we moved . . . In compensation, the Arabs are still waiting for us, just like before . . . Actually, now they're ready because they know we're about to attack!'

'Birch, we order you to follow the assault units in zone B14! Confirm receipt!'

'Receipt confirmed, 102! Zone B14, we're heading for the position now!'

'Over and out!'

So we went back to our burned-out positions.

Everything was black and covered in ashes; a light dust lingered in the air. There was a strong smell of explosives and acid that made our noses itch and went all the way down to our lungs. Our eyes burned, as teary as if someone had sliced up a giant onion.

We went onto the street and joined the paratrooper assault unit, whom we had been ordered to follow. They were all ready and couldn't wait to begin.

A few minutes later came confirmation of the operational order and we set off for the first enemy-defended route. Between us, behind the assault unit, three tanks followed. On the other side of the block, a group just like ours was entering the enemy zone. We heard the first shots; they were coming from the top of our column. It was the paras firing at the Arabs, and then they moved to the next point. The tanks would come to the places to be liberated, launch a few rounds and then continue on their way, while we covered their retreat.

One of our tanks fired five rounds at a three-storey house where some machine guns were firing. Right after that came a missile from behind a fence that hit the tank full on. The explosion was extremely loud; we were twenty metres away and the powerful wave of heat blew us to the ground. This time nobody was going to deny us a nice fat shock . . .

The turret exploded, and after flying a long way it plummeted into a half-destroyed house. The chassis was in tatters. It was remarkable seeing such a powerful vehicle catch fire so quickly, like a box of matches. The guys inside had burned to death in less than a second.

Nosov stood up and shouted:

'Onward, onward! Don't stop! Everyone move!' Then he crossed the street and unloaded a blast towards the gate from where the enemy had fired.

Moscow, from behind him, threw a hand grenade, while Zenith fired the machine gun. From inside they responded with a loud RPG blast, but it hit the inside wall of the courtyard. A piece of the wall blew up, raising a cloud of dust, and the broken bricks flew into the street. We rushed into the courtyard, shooting in the smoke and dust, and we took out the enemy.

That's what we did, house by house, following the

paratroopers. They moved very quickly, doing the majority of the work and leaving the survivors to us, tightening the ring even more.

By noon we had liberated almost the entire neighbourhood. The radio announced that the enemy had tried twice to break the ring at multiple points but both attempts had failed. Their losses numbered about five hundred men.

To conclude the operation, the infantry units joined us.

The infantry soldiers in that war were treated like beasts at the slaughterhouse. The commanders over at headquarters didn't give a shit and used them as pawns. Fallen infantrymen surpassed the fallen in all the other units combined. Not because they were incompetent or their officers disorganised – no; simply because in Moscow they were scorned. In Russia they always say the infantry is the queen of the army. Well, if that were true, then the guys in the infantry paid too high a price to maintain that regal title.

Our group, meanwhile, had been given a street to clear. Nosov was talking on the radio with the tankers' colonel, the one with the sad eyes who I had talked to before the beginning of the operation.

'How goes it, Birch? Your men all healthy?'

'Yes, all fine, it should be over soon . . .' Nosov replied.

'Did you see what happened to my "little box"?*

---

* A tank or other armoured vehicle in radio code.

The paras say that my guys exposed themselves too much . . .'

'I saw it, we were right there . . . They stopped on the crossroads for too long; they should have fired fewer rounds and hidden behind us . . .'

'Whore of a war, those were good boys . . . Well, good luck. I've sent you three light tanks for support, with ammo and food. They'll be there within fifteen minutes . . .'

'I'll expect the tanks. Confirm receipt . . .' Our captain was about to end the conversation.

'Such shit, my friend . . .' the colonel said suddenly. I could picture the melancholy look he had at that moment.

'What shit?' Nosov asked, knowing very well what he was referring to.

'Fucking constitutional order . . .'

'You know the only place where the constitutional order counts?'

The colonel was silent for a moment.

'No, I can't say that I do . . .'

'It's simple, old man: the cemetery!'

Hearing a conversation like that between two officers was like being splashed in the face with ice water – your mind began to replay the events of the last few hours and see things in a much simpler way. We were the ones who established the constitutional order, the ideal we were ready to lose our lives for, the ideal we all hated . . . But we knew that, in reality, such an ideal didn't exist. At least not for our officers, not for our fallen and wounded, not for the families of the missing in action . . . Because if a soldier is 'missing', the government doesn't pay anything for the transport of the body or for the funeral – but a missing person could also be a deserter or a traitor who abandoned his unit and went to the enemy side. Those who were truly missing were few, because in the large units the majority of the fallen were left on site – they were referred to as missing because the bodies ended up in common graves and nobody could find them. That was why we no longer had respect for the constitutional order – because we knew there was no order, the entire Nation had plunged into chaos.

About twenty minutes later three BMP-2 vehicles arrived with a group of soldiers sitting on top – they were Cossacks who had come to back us up. They were coming from the other part of town; they must have just finished an assault. The cars were dirty and the men were tired; one had a bloody bandage around his left arm. They were all veterans – there wasn't a single young soldier among them. In order to be a little more comfortable riding on top of the tanks, they had put some old car seats on the armour.

As we approached, they came down from the vehicles and the first thing they did was have a cigarette. After smoking and eating the food they had brought, we restocked our ammo. As we reloaded our rifles, we exchanged information on how the operation was going. Then Nosov briefly explained the situation, showing them on the map the places where our intervention was needed. The Cossacks listened to him attentively, without asking useless questions, and when he finished we set off.

Within a couple of hours we had liberated three enemy-controlled positions, eliminating their scattered units, who tried to run away by hiding in the cellars.

We came to a very well-defended house and found a terrible spectacle before us. The bodies of our infantry were scattered everywhere; there must have been about thirty dead.

From the way they were positioned it was clear that the enemy had taken them by surprise. Maybe they were tired, and had made the mistake of not inspecting the area well enough, thus exposing themselves without having anyone to cover them. Many soldiers had had their throats cut and no longer had their vests, a sign that the enemy had already come out from their position to pillage them and finish off the wounded.

We stopped in a courtyard, a hundred metres from our dead men.

I examined the situation through my scope. I could see a yard blocked by three cars arranged in a row, and I could see movement in one of the windows.

'They're waiting for us,' I said.

'Zenith,' Nosov ordered, 'go with two Cossacks and two explorers and find a position to place a heavy machine gun across from the house. They don't know what we're capable of . . .'

Nosov, Moscow, Shoe, the rest of the group and I broke into the house next door. We went up to the second floor. Nosov loaded a round into the RPG and fired directly at the window where I had seen someone moving. After that we opened fire too.

Then Nosov moved to the first floor with Moscow; from there, he fired another two RPG rounds. One hit the wall and made a huge dust cloud, the other one went right into a window and we saw a wave of smoke billow out from inside. Then the Cossacks and explorers went out into the street and fired as they ran towards the house.

We followed. Nosov threw a hand grenade inside the house, then I threw one and Shoe another, each of us shooting at the same time we burst in. Someone responded to the fire; I could hear the bullets very close. Nosov jumped in between us and fired a long blast; Shoe and I covered him, shooting, while he reloaded the magazine.

Room by room, we went on our way; all shouting to identify ourselves so we didn't kill one other. When everyone had stopped shooting, silence fell: we had got rid of them all.

Our men went to help the wounded. One of the Cossacks called for a tank on the radio to take away one soldier who was more seriously hurt than the others. I checked the halls. One explorer was on the ground with injuries to his face, another was the enormous sergeant who had killed the girl. He was lying down, motionless; both of his legs were bloody. Someone from his unit was opening a medi-kit to treat him.

We went into the main room, a sort of parlour with big windows overlooking the courtyard.

The silence was absolute – it was as if I had entered a church. In the middle of the room there was a table covered with open cans, pieces of fried meat, a few overturned glasses and two big bottles of vodka. There was also some fresh bread, wide, crisp and thin, which was delicious, especially with wine. On one of the chairs at the table sat a dead young Arab, his head bent down unnaturally, his chin almost touching the gaping hole in the middle of his chest. A wide dark red stain spread from the hole down to his trousers, pooling on the seat, then slowly dripping onto the floor, forming a puddle as thick as honey. Under the table there was the corpse of a dog. It was an animal with a large head, a Caucasian shepherd. The fur on his belly and neck was drenched in blood, the tongue that dangled from his open mouth was so long it looked fake.

Past the table there was a sofa; on it sat three corpses. One of them was a boy, no older than fourteen. He was wearing a shirt with American cartoon characters on it, Mickey Mouse and some others; it was bloodied, except for the sleeves, which were white, spotless. He was full of holes at the heart and the belly. He had a wide cut on his neck, like a tear – he must have been hit by several bullets there. His face displayed an expression of slight surprise, like a little boy about to burst into tears. Next to him was a young man. His chest was one gaping wound. His hands lay at his sides, as if he were sleeping; his legs were clenched together. On his right cheekbone he had a large hole; his face had become completely deformed – it was swollen, his eye bulged from its orbit, ready to pop out. A little blood was still trickling out of his open mouth, thick and black. On the floor in front of them, on his belly, was a man who looked about fifty years old. On his back you could see a series of holes; the bullets had pierced through him from one side to the other. From the position he was in, you could tell that he had been sitting next to the others. Before dying, he had tried to crawl on his hands and knees; there was a long trail of blood that went from his body to the sofa and on the floor were the marks of the bloody handprints he had left trying to drag himself along. Not even a centimetre of the tapestry behind the sofa was left intact; the whole thing had been punched out by bullets. The tapestry had caught fire in some spots; the black burn marks made it look like a work of abstract art . . .

At the head of the table was a chair with worn armrests and a high back. Sitting there was a man with a white beard. His eyes were closed, his head was turned to the side and his arms dangled at his sides. Next to him, leaning against the table, was a Kalashnikov. On a saucer in front of him there lay a half-smoked cigarette, still burning; a wisp of smoke wafted upwards. The man's chest was so soaked with blood you couldn't see the bullet holes.

Shoe went over to the table and began to eat raven-
ously. His jaws made a very loud noise, as if they were
about to snap. He chewed on the meat and tried to shove
a thick slice of bread in his mouth at the same time.
Moscow went after him; he pounced on the table and
took a piece of bread too, chomping on it violently, almost
as if more than eating it he needed to kill it. He turned
to me with his mouth full, gave me a smile, and grabbing
a piece of meat off the table threw it across the room to
me. I felt as if I was drunk, without my reflexes, and I
didn't put my hands up in time − the piece of meat hit
my face and fell to the floor. I took a deep breath and
freed myself from the straps of my bulletproof vest.

Just then the corpse sitting in the chair jolted, and then
from his mouth came something that would have been a
yell, but it drowned in the blood he had in his throat.
The man spluttered blood on the floor and the table,
started to cough, and then opened his eyes. Moscow, who
was closest to him, pulled his gun out of his pocket and
fired a round right in his head, without stopping eating.
Then he put his gun back in place and grabbing a bottle
of vodka said, his mouth full of meat:

'Get a load of this Arab arsehole . . . He won't even
let me eat in peace . . .'

Shoe started laughing and looked out the window.
Another unit of ours was approaching quickly. He leaned
out and signalled to them.

I didn't feel well. My head was exploding. I knew
what I needed to do: clear a place where I could rest. I
went past the table to the sofa and grabbed the two

corpses sitting there by the legs. I pulled them until they fell to the floor. The body of the boy made a dull sound when it landed on the wooden floorboards, like wood against wood. The other dead man fell on top; his forehead hit the ground, making a sound like bones breaking. I examined the sofa; there was a huge bloodstain in the middle. I looked around. On the floor by a window, there was a small rug. I picked it up; it was covered in fur and stank of wet dog. I threw it on the sofa and lay on top.

The pleasure of reclining on a sofa was enormous. I knew I couldn't stay for long, but I wanted my body to remember how it felt to lie down on a soft, comfortable bed, at least for a few minutes. It immediately gives you the impression of just having come out of a nice hot bath, being under clean, sweet-smelling sheets . . . I yawned savagely and tears sprang to my eyes. For a moment even the ringing in my ears went away. I felt a light tingle go through my fingertips, which then spread to my spine. My body responded with a long groan; relaxing, the muscles rebelled, it was almost like I was paralysed. I was wrecked; all I wanted to do was sleep . . .

But I knew I couldn't keep my eyes closed; I kept looking at the corpses that were by the window, right in front of me. There were two Arabs and a Chechen, well armed, with two Kalashnikovs and a machine gun, some American vests and a load of other valuable stuff. So far nobody had touched anything, but I was sure that as soon as Moscow and Shoe finished eating they would pillage them . . .

Suddenly Nosov arrived, and threw a pair of shoes at me.

'Here, take these. Yours are rotten . . .' he said, sitting down at the table with my comrades.

It was a pair of trainers, practically new, with barely a few drops of blood. Without getting up off the sofa I took the old ones off, which were filthy, and put on the new ones. My feet felt nice and comfortable; I was content.

'So, how are they?' Nosov was eating some meat and had a glass of vodka in his hand.

'Thank you, Captain, they're perfect.'

'Well then, don't forget how generous I am . . .'

The others broke out into laughter.

The siege on the village was over. Our assistance was no longer needed, and in two light tanks we headed for our positions.

The tanks went along, shaking, shooting black smoke into the air, and we shook too, from the pounding of the tracks. We passed by the burned-out cars and the bodies of the fallen, moving down the streets where a moment earlier we were about to die.

Once we were outside the town we looked at what we had left behind: collapsed houses, smoke rising into the air . . . total destruction, as if every inch of the town no longer existed.

Nosov observed everything, a strange look on his face, neither satisfied nor dissatisfied; if anything, he seemed lost in a strong nostalgia, like when you see something for the last time.

Our captain stood firm, still, holding on to the turret

of the tank. At some point he said, under his breath, to himself:

'Anyone who doesn't want to be under us will end up underground . . .'

BREATH OF THE DARK

Do evil and evil will come back to you.

Old Russian proverb

Can't get used to the stillness
in war, in the war, in the war.
Stillness is only a trick, just a trick.
On the steep path
in a strange land
we head for the caravan.*

Caravan – the high of triumph, the pain of defeat
Caravan, I wait to meet you again
Caravan, red with the blood of Afghanistan,
Caravan, caravan, caravan . . .

'Civil' life will never grow on me,
war is so clear, it's friend or enemy.
Here you can't see anyone's soul
through all the fog.
It's a shame that friend is gone,
another one
taken for good by the caravan.

Caravan – a flask of water
without which means death.
Caravan – it means we can.
Caravan – kill the infidels, says the Koran.
Caravan, caravan, caravan.

Can't quite get used to
no AK on my back
no mines in roadside bushes
no lurking Muslim packs.
I just know that somewhere
following in my tracks
someone's after the caravan.

---

* The saboteurs of the Russian army, during the war in Afghanistan, used the word 'caravan' to indicate an enemy group transporting arms or drugs.

Caravan, hundreds of missiles
that will not reach their goal.
Caravan, salt in our faces
Caravan, at the third drink a moment of silence
for who is lost and who hung on.
Caravan, caravan, caravan . . .

'Caravan' by Alexander Rozenbaum

Here during the war I once met a really interesting person.
Too bad that by the time we started to become friends, he
was dead.

Surgeon R. Krasnov, a medical service officer
I met in military hospital

The Jew knows it, the Chinaman too
the Red Army's the best.
Berlin remembers how in '45
it took the red star in the arse.

The boots stomp hard,
subs swim under the ice.
Fuck the guns and the gas,
we'll take the enemy fast.

Planes roar and tanks smoke—
combat father, father combat.
From north mountains to south seas
we'll take and break the enemies.
Combat father, father combat
from north mountains to south seas
the Red Army's the best.

To scare off our faggot enemies,
our destroyers shoot through the skies.
Screw America, screw NATO too
even with our worst shot they're through.

But if the enemy really steps up to us
the spetsnaz will take on the cause.
Say goodbye to your planes and your tanks
nothing will be left but their shit and socks.

Planes roar and tanks smoke—
combat father, father combat.
From north mountains to south seas
we'll take and break the enemies.
Combat father, father combat
from north mountains to south seas.
the Red Army's the best.

In thirty seconds our missiles can hit
anywhere on the planet.
We'll show all those pieces of shit:
Glory to Russia, our homeland!

'Red Army' by the pro-nationalist punk
group Krasnaya Plesen*

Surely only the fish in the sea and the birds in the sky know
     who is right,
but we know the important things aren't in the papers,
we'll never hear the truth on the radio . . .
The name of the town doesn't matter
but out of all those people who went there,
none of them ever came back.

So we have no reason to cry, to have sad thoughts,
now only the heart can save us, because reason fell short.
But the heart needs sky and roots, it can't live in nothing,
and as once said a boy who was there by chance,
'From this moment on we'll be different . . .'

From Boris Grebenshikov's 'Captain Voronin'

On my shoes the dust of hundreds of streets,
on my shoes the ash of hundreds of wars,
my hands have turned to dirt . . .
I'm coming home.

From 'I'm Coming Home' by Russian
singer-songwriter O. Balan

---

* Russian for 'red mould'.

At the end of my second year of military service the saboteur unit transferred to the mountains. Along with some of the Ministry of Internal Affairs' special units (called the OMON), we went through the villages to conduct what in our operation order was called 'clean-up of residential areas'. Obviously this had nothing to do with maintaining sanitation in the mountain territories; it was a very specific and sensitive phase of the counter-terrorist operation intended to 're-establish respect for the laws of the Russian Federation'.

We went through the areas controlled by federal forces in order to 'ensure the presence of the necessary conditions to enable the recuperation of the Chechen community'. It was May, and it was very hot.

By that time, the Chechen plain had been almost completely liberated of enemy forces, but many terrorist groups had survived in the mountains. They had regrouped into small units and continued to attack our military convoys and put any representative of the law to death. They terrorised civilians, too, but more often found them to be sources of support in the fight against the Russian Army and state power. Many families had lost someone during the war and blamed the army for their losses, which is why they gave provisions to terrorists, harboured them secretly or hid arms and ammunition. To us, the Chechen mentality was incomprehensible – it seemed absurd for them to help foreigners from Africa or the former Yugoslavia but to want nothing to do with us, their neighbours, with whom, for better or worse, they had a shared history. They saw the terrorists as heroes, as people who had sacrificed themselves for the good of the Nation – Muslim Robin Hoods.

Obviously we soldiers knew that both Chechen campaigns had been tainted by political and economic interests. As Captain Nosov had often told us, practically branding it into our minds: 'Always remember that the feared Shamil Basayev, like many other Chechen Islamic terrorist leaders, was trained by our own secret services – we Russians were the ones who taught him to defend himself.' We had learned from experience how the terrorists were linked to the corrupt officials working in our Command, but no one ever dared to bring up those stories; no one ever released the findings from the investigations conducted by the FSB. If we found out that there was a mole it was because of his comrades, who had reported him or in some cases simply eliminated him, since accidents happen in war every day anyway. These affairs, even if they didn't reach the ears of the media, circulated widely among soldiers and officers. They were shared in whispers, during pauses between one battle and the next. Often the whispers were about an officer from Command dying in an accident: 'He fell from a moving tank,' they would say, which meant that he had been beaten to death by his own men. These stories were always concluded with a statement full of scorn and malice, spat out with cigarette smoke: 'He liked *shawarma** too much . . .'

It was very difficult to communicate with the local people. Up in the mountains they were especially aggressive; even routine operations in their villages risked ending in bloodshed. We would capture the terrorists who hadn't been able to escape before our arrival and execute them right in the streets. At that point the entire village would give voice to a single sentiment – the women hurled shouts and curses of all kinds on us, old and young alike sent us promises of Apocalypse . . . We had to be very careful, because sometimes bullets would come from the mob, where the instigators, who expected nothing less than for us to raise arms against the civilians, would hide. Then the commanders would oblige us to quickly withdraw, to avoid being caught in a fire fight with women and elderly people present. We would shoot a few bullets into the air to scare people and then be on our way.

Often, on the way back from those operations, our columns would be attacked. If we were lucky the attack would be limited to a few machine gun blasts at the men on the carriers. In the worst cases, when our attackers

---

* A common dish from the Caucasus, similar to kebab – this was a way of referring to traitors.

were better equipped, they would torch the carriers with
RPGs or scatter homemade mines made from large-calibre
cannon rounds along the road.

Some strange and sad things happened too.

One time, as we were returning from a mountain village,
an old man planted himself in the middle of the road
in order to stop our cars. He pointed a hunting rifle at
us: a real antique, all rusty. The old man was desperate;
he was crying and shouting something incomprehensible.

According to military regulations, a column of armoured
vehicles could not stop for any reason outside the scope
of the operation. Even if we went past a person who had
been wounded, we had to go on, either evading him or
going around him – the important thing was never to stop
the cars. It was also prohibited to slow the speed of the
convoy, which had to proceed at a minimum of ten kilometres per hour; if we slowed down we could all become
easy targets for potential aggressors.

So when we saw that old man, the boys signalled for
him to move. But he kept standing in the middle of the
road, as if his feet were glued to the ground, making his
choked cries and waving his gun, which he kept pointed
at us. The column slowed its pace, and one of the men
sitting on the first carrier shot a burst of rounds in the
air to scare him, but it didn't work – he refused to move
and kept threatening us with his pathetic rifle. I was on

the third car in the convoy, and I watched as the old man's figure grew bigger and bigger.

When the first carrier approached him, the driver manoeuvred, trying to avoid him, to pass by him. But the old man gritted his teeth and placed his rifle to his shoulder, aiming at one of the boys sitting on the car, as if he were going to shoot him. At that instant a series of rounds went off – everyone sitting on that carrier opened fire on the old man, who with one insane act had suddenly turned into an aggressor. I saw scraps of his suit go flying, along with pieces of flesh as the bullets pierced his body. In a second they reduced him to tatters. He fell to the ground next to his rifle.

The column didn't pause; the cars resumed their course. When my carrier passed the corpse, I saw that on his jacket the old man had a row of medals from the Second World War. As a young man he had fought to defend the Great Soviet Nation against the Nazism of the Third Reich, and here's how the Nation repaid him for his sacrifices, years later.

This is how, in the complete chaos of post-Soviet history, the power of the Russian Federation was restored in the mountain areas of Chechnya. And we couldn't do anything to oppose it – our personal stories were worth nothing in that great river of time and fate that mixed wars and men, innocent people and criminals. But the current has always stayed the same. It hasn't changed in the least . . .

*

In late May we received an order that was very unusual: to search a mosque in a mountain village. Apparently, after a mission had been carried out by our artillery, several weapons and the bodies of some wanted terrorists had been found in the ruins of a mosque. The army never set foot in places of worship, but now, suddenly, the operational units were changing their strategy and ordering us to search them. None of us, however, believed the stories anymore.

'And so, all of a sudden they discover terrorists hiding in mosques,' Shoe commented sarcastically.

'It's obvious,' Zenith chimed in. 'The Russian secret service has decided to sacrifice one of their "bridges" with the Islamic world, breaking some old pact that called for the protection of the mosques . . . And it's up to us to do the dirty work!'

Before then, none of us would ever have dared to search a sacred site. The Russian military was capable of committing many injustices and of proving itself even crueller than the devil, but they would never dream of sending soldiers to go and fire their weapons in a place of worship.

It wasn't a question of respect, but a kind of superstition. We believed that profaning what other people venerated, such as the house of their god, would bring us nothing but misfortune. In the course of the war, many of us had become believers. To get through the more difficult moments, we often turned to God; He was a haven for our souls, the only place not regulated by military code. We all thought of our mothers, who went to church every Sunday to light candles by the orthodox icons for their soldier sons; certainly Chechen mothers prayed in the mosques for their children's survival. Either way, we had always respected those places. Even simple people, or people with little education, can understand the importance of hope, but this is a feeling experienced only by those who fight war – although of course not by those who wage it . . . As always, however, the only voice our Command wasn't willing to listen to was ours.

And so we left our base on a mission with five armoured vehicles: one for us, one for the infantry explorers, and the other three for the OMON special teams; all together, there were forty-two of us, including drivers. We also had two dogs, German Shepherds trained to sniff out drugs and find explosives.

It was unbelievably hot, and the wheels of the cars on the dirt roads flung up a clay-like dust that stuck to our faces, mingling with our beards and our hair. That was why we saboteurs all wore sunglasses, shorts and no shirts, our bulletproof vests against our bare chests. As always, we knew we were the envy of the other units because of our freedom in dress, even if amidst the pandemonium of a counter-terrorist operation like the one that awaited us, there was really nothing to envy of anyone.

Going up the mountains, we came to the little town where we were supposed to conduct our search. There was a wonderful peace; old men sat on the benches chatting, children ran through the streets, women were doing housework in their yards . . . It seemed impossible that there was anything threatening there. When faced with situations like this I felt uneasy; we were there to ruin the lives of people who had nothing to do with the war, or with the dirty business in which we were immersed.

My group and I hopped off the cars and marched ten metres in front of the vehicles, which advanced slowly, at walking pace. We walked in the middle of the street with our weapons in hand, prepared for the worst. As soon as they spotted us, the women grabbed the children and all the civilians ran inside. They were used to military operations; they knew they had to leave their gates and front doors open, come out into the yard, keep their hands in full view and have their papers ready. We went down the road without stopping to do any checks, but we glanced at the yards anyway. When they left a house quickly to avoid a search many terrorists would leave something behind − a clip or a grenade might fall out of their jacket − so it was necessary to look carefully at everything on the ground and search for any clue that might reveal the presence of an enemy. The terrorists had learned to comb every corner, to find out where the deeply worn foot paths led. Often civilians hid terrorists in underground pits they had dug; sometimes the entrance to a hiding spot was concealed by a kennel or a tool shed. Regulations stated that it was also necessary to inspect people's hands, to check for traces of gunpowder, calluses or unusual burns, to see if they had ever shot a gun or done so recently.

On this occasion, though, we didn't have time to look

for these things. We were headed for the mosque, a large building in the centre of town, surrounded by a white stone wall. There was a high green gate at the entrance, with yellow writing in Arabic at the top. According to the operational orders, we had to conduct a raid, which meant that one of our cars was supposed to break down the gate, bursting through at full speed, and once inside the building we were supposed to inspect every room, first with polite requests and then, if the people didn't understand or didn't want to understand, with a nice fusillade. Usually a raid lasts a few seconds – the enemy shouldn't have enough time to react. If he has the chance to organise himself and start shooting, it's common for soldiers to say 'the ping-pong game has begun' – and it's a game that's hard to win.

Our car approached the boundary wall, and we saboteurs jumped up on it with ease. The white stones were nice and wide, and after running a few metres along it, we leapt down to the other side, into the courtyard of the mosque. Everything was calm. There were well-manicured trees, freshly varnished benches and whitewashed walls with mosaics depicting religious scenes; the human figures were disproportionate, as if they'd been drawn by a child's hand. From the spout of the fountain in the middle of the yard water dripped, a sign that someone had taken a drink not long before. There was no one around the mosque, but the doors were open.

Our captain signalled to us to position ourselves along the wall under the windows. Then he took a stone and threw it at the gate, by the road; that was the sign to alert our men. The infantry explorers' carrier charged full speed ahead, levelling the gate and knocking down part of the wall. Behind them ran the explorers and the OMON.

At that same moment we smashed in the windows. Moscow and I were the first to enter, and in a few seconds we were all inside.

The building was even bigger than it had seemed from outside, with high ceilings and decorated rooms. On the walls hung photos of holy places, other mosques and portraits of Islamic clerics. On the floor there were some valuable rugs yet there were fake plastic flowers in the corners. Arranged among the flowers were photos of armed men; evidently these were the dead terrorists, stuck amidst that plastic green that symbolised their eternal life in Islamic heaven.

When we reached the hallway, we ran into a group of men, who were simply dressed, with long beards.

'Lie down, on the floor,' Moscow said, curtly. 'Arms open wide.'

They obeyed the order without opposition. We could hear the first interrogations beginning in the courtyard; it was the OMON trying to get as much information as possible.

We inspected the rest of the rooms without finding anything of interest. There was the same stuff everywhere: rugs, fake flowers and potted plants, photos and a few books in Arabic.

Nosov came out into the hallway and took an old imam aside.

'Where is the kitchen?' he asked him politely.

The old man lifted an arm, indicating a small structure on the other side of the courtyard.

'Kolima, Moscow,' the captain said to us, 'come with me.'

We took a young man with us who must have been a mullah. He was wearing a tunic and he was well fed, too, with a nice round belly and jowls like a bulldog. Nosov took him by the elbow and, in a friendly voice, like a curious tourist, he asked for information about the mosque's activities, the people who attended it, and many other questions that had little to do with our operation. The man tried to respond calmly, but he was nervous. He spoke very slowly in Russian, attempting to pronounce the words in the most correct way possible − he must have been educated.

We went into the kitchen. There were foodstuffs piled along the walls: bags of cereal and sugar, tins, plastic plates and cups, and some small camp stoves. On the table there were several pots, oil lamps, and bags full of American, Turkish, Swiss and German medicines.

Nosov examined the pots, grazing them with his finger-tips; he almost seemed to be measuring them. He waited a little, as if he knew that sooner or later the man would begin to talk. But he was silent, with a slight, innocent smile stamped on his face.

Nosov looked the mullah straight in the eye and, in that tone we all knew well, the one he used when he didn't feel like playing anymore, he asked:

'Where are your wounded?'

The man suddenly went pale, and his hands began to

tremble. Trying to keep calm, he raised his hands to the sky, as if he were asking for divine forgiveness, and addressed the captain in a humble voice:

'What wounded, commander? Perhaps I do not understand the meaning of your words. We are only servants of God. We help the people of the village . . .'

Nosov smiled with the politeness of an English nobleman, went up to him, and without removing his gloves – he was wearing the tactical Kevlar ones, which are stiff and heavy – gave him a hard slap in the face. The man let out a cry and then crumpled to the floor, sliding down the wall as if his muscles could no longer support the weight of his body. His nose immediately swelled up and started to bleed; his eyes filled with tears.

Nosov pulled out his gun from under his vest and pointed it at the man's head.

'I need your wounded, now. If you prefer, I can find them myself, but by that point everyone will be dead: old, young, women, cats, dogs . . .'

The man started to whimper, hugging his knees to his chest. Breathing hard, big reddish bubbles came out of his mouth, saliva mixed with blood.

Nosov took a lamp from the table, broke it apart and poured the kerosene over the man, who started to squeal like a pig at the sight of an executioner's knife, while trying desperately to unwind his kerosene-soaked turban. His dirty hair poked out from the strips of cloth.

Our captain took a box of matches and lit one, holding it over the man.

'If you don't tell me where you keep the wounded I'll

burn you alive,' he said cruelly, holding the match in one hand and the gun in the other. 'I don't give a shit about your fucking religion; I think you should all be killed . . .'

Sobbing, the man sputtered out a storm of incomprehensible words, among which we could just make out:

'In the garden . . . around the back . . . under the tent . . .'

Nosov pushed the point of the pistol into the cloth of the turban hanging off the man's head and fired; the bullet was muffled, as though he had used a silencer; a cloud of gunpowder spread all around. The man's head had been pierced by the bullet from one side to the other; the wall he had been leaning against a moment earlier was covered in blood and bits of brain. For a few seconds the dead man's left foot kept moving over the kitchen's rough floor, scraping the cement with his fake leather shoe.

Nosov spat on the ground and pointed us to the exit.

'I'll be right there,' he said.

As I stood by the door, I saw the captain dropping the lit match on the corpse, which immediately caught fire.

At that point Nosov looked right at me:

'I'm really fucking sick of these Muslims . . .'

When we went out into the courtyard everyone was staring at us with curiosity. One of the OMON men ran up to give Nosov a report:

'With the dogs' help we found three hiding places,' the man stated. 'Crammed full of—'

'Very good,' Nosov cut him off. 'There should be a tent somewhere – find it.'

Along with the explorers we scattered across the yard. Behind the mosque there was a garden that looked out to a view of the mountains. In the middle of the garden there was a wooden gazebo; it didn't seem very sturdy. Underneath, in the shade, was a small table and chairs. An infantryman took down the structure with a shove of the shoulder, and cleared away the table and chairs. When the gazebo collapsed, we could see an iron trapdoor poking out from underneath. It was the entrance to a transport truck container. The Arabs had buried it, turning it into a refuge for the wounded.

The soldier lifted the door and then jumped back immediately – a blast of machine gun fire had come from inside. The head of an armed man with long hair peered out. We didn't give him time to emerge – we shot him on the spot, and he fell back down. We threw two hand grenades into the container; the explosions spread scraps of human flesh, supplies and cloth everywhere. After an operation like that, the officers back at base would write in their reports: 'A secret refuge harbouring terrorists was discovered and liquidated. Due to the nature of the injuries sustained, the bodies are not fit for identification.'

The OMON guys found many items of interest in the three hideouts: arms, ammo, money, drugs (almost a hundred kilos of heroin in brick-sized blocks, which we all called 'Afghan bricks'; I had never seen so many drugs in one place before, and I definitely hadn't imagined I'd be seeing them at a religious site), books on Islamic extremism, flags and other materials intended as propaganda for the holy war against the infidels, plus instructions for making explosives.

There were some videocassettes and DVDs showing torture being inflicted on our soldiers who had been taken prisoner, along with clips of attacks on Russian military convoys. They also had lots of identification papers belonging to dead or missing terrorists, and they had an entire archive (from the Chechen capital, as we later discovered) with the names of the heads of the various terrorist movements in the country.

We piled it all into our cars and then began loading the prisoners on one by one, among them the old imam and his companion, and a woman in her fifties who wouldn't speak to any of us. To get her into the car an explorer had to hit her on the back with the barrel of a rifle. To begin with, the prisoners resisted, but after the first blows they gave in. There were three young Arabs in particular who kept on shouting, threatening us and refusing to get in the car. One of them grazed an infantryman on the neck with a kitchen knife. The cut wasn't serious, but the act was: we had to shoot him and his two friends.

We had taken seven prisoners. We tied everyone's hands and legs together for security, and to keep them from moving we cut the men's trousers at the waistband. Then we left for our base.

Alerted by the shooting, the local inhabitants gathered around the three corpses. To them, the men on the ground were martyrs.

As our vehicles passed through the village, the streets filled with people, and many inhabitants peered out from behind their front doors – the eyes of the women and the old men, full of hate and a desire for vengeance, were more piercing than plated bullets. No one dared to shoot us, because they knew that if there were even one attack on representatives of the Russian Federation Army, the next day the residents would be awakened by cannon blasts from the artillery or, even worse, by the sound of helicopters, ready to generously drop their surface-to-air missiles. In just a few hours, the entire place would be swept away like the wind scatters leaves in the autumn, without even a memory left behind.

Once we left the village we took the road that led down from the mountains. Our convoy was slowly snaking through the woods along a steep, narrow path, when the terrorists showed up. Usually they would attack the head and the tail of a column, trying to trap the cars in the middle. A few bullets hit the first carrier, where the infantry explorers were; that was the car on 'detachment', or further ahead compared to the rest of the line.

The enemy was hiding among the trees of the forest, and by taking that path we had offered ourselves up on a silver platter to their bullets. When we heard the first shots we jumped to the ground, to the opposite side from where the shots were coming. The drivers came out of the carriers too, rolling along with us to the edge of the road, the only place where the Arabs couldn't see us. According to military regulations, at times like these leaving the car is prohibited − the unit is supposed to defend the vehicle, using their personal weapons as well as the ones the car is equipped with. But in reality, none of us ever followed this rule. An RPG shell travels very fast and can destroy an armoured car in three seconds. In just a few minutes a marksman can torch up to five standing vehicles, and if there are three or more marksmen, the crew doesn't stand a chance. That's why active units led by good officers who knew what they were doing would leave the vehicle immediately, to try to organise a counterattack.

The Arabs were shooting with three light machine guns and about ten Kalashnikovs; once in a while, like cracks of a whip, the sound of two precision rifles could also be heard. The car that had been hit was in flames, but the enemy continued to fire an impressive number of projectiles into it, trying to blow it up. Usually the Arabs would shoot a grenade launcher shell under a car, between the tracks. The explosion would break the transmission and the vehicle wouldn't be able to move; that way, after the battle, the car could quickly be repaired and used as if it were new. But it was a different story with the armoured cars that had wheels, like our BTRs − they couldn't easily be disabled, so the enemies were forced to burn them or blow them up.

Every so often a few long blasts of machine gun fire came near us; when the car finally exploded, the terrorists moved, probably to take care of the last one in the line.

The fact that they were changing positions was positive; it meant that there were only a few of them, so few that they couldn't handle more than one point of attack at a time. While the majority of their group was going through the woods above us – covered by a few single shots that tried to keep us under the effect of fear – Nosov gave the order to move out of the road towards the hill.

'Let's go past the burned car, cross the road and get into the woods,' our captain said, amid the pandemonium. 'We'll take those bastards by surprise, while they're on the move . . .'

Nosov hadn't quite finished his plan when one of our prisoners jumped out of a carrier. The plastic bands we used to bind prisoners were occasionally defective; the man had evidently managed to free at least his feet. He ran for the woods as best he could, holding up his trousers, which kept falling down, with his bound hands. Suddenly the terrorists stopped shooting. In fact, we could hear their shouts of encouragement – it almost felt like we were watching a sack race. But one of the OMON officers shot a powerful blast into his back, putting an end to the show. The prisoner fell face down on the ground, his trousers around his ankles, and one of his arms – riddled with bullets in the shoulder – came away from his body yet remained hooked to the other arm with the plastic band.

'Shit, just when I was starting to have fun . . .' Shoe commented.

We set off down the hill. It was very steep and at some points we were in danger of slipping. To keep our balance we went almost on all fours, hanging on to every stone, every patch of grass, every little root poking out of the ground. Some of the OMON team came with us, while the others stayed behind; their task was to respond to the fire, to make the enemy think that all of us were still there, following the classic army tactic of protecting the vehicles.

When we got to the first car, we heard not only the sound of ammo exploding inside it but also the voices of our explorers, cursing. So they were alive! Somehow they had managed to get out of the car before it caught fire.

'Come on, strays, let's get to this fucking forest . . .' Nosov had his own way of encouraging us.

An infantryman rushed up to us, and stopped in front of our captain. I glanced at his uniform; he was a lieutenant major.

'They got my machine gun and two drivers. Fuck . . .' he said, breathing hard. 'And my radio man has a hole in his stomach . . . What are you guys doing?'

He didn't seem scared or worried, but he was angry, and somehow surprised, as often happens to people taken body and soul by war.

'Bring the wounded down here away from the vehicle and the road. Leave three men with them, get the rest of your guys and follow us – we're going into the wood . . .' Nosov gave him a light shoulder tap, to demonstrate his support at that difficult moment.

'All right, Captain,' he replied. Then he pulled out a cigarette, lit it, and took in a long drag of smoke. 'Just give me a moment!'

He went back onto the path. You could hear his shouts amidst the shooting, then gradually his soldiers joined us, transporting the wounded and the dead. The radio man had just died – the mask of suffering was still plastered all over his face; they say that stomach wounds are some of the most painful. He was very young. He had delicate features; he looked like a young girl.

We kept moving. Three explorers and their lieutenant had joined our group. The OMON guys passed a ciga-rette around, each taking a drag and then handing it to his neighbour, like people do with joints. Despite every-thing, some even managed to joke around. One man asked, 'How's it going, little brother?' and the other replied, 'Great, just like when you have diarrhoea. Be careful not to sneeze or else you'll end up with your arse in the shit!'

We had got far enough away. Nosov jumped up onto the road and we followed his lead, running across with our weapons in hand, keeping far apart from each other, to avoid being hit as a group by likely enemy fire. Before us were the forest and a hostile, rocky hill, wet with all the humidity.

Once we were all in a huddle, Nosov reminded us of the tactics to employ in forest battles.

'We'll take that route,' he said, pointing to a spot on the mountain. 'It's important to maintain visual contact, otherwise we risk killing each other if some of us arrive at the battle site early . . . When you see an enemy do not wait for a command, fire immediately. Just make sure your position is safe. Don't shoot in the open – conceal yourself behind a tree or lie on a rock, and remember that your primary objectives are the terrorists armed with optic rifles or RPGs. If someone gets wounded, don't all jump on him, only his neighbour helps him. The others must continue fighting. If you decide to retreat, don't shoot behind you while running, you could hit one of your comrades . . .'

Nosov went into detail because he knew that the OMON guys weren't used to fighting in operations like this one – lots of them had come to Chechnya directly from their local police force. They didn't have any experience of war – they shot badly and they weren't trained, but they were good men, courageous and full of a great desire to serve the Motherland. Many of them would later become career soldiers, joining the FSB or special counter-terrorism teams.

'If you decide to use hand grenades, never throw them upward. They can bounce off a branch and fall back onto you or your comrades. Only throw them from high to low, or at human height. Try to shoot single rounds – in the woods, the more chaos there is, the more confusing it can be, and often under violent fire it's easier for the enemy to retreat. Shoot one or two rounds and then correct your aim, but if you can't see your targets anymore save your ammo, change position instead, watch carefully for the enemies to come back into your field of vision. Don't trust any sounds. Don't believe everything you see or hear – the woods can play tricks on your senses, don't forget . . . Are you ready?'

We all nodded, and so Nosov added:

'Come on, let's waste those monkeys . . .'

We climbed up the hill following a tactic called the 'avalanche', which was used in patrolling mountain areas, when it was necessary to keep watch over a very steep incline. This is how it works: everyone moves at a distance of five to ten metres apart, but the ones who are up higher move slightly to the right while the ones down lower slightly to the left, in relation to the vertical line of the mountain. That way everyone can fire in the same direction. The ones up higher shoot lower and lower, down to the last person in the line. No one shoots upward, because he knows that there's someone covering him above; that way they avoid the risk of getting caught in friendly fire or more than one of them shooting at the same target without being aware of the others. The avalanche works well if everyone follows the rules, forming a chain of soldiers who have one another covered.

I was one of the first to go up, as the upper position is more useful for precision shooting. To be honest, it's the least dangerous part of the avalanche – the risk is much higher if you're in the middle, where my other comrades and the explorers were that day. Above and below them were the OMON guys. I stood next to one of their snipers; he was probably about five years older than me. He was armed with a brand new Dragunov, but it worried me that he held it to his shoulder as you would with any old assault rifle. I could tell he was nervous; at every little sound, his finger leapt to the trigger like a crazed grasshopper. There was a risk that he would reveal our position.

I went over to him and said:

'You don't need to hold this like an AK. Put it in front of you. Bend your left arm, so you can use it as support. When you need to shoot, you just straighten your arm and the gun will bounce onto your shoulder by itself, like this . . .' I showed him what I meant. 'When we hear the first shots we have to be ready to move forward and set up a well-concealed position to fire from. Our bullets have to be in the background of the gunfire . . .'

The kid was all ears.

'Is this your first time in Chechnya?' I asked, in a tone of solidarity.

'Yes . . . Shit, I've fired a few bullets at the range, but I'm not sure I can aim well here, in the middle of all these trees . . .'

He was being sincere; he cared about doing his part but didn't feel confident enough of his ability. A man who finds himself in the middle of a war for the first time suddenly has the realisation that human lives depend on his actions, and every personal failing takes on the magnitude of real tragedy. These men need to be talked to, they need to be helped and kept under watch, otherwise in the middle of combat there could be a bad surprise.

'Don't worry,' I told him, smiling. 'When we get started, stay with me. I'll tell you who, how and when to shoot. You just need to aim, breathe slow and stay calm . . .'

When he moved I couldn't help but hear all the noise the metal hooks on his rifle sling made, or the thousand other sounds coming from various parts of his jacket, or the poorly attached ammo . . . This was something that we saboteurs couldn't stand – we would rather be on our own than in the company of people who made more noise when they walked than the tracks of an armoured car. Fortunately, it was loud as hell – the enemy was shooting wildly at the last car in our convoy, so they wouldn't have noticed if an elephant had come up behind them.

The bullets were getting closer and closer – it seemed like they were shooting right in our ears. And then I realised that we could also hear the enemy's voices. I went down to the ground and motioned to the sniper to follow my lead.

We crawled over to an enormous tree that had grown next to a wide, jutting rock that formed a kind of terrace. I stopped a few metres below, in the bushes. My observation point had an excellent view down below. Between the trees I had a clear sight of part of the road – there was our car and the other two OMON cars which hadn't yet been attacked. I couldn't see the last car in the column, but it must have been hit too because black smoke was rising into the air.

I focused on a cluster of bushes that was moving

strangely. Since there wasn't much wind that day and all the animals of the forest had certainly run away already, it was obvious that there were enemies hiding in there. When our comrades shot a few rounds, further down, a young man leapt out from one of the bushes I had been watching, armed with a machine gun and an empty RPG around his shoulder. There were fewer than a hundred metres between us; I aimed at his chest and fired. He grimaced with pain and, bringing both hands to his chest, he tumbled to the ground, as if he had lost his balance. I aimed a second round at his head, and he fell backwards, vanishing into the grass.

I showed my neighbour a well-protected spot between the roots of the tree.

'Go and lie flat over there. Hide so that you can't see the barrel of the rifle poking out from the other side. Stay low, don't move and observe everything carefully. I'll cover the right side, you do the left. If you see a target, take a nice deep breath before shooting. Pull the trigger slowly, almost gently, and when you let go don't close your eyes. Can you handle that?'

He nodded, then went over to the position I had pointed out to him.

We could hear shots and the explosions of the hand grenades below, interspersed with the shouting of our men and the enemies − the violence of the battle was increasing at light speed.

'Down here, down here! Help!' one of the OMON boys shouted, from the group that was the furthest down, almost at the foot of the mountain. 'They're pushing, trying to come out into the road!'

'Zenith, Deer, Moscow!' Nosov's voice was agitated, but filled with the desire to win. 'Get down there, stop those arseholes – don't let them come out otherwise they'll be right on top of us!'

As usual, even at the most difficult moments, our captain showed the gusto for danger that a pirate might have.

From somewhere behind the trees the enemy shot an RPG round.

'Oh God, they shot my leg off, they shot my leg off!' one of the OMON boys started screaming in desperation. His screams were so loud and high-pitched that they almost drowned out the sound of the shooting.

I tried to spot the place where the Arab with the grenade launcher was hiding, but the trees were obstructing my view. So I fired a few shots at random, near a clump of bushes that seemed to be moving. I immediately heard a bullet fly over my head – they had a sniper too.

'Let's go down lower,' I told the other man.

It was an inferno down below. The soldier who'd been hit by the grenade kept screaming, while Nosov let out a string of curses, trying to call back one of the OMON boys who had gone out of formation and had started shooting uphill:

'Come back here, you fucking idiot, get back here now . . . or stop shooting! Fuck, you're going to hit us!'

'Reznyak, you filthy bastard, take your position or I will kill you myself!' the OMON officer commanded. 'Either come back here or I'll shoot you in the face!'

We went a few metres further down. I positioned myself next to a brook and sent my comrade a little further ahead. From that position the area could be surveyed more easily – I saw a man armed with an RPG almost immediately – but I couldn't locate their sniper.

My comrade aimed at the man with the RPG, getting him with the first shot, full in the chest. But the Arab fired as he fell, and hit a tree in front of him.

After the explosion, a young man with a Dragunov on his arm emerged from one of the nearby bushes. He was covering one of his ears and was making strange movements with his head, as if he had a bug stuck in his hair and was trying to get rid of it by shaking his head wildly. He must have taken a hit; the shell had exploded too close to him.

Without a second thought I shot a few rounds and he fell to the ground; the rifle came out of his hands and sailed through the air like a feather carried by the wind. Two other men came out behind him, one with a machine gun and the other with a Kalashnikov. I aimed at the one with the machine gun and fired, and then he leaned against a tree and responded with such a long blast in our direction that his weapon started to smoke. He was shouting like a madman, but his voice was drowned out by the sound of his own weapon. I fired again, twice, because I couldn't tell if I had hit him. He dropped to his knees, but didn't stop shooting, even though his bullets were going too high – he was probably wearing a bulletproof vest. I pinpointed his head in my sight; he kept shaking it like a wounded animal that senses the end is near.

Without pity, I planted a bullet in his face. The tree behind him was splattered with blood; through my scope I could see a dark stain spreading over the bark like a moving, living substance.

The young sniper took out the guy with the Kalashnikov, landing two bullets in his back as he was trying to run away. The enemies hadn't expected this kind of attack.

'Excellent work, friend,' I whispered.

He flashed me a big bright smile, like a little kid.

We moved again – we needed to move together to push the enemy further down and surround him. And we had to be quick, so as not to give the Arabs the chance to flee in the other direction.

'Close in on the area, don't let them get away!' Nosov ordered.

Our avalanche began turning towards the road. We went downward, inspecting every tree in search of hidden terrorists. The air smelled of freshly cut grass, newly split logs, mould and burned flesh.

'Don't touch the corpses – they could be hiding some nasty surprises!'

We knew exactly what our captain was alluding to – often enemies would leave hastily made traps as they fled. They would put bombs under bodies, hiding them between the legs or beneath the backs of their dead, so that if anyone moved them to take a weapon he would get blown up.

'If you see anything on the ground that attracts your attention, do not go near it!' Nosov yelled, continuing the accelerated survival course for the OMON team.

The enemies resumed shooting at us. It didn't seem like they wanted to flee; they were really trying to wipe us out. We dropped down, sticking as close to the ground as possible. When someone shoots at you from that close and you don't have anywhere to hide, you start to see the ground as a magical substance, ready to change its form just for you, as if it were a blanket that could mould itself to your shape to protect you. A hole, a small pit, becomes a world.

Nosov shot a blast in response to the enemies and hit one; a few metres away from me I heard a short moan, the kind we called 'the last breath' – the unmistakable sound someone makes just before he dies.

I stood up and took cover behind a tree, followed by my comrade from the OMON. The enemy fired a series of short blasts, and a few bullets hit our tree – I could see the wood exploding all around.

'Christ, what do we do now?' the kid asked.

'We can't do anything but kill them . . . They feel trapped and they're trying to come out, but there aren't many left and we can crush them . . . Now, let's move ahead and get them from the side . . .' I tried to give him a little faith in himself, even if in that situation I needed it just as much.

We scrambled further down and positioned ourselves behind a tree from which we could see three terrorists trying to get to the road. Two of them carried a wounded man on their shoulders. The man had lost consciousness – his head dangled forward, his trousers were completely soaked with blood.

I pointed out the targets to my comrade:

'You take care of the lone one; I'll handle the two carrying the wounded guy.'

In seconds we had taken out the entire group. One man, however, didn't die right away – he was on his knees, screaming. Nosov threw a hand grenade to finish him off. As soon as the bomb went off we raced down.

Our captain, Moscow, and my other comrades were getting closer and closer, the ring was tightening. For an instant I felt like the fight was over – it was a sensation I felt when a moment of calm suddenly occurred during a battle. You don't hear anyone else shooting around you and you feel as though you're the only agitated, vengeful person left in the whole universe. Everyone else is calm and peaceful . . . It only lasts a few seconds, but it's enough to make you feel a sort of shame, as if the blame for everything that was happening lies on you alone – and that's the moment when you're most in danger of losing touch with reality. That's what happened to me. As I ran I began to overthink the situation, and I passed a live terrorist without even noticing.

He was a young Chechen armed with a Kalashnikov, with a shadow of a beard on his face and a strip of green cloth affixed to his wool cap. He was sitting against a tree, and when I passed beside him he decided to shoot me in the back. Unlike me, my comrade had seen him and stopped to shoot him. But the Chechen moved faster, and emptied his clip into him.

I turned, and without hesitation fired my entire magazine at him, keeping the rifle at my right side. He tried to respond but the rifle fell from his hand. His face was white, his eyes startlingly open, and his mouth kept opening and closing – he looked like a fish that had flopped out of the water. He tried to remove the heavy jacket he had on, as if it were suffocating him. I kept shooting, and as I shot him he tried to shield himself – he put a hand in front of his body, as if to protect himself from the bullets, but his arm immediately lost its strength and his hand flailed, groping in mid-air. At last a bullet crushed his chin and part of his jaw; his head whipped to the side and froze in a surreal position. The broken bones of his face, the shattered teeth, the blood pulsing from his open veins and uprooted tongue: all these details made the wound look like a flower. Seeing that macabre botanical composition above a man's shoulders had a strange effect; it seemed as though he had not died but had transformed into something new, something that, for those of us still in this world, was impossible to comprehend.

'Kolima, that's enough,' Moscow said, placing a hand on the rifle to make me stop. I hadn't noticed that he had approached. 'He's dead.'

Only then did I look at the OMON officer. He was lying on the ground next to his rifle. His eyes were still open, but he was no longer breathing – he'd taken a bad hit directly to his chest. His mouth was full of dark blood; his stomach and lungs must have been pierced by the bullets. I bent over and checked his vest; the iron plates weren't there. He had probably removed them so as not to carry any extra weight.

It was terrible to discover that the boy had died in such a stupid way, because of my mistake – one moment of inattention had cost another man his life. A man who was now a piece of motionless flesh at my feet, without wants, fears, loves . . . everything that had connected him to this world. Who knows what his last thought had been before dying, or what words had died on his lips, caught in that mouth filled with black blood.

Moscow ran off towards the others. I told him I would be right there.

I inspected the corpse. I found four rifle magazines, and I took his gun. I hadn't even had the time to ask him what his name was.

The fire fight was still raging. I could hear Nosov giving orders while someone from OMON was busy talking on the radio. None of us had been carrying a field radio, so that meant we had finally made it back to the road.

I was heading in the direction of the gunfire when I came upon Shoe. He was lying on the ground behind a tree, looking at the sky, oblivious to everything that was happening around him.

'Hey, what are you doing over there, taking a nap?' I positioned myself not far from him, trying to inspect the area below us.

'There are four spirits. I'm waiting for Nosov's signal to throw the hand grenades, then they'll hit them again with the machine guns . . .' Shoe was relaxed; he seemed far away from the war, like a tourist who'd dropped in from some Caribbean beach, sunbathing and sipping on a nice cold drink.

'There's the body of an OMON guy in the woods, their sniper . . .' I said, peering out a little to observe the situation better. 'An enemy shot an entire clip into him. We have to take him down to his men . . .'

'Hey, quit sticking your damn head out,' he scolded me with a little kick on the leg. 'In a few days you'll be discharged, isn't that enough for you? You want to leave the army in a coffin with the band behind you?'

'Relax, brother, I see them.' I took my rifle and got into a comfortable position. 'I'll take care of them; there's no need to pollute the wilderness with your bombs . . .'

The men were hidden in a deep pit, with their backs to us, about fifty metres away. I shot an entire clip at them. Three fell immediately. One managed to move in time and began to fire in my direction, but I shot him in the forehead.

We heard shots coming from the other side – our men were attacking the same enemy position, which no longer contained any live Arabs.

'We already handled it, Ivanisch!' I yelled.

'Why do you always have to do things your way?' Shoe asked me, smiling. 'So, where's this kid's body?'

We went back up to get it. Shoe took his rifle; I took the young Chechen's. I inspected the enemy's body and found army documents, a plastic card and a piece of paper covered in Arabic handwriting and various stamps. I took everything, because our commanders and secret service agents loved playing with the paperwork – when it came to tracking down our soldiers killed or gone missing in the war they'd beat around the bush, but when it came to terrorists they were always at the ready. They would even send entire investigative teams to find the body of some Islamic extremist.

Shoe and I picked up the sniper's corpse, and, holding him by the jacket and feet, we went down to the road.

When we arrived the fighting was over. Our men stood beside ten or so enemy corpses piled up at the edge of the road, while the OMON dogs ran in circles, agitated, sniffing the air and growling in the direction of the dead.

One of the OMON men sat on the ground; Spoon was treating a hole just above the knee on his right leg. Another was already on a stretcher; his comrades were trying to make room for him inside their car. The driver stood next to them, and he kept repeating, like a prayer, the phrase:

'Put him in feet first, remember, feet first . . .'

This had to do with an old Russian custom, according to which only the dead should be transported with their heads towards the front, so that they come out feet first. Drivers and pilots always made sure the wounded were loaded feet first, so that when they reached their destination they would come out like the living, head first – this was a kind of insurance, a good luck charm that prevented the wounded from dying during the trip.

An OMON soldier was fiddling with the radio while Nosov spoke on the handset. Before going into the woods, Nosov had given the order to call in reinforcements to ensure the transport of the wounded and the prisoners, since two of our vehicles had been attacked. The reinforcements had started on their way, but they had run into enemy fire on the road. It sounded as though they were still in the middle of a battle; you could hear shots and explosions through the radio.

'Comrade Captain, we've been hit . . . On the rise at the twentieth kilometre from the inhabited area . . .' In a weak, shaky voice a young soldier was trying to provide useful information.

'Let me speak with your commanding officer, private!' Nosov yelled.

'I think Lieutenant Kuznecov is dead, sir. I think . . .'

'Son, you *think* so or you *know* your lieutenant is dead?' The captain tried to enunciate his words. 'Can you confirm his death for me?'

'Yes, sir, I confirm; he has a hole in his chest and he's not breathing . . .'

'Then find me the highest ranking soldier among you. I need to speak with him immediately!'

The sound of confused voices amidst gunfire came through the handset of the radio. The soldiers were calling to each other; all signs indicated that chaos had taken over.

Then an awful voice, raspy and low, came on:

'Sergeant Major Kopchik, at your service!'

'Sergeant, gather your men and get the fuck out of there, now,' Nosov growled. 'If you can't respond to the attack get down to the road. If your vehicles are still intact, take them and return!'

'But I'm not authorised to give the unit orders, sir! Lieutenant Kuznecov is in command here!'

'Well, it appears that you are not very well informed, Sergeant. Your lieutenant died in battle. If you take a look around, his body should be somewhere nearby . . .'

There was a long pause at the other end, then in the distance you could hear the sergeant spit out a vile epithet, cursing everyone and everything. Then he picked up the handset again:

'I confirm, sir, our commander has fallen in battle! What do I do?'

'Take your unit to safety, Sergeant. Clear the road – we'll come down to you, but make sure we don't have anyone in our way!'

'But the terrorists in the woods have . . .' the sergeant tried to protest.

'You have no chance of sustaining a fire fight against the terrorists . . . Get out of there while your cars are still in one piece. Retreat immediately, that's an order!'

'Yes, sir, I'll initiate retreat!'

'And hurry up, otherwise they'll get all of you!' Nosov replaced the handset, looked at us in desperation and said:

'Someone explain to me . . . Trapped by four fucking shepherds shooting a bullet or two . . . I mean, they don't even have an RPG to hit the cars. But our heroes are already in trouble – they don't know what to do and they've even lost their lieutenant . . . How the fuck are we fighting this war?'

Nosov ordered us into the cars. We had lost six men; five others were wounded. We loaded everything into the three functioning vehicles: the wounded, our dead, the ammo, the drugs and everything else we had found in the mosque. We put the prisoners, however, on top of the cars, binding them to the side hooks on the armour – that way, we hoped, nobody would try to attack us again.

We left quickly, watching the surrounding woods and mountains with suspicion, as if we were expecting them to start moving at any second.

Once we were back on base we realised that one of the prisoners had died; it was the old imam, who hadn't been able to endure the discomforts of the trip. The others weren't doing so well either, but they still gave signs of life.

The OMON guy who'd been hit by a grenade during the avalanche had fainted, and the helicopter whisked him off to the military hospital that was set up for the most serious cases – he had lost a lot of blood.

We saboteurs shut ourselves up in our container to rest.

I took a long bath in the iron vat behind the kitchen, and then I climbed into the bunk next to Spoon, who had already been snoring for a while.

I slept for a long time, and when I woke up Nosov was sitting at the table, eating out of a pot and drinking cognac straight from the bottle. Moscow was next to him, chewing on a piece of bread. He looked like a little homeless kid.

I got up, opened a jar and, using my fork, pulled a hunk of stewed meat from the pan, where it was mixed with fat and God knows what else. I dunked it into my jar before taking a bite.

I was standing up, enjoying my food, when Nosov looked me in the eyes, serious, and said:

'Today the order from the division commander came: you're fired, criminal . . .'

I set the jar on the table and sat down with them, unable to say a word. I felt soft, as if I were made of cotton inside.

'Starting today you're free again. Live, do whatever you want . . .' Moscow smiled. 'But never forget your brothers . . .'

Just then Zenith came in. He was walking with an arm over his stomach; it was obvious that he had something hidden under his jacket.

'So, you're abandoning us, I hear. Well, how about one last bender first?' He opened his jacket and pulled out some bottles of vodka, uncorked one with his teeth and took a long drink.

'Hey, leave some for me too!' Spoon shouted, leaping up from his bunk.

Shoe and Deer came over too, laughing like a couple of fools.

'What's so funny, soldiers?' Nosov asked, pretending to be angry, still chewing.

'I think we won't be alone at Kolima's goodbye party,'

Shoe said. 'Our Deer has made quite an impression on the cook!' and he shouldered Deer so hard he fell down. Everyone burst out laughing.

I really didn't know how to act. It was the last time I would be with my team; the last time I would see all the men together. Over the months I had often thought about the fact that my discharge day would come, but I had never imagined what it would be like. Sure, I had seen it happen other times, when friends or other people I knew only by sight left, but I'd never believed that one day I would be in their place. I seldom thought of the future; maybe somewhere inside I believed that I was never going back. I had expected to die in that war . . . And yet here I was with my friends, celebrating the end of my military service.

It didn't occur to me that it was a special occasion, the last chance I would have to ask my comrades about their lives, or to tell them the stories I'd always wanted to . . . Thinking back on it now I realise that, like an idiot, I wasted that moment, as if I didn't know that the next day I was going to be far away, far from my comrades with whom — because of the war — I had formed an intense bond. I don't know why, but at that moment I didn't have any of these thoughts in my head; I drank, I got drunk and I watched my friends' faces grow blurry and distant until I passed out.

At five in the morning a military car would take me to another camp, and from there I would get on the plane that was finally going to take me back home. That was the last thing I remembered from the night before . . .

At five in the morning, however, I was still so drunk that I couldn't drag myself from one bunk to another. My head was spinning like a giant propeller, my comrades' voices, shouting and joking, throbbed in my ears. The moment a thought appeared in my head, vomit lurched into my throat, as if the workings of my brain somehow irritated my stomach.

I could hear Nosov describing yet another of his adventures in one of the many wars he had been in, while a few bunks away Deer was making love to the young cook, and Shoe and Spoon were teasing him, throwing empty clips at him, for a few laughs . . . I was in an endless delirium, like a sudden fall off a precipice, like a feast in a time of plague.

I remember that at some point two soldiers I'd never seen before lifted me up from the bed; one of them took my papers, the other my bag, and they carefully dragged me to the door of the container. One of them suddenly dropped me − I fell to the ground and hit my head. I didn't know if he'd done it on purpose or not, but either way I didn't feel any pain.

The captain got up from the table, where he was still sitting with Zenith and Moscow, took a bottle of vodka and a pack of cigarettes and gave them to the soldier with these words:

'Be careful, boys, make sure you don't harm this soldier. He has saved many lives. He's a good sniper . . .'

One of the soldiers took the offering from Nosov's

hands and slipped it under his jacket. He and the other guy lifted me to my feet, made a show of dusting off my uniform and addressed Nosov in a pleasant voice:

'Don't worry, Comrade Captain. Your sniper will reach his destination safe and sound, I will see to it personally. May we be dismissed?' He asked Nosov's permission before leaving, as military regulation demands. My captain looked me in the face and said:

'Have yourself a peaceful life, Nicolay, without too many worries . . .'

Then he turned to the two who were holding me up and saluted:

'Soldiers, you are dismissed!'

They saluted back and I tried to as well, but my arm wouldn't hear of travelling all the way to my head, so I must have just jerked it awkwardly. I was a mess.

I remember Nosov's words and the look he gave me perfectly, and I often find myself thinking about it. But I can't remember if or how I said goodbye to the guys in the group before leaving, what I said to them or what they said to me. All I remember is that phrase of the captain's, the last thing I ever heard him say: 'Have yourself a peaceful life . . .'

Then I had a surreal ride in the car. I wavered on the border between sleep and waking, each time thinking that I was in a thousand different places – at first I felt as though I was on the armoured car with the rest of the team on our way to a mission; then I thought I was wounded; finally, I was sure I'd been captured by the enemy − I looked for my rifle and despaired when I couldn't find it . . . Then I realised I wasn't wearing my bulletproof vest, and I got so scared I started shaking. I was on the verge of tears. I don't remember if I was delirious or not, but when we got to the camp I heard one of my escorts who was smoking outside the car say to the other that it would have been better if I'd been shot in the war, because returning a person like me to society was a real crime.

There was no plane waiting when we stopped, so I thought that it was just a break and we hadn't yet reached our destination. But I was wrong − I was taking the train home, not a plane. At that point even if they had told me I had to ride a donkey home, I'd still have been happy − without arms or ammo, without my precious vest, I felt naked. I wanted to go home as soon as possible, in peace.

They showed me to a barracks, where I had to have a physical examination. A military bureaucrat, without asking me a single question, without even looking me in the eyes, filled out a few forms and wished me luck. The examination was already over. Then they asked me to take off all my clothes, and gave me a chance to take a hot shower, in a barracks-cum-bathroom. Then they gave me a new uniform, which stank of mustiness; it was the typical smell of military depots. All the army stuff smelled like that.

I got dressed, took my bag and left for the station, accompanied by the same two soldiers. In the car with me were three other soldiers, who had just been discharged: an infantryman, a paratrooper and an artilleryman. None of them had any desire to talk or joke around; they were as desolate as I was, lost in thought, wearing the signs of their farewell celebrations from the night before. For the whole trip my three companions smoked like it was their last, and so I arrived at the station half-cured, pissed off and with a pounding headache.

The train trip was long and boring. The carriages were full of other discharged soldiers, officers on temporary leave and OMON officers who had finished their war service and were returning to their police precincts. As the wheels of the train ate through the kilometres of tracks people gathered in small groups to drink, tell stories and complain about everything and everyone . . . There was a lot of anger, but it was softened by the fact that we were alive, returning home in one piece, thinking of the future. I for one couldn't wait to lie down in my bed and sleep in peace for as long as I wanted, without anyone interrupting my rest.

As soon as I stepped off the train I took a walk around my home town, and I realised that I had an inexplicable impulse to shoot everyone I saw on the street. I felt a lethal charge of hatred: it was eating me up inside, making me scorn everything that represented peaceful life.

I ate an ice cream but the feeling didn't go away, so I bought a bottle of vodka and once I got home I started to drink. But even drowned in alcohol, my state of mind stayed the same – it was as if peace bothered me, as if I sensed something false, something *wrong* with people, and their polite behaviour. I left the house; it was hard for me to stay in one place for too long.

I looked at the houses, searching obsessively for signs of destruction, but everything was too nice. The window frames and panes were intact, and behind the glass, signs of a life of comfort and peace. Everything was in order: the light bulbs in their places, the brightly-coloured curtains, the flowers on the windowsills . . . it all seemed horrible to me. At night people would drink tea and watch television, laugh at some comedian's idiotic jokes, listen to pop songs by singers decked out like living Christmas trees . . . And as the star machine cloned new idols, everyone wanted to be like the famous figures. Young people competed to see who was the most ignorant, because ignorance is something that's always in fashion – running to the nightclubs to dance at desperate parties that went on until dawn, finally feeling like they were the stars of something. If you're rich, you can do anything; if you're beautiful, you should exploit your beauty to manipulate everyone – this seemed to be the only valid rule, besides unwarranted, limitless violence, because being violent is fashionable too.

The chaos of war seemed more ordinary and comprehensible than the so-called morality of peaceful society. I thought back to everyone I had seen die in the name of peace, and I was increasingly convinced that this kind of peace didn't deserve to exist. Better the bloodbath I'd known, where at least we knew what the enemy's face looked like and there was no chance of getting it wrong, where everything was as simple as a bullet. But now I had been returned to a peace that enabled me to be a consumer of the beauties of the universe, making me believe that they had been chosen just for me, even prepaid: packaged food and virtual sex, and after those fake orgasms you're left with nothing but contempt for yourself and for the world.

Back at home, trying to calm down, I turned on the television, but all the news I heard seemed like a joke to me: in some cellar four Azerbaijanis had mixed tap water with a little alcohol and sold it as vodka, for the price of a stabbing during a fight in a nightclub car park; the former attorney general had been filmed doing drugs and having sex with an underage prostitute, later claiming that it was just an evening of fun, his civic right; politicians made lots of promises, then would get into ridiculous arguments that amounted to 'who's the more disgusting', while on another channel the President spoke like a genuine criminal, openly threatening anyone who got in his way but at the same time so charismatic and reasonable that even I wanted to applaud his speeches . . .

When I saw a news feature about a group of our soldiers who had recently died in a battle in the mountains during a terrorist operation in Chechnya, I unthinkingly grabbed a clock and hurled it at the television, cracking the screen. The piece dedicated to our fallen soldiers had come on after two other stories: one on breeding pigs in southern Russia; the other on some young models who had won international beauty pageants and were ready to take on the world, thus making an enormous contribution to the cause of Mother Russia.

I sat there in front of the broken television all night, thinking of how, like sheep to the slaughter, we had obediently gone to sacrifice our lives in the name of an ideal that the rest of the country cared nothing about. By the time I got up from the chair it was already morning, and something that an Arab prisoner once told me kept going through my head: 'Our society doesn't deserve all the effort we're putting into this war.' Only at that moment did I comprehend how right he was, this person, this man whom I had continued to call an enemy.

In the subsequent days I wandered around the city, and I saw some absurd scenes. On the streets, groups of police officers, out of their minds on drugs or alcohol – people who were so ignorant they were incapable of reading the information on the passports of the people they stopped – vented their frustrations by beating up anyone that came within range. Even the conversations on the bus scared me – the night before, on a reality show, one of those tarts who enjoy being thrown in a house with a bunch of other idiots had pulled down her pants on live TV, showing the whole country her privates. Some young women sitting next to me were debating whether this girl waxed or not . . . Nowhere was spared from this lunacy. Even in church, at the door, the first thing they offered you was the chance to donate some money, as if your relationship with God could be condensed into some sort of restaurant menu, just like at a fast food establishment, the church had become a fast faith establishment: 'Today only, a menu fit for a saint on his way to Heaven. Try it!' Even love for God had become a privilege . . .

With every molecule in my body I could feel the hypocrisy of peace, a forced peace, taken to the limit of human possibility; a contest whose prize was the right to get bitten by one of those many chimeras. I had better keep to myself.

Living in a house once again, *my* house, I decided that the light coming through the windows bothered me, so I covered them up with blankets.

I needed to hold a weapon in my hands; I felt a physical lack, as though I couldn't breathe properly. I took an AK out of a hiding spot – it had come directly from Chechnya, thanks to some of my driver friends in the army.

At night I couldn't fall asleep. I stuffed myself with pills and alcohol, trying to get at least a few hours' rest, but it was futile. After a month of insomnia, I realised what was wrong with my house: silence. There was too much silence, and I wasn't used to it anymore. So I turned the television up as loud as it could go, and I fell into a sort of trance, a dark, empty space that erased everything, for four or five hours . . . Every time I woke up I had cold sweat on my face and I felt as though I were in imminent danger, as though I were sitting on a box of explosives about to blow up.

During that period it was very hot and I often went around the house naked, with a Kalashnikov in one hand and a bottle of vodka in the other; I wandered the rooms without any particular purpose, just to keep moving. Once in a while I'd sing a song or talk out loud, in an effort not to feel so alone. At night I would gaze out of the window. Turning off the light and aiming my rifle at the nearby houses, I would observe people; frame them in my sight and then shoot, pulling the trigger of my unloaded weapon. This gesture – shooting at real people with a real weapon, even if just in pretence – brought me some serenity and peace, and led me onto the right track. I was able to put my thoughts in order, just as some people relax by doing crossword puzzles.

I had shaved off my beard but grown sideburns, even though seeing my face clean-shaven had a negative effect – a stranger staring back at me from the mirror.

I had a hard time getting reaccustomed to having hot water, being clean – even eating fresh food. Every morning my grandmother came over and prepared the whole day's worth of food for me, and I would give her a hand in the kitchen. We talked a little, but I got tired very easily, and I would get headaches, as if I were doing work that took great concentration. Then my grandmother would say goodbye, and leave me by myself. The rest of my family was very good to me, very understanding, but I didn't feel like seeing anyone.

And this was how I spent my days, shuffling back and

forth in my apartment, in the dark, with the TV turned all the way up, naked as the day I was born, my Kalashnikov on my arm and my face shorn and sad. I thought of the war, imagined what was happening to my team at that moment, and every one of those thoughts triggered a fit of rage against myself – it was as if by accepting my discharge papers I had betrayed my comrades.

One afternoon I went out on the river. I took my boat and pushed off towards the area where the most affluent residents had their second homes. I took up a position in the woods nearby and started aiming at their flowerpots with my rifle. I went on like that for a few days. Before sundown, I would wipe out the flowerpots at the mansions of the wealthy. It made me feel good.

The following week the weather was bad; it was a good opportunity to go back out in the city. I put on a cap with a brim and some sunglasses so I wouldn't be recognised – at the time it bothered me to run into old friends. I would pass by people I knew, but usually they seemed to not even see me. Maybe I had changed too much. Once at the market I saw an old friend of mine; when we were teenagers we thought we were in love. She was right in front of me, and I took a step forward to say hello, but she bolted, pushing me away cruelly, with a look of anger on her face. I was taken aback by the malice I had seen in her eyes.

Walking through my city, I stopped at an old shop with

a wide window display, which reflected everything like a mirror. When I was a little boy, I often passed by that shop, because I liked the way my reflection would follow me as I walked. A thousand times, growing up, I stood there frozen as if under a spell, studying the details of real life reflected in that window; it was nice to observe things in reverse, as though I wasn't really able to perceive their true character when I saw them in their actual dimension. I even went to the shop at night. I would sit down in front of the window and watch the reflection of the stars at the top. They seemed so close it took my breath away.

And now there I was again, at that window. I looked at myself and in just a few seconds I knew that I was going crazy. I don't know how it happened, but suddenly my thoughts became fluid and clear – there was no longer anything stopping them, no obstacles. I observed how I was dressed and I reflected on how I had spent the last few months, as if before, as I was living my life, I hadn't been able to think. I had the impression that someone had stolen time from me, manipulated my life and reduced me to a zombie. An unpleasant sensation, but powerful and liberating, and it pushed me to start over again . . .

At the end of that week I was on the train. I was going to my grandfather Nikolay's home in Siberia. I had a backpack filled with heavy clothes, along with the essential equipment for the woods: a rifle and ammunition.

As the train rattled along, the immense landscapes of Russia flashed by. I imagined the life that awaited me in the forest: my grandfather's house on the lake, the smell of the wood, the purr of the lazy cat, a pack of dogs who looked like wolves, the dry trees to cut down, their logs stored in the woodshed in preparation for the winter; the days of hunting and walks in the *taiga*, the game prepared by Grandfather, the evening chats in front of the wood stove fire, the sauna full of boiling steam and the sharp scent that burned your lungs inside, like fire . . .

The closer I got to Siberia, the more I felt like I was a part of the land. It was as if it were calling out to welcome me, to help me get past all my troubles, to give me strength. I knew that I was going home, to the place where I belonged and where I would be able to find peace.

It was a reawakening, a moment of connection with the real that makes you want to get out of bed, to do something with your day, to live.

Like jumping out of an airplane in flight, and savouring the free fall before you open the parachute.

I found out from some friends in the army that Captain Nosov and Moscow fell in battle – a few months after my discharge – in a mountain area between Chechnya and Dagestan. They had gone on reconnaissance and found themselves surrounded by a large group of terrorists.

The infantry night explorers who went to recover the dead that day said that Nosov's and Moscow's bodies had been mined. Evidently one of the two, before he died, hadn't wanted to give the enemy the chance to commit dishonourable acts on their remains.

I visited their grave, in the military cemetery of the city of M—. According to army tradition, friends who have fallen together are buried together.

Shoe was wounded, but not seriously, a few months after my discharge. Nobody knows how, but he was able to get into the secret service and over time has climbed the ladder in the FSB. Our paths have crossed many times; we have remained good friends.

Zenith decided to stay on contract. I didn't know much about his whereabouts; once in a while I would hear some story from mutual friends in the army who had run into him during a mission. He also went into the counter-terrorist wing of the FSB, the secret service.

Last spring, as I was beginning to write this book, I found out that he was killed during a counter-terrorist *operation in a small town in Dagestan. Nobody could tell me anything about his death, only the place where he was buried.*

I lost track of Deer. Some say that after getting discharged he went to live in southern Siberia, where he got married and works in the forest service.

Spoon is still part of the saboteur unit today. He was wounded twice, earned a few medals and, as far as I've been told, provoked the ire of a powerful general after courting his young wife.

　　A few years ago I came across him by chance while surfing on the internet, on a recorded television show about the war in Chechnya – he recounted the details of one of our missions. It struck me that he was losing his hair; he was almost bald. Then I realised that we were exactly alike.